Byung S. Lee

SOFTWARE CREATIVITY

Robert L. Glass
Computing Trends

Prentice Hall PTR
Englewood Cliffs, New Jersey 07632

Library of Congress Cataloging-in-Publication Data

Glass, Robert L., 1932–
  Software creativity / Robert L. Glass.
    p. cm.
  Includes bibliographical references and index.
  ISBN (invalid) 013147364
  1. Computer software—Development. I. Title.
QA76.76.D47G57 1994
005.1'01'9—dc20   94–20170
                                CIP

Editorial/production supervision
  and interior design: *Mary P. Rottino*
Cover design: *Bruce Kenselaar*
Cover illustration: *Don Martinetti*
Buyer: *Alexis Heydt*
Acquisitions editor: *Paul Becker*
Editorial Assistant: *Maureen Diana*

The publisher offers discounts on this book when ordered in bulk quantities.
For more information, contact:

Corporate Sales Department
Prentice Hall P T R
113 Sylvan Avenue
Englewood Cliffs, New Jersey 07632
Phone: 201-592-2863,
FAX: 201-592-2249

Printed in the United States of America
10 9 8 7 6 5 4 3 2 1

ISBN 0-13-147364-6

Prentice-Hall International (UK) Limited, *London*
Prentice-Hall of Australia Pty. Limited, *Sydney*
Prentice-Hall Canada, Inc., *Toronto*
Prentice-Hall Hispoamericana, S.A., *Mexico*
Prentice-Hall of India Private Limited, *New Delhi*
Prentice-Hall of Japan, Inc., *Tokyo*
Simon & Schuster Asia Pte. Ltd., *Singapore*
Editora Prentice-Hall do Brasil, Ltds., *Rio de Janeiro*

This book is dedicated to all the creative software professionals in the world. It is my belief that this means all software professionals!

I wish to thank Linköping University, Sweden, where I was a visiting professor during much of the creation of this book.

CONTENTS

PREFACE

The title of this book is *Software Creativity*. It is written from a powerfully felt personal perspective:

- That software construction is primarily a problem-solving activity
- That all problem-solving requires creativity
- That software problem-solving is deeply complex, perhaps more deeply complex than any other such activity
- That, therefore, software problem-solving requires the ultimate in creativity

When I began the book, I had the wrong reasons for writing it. I was tired of, and angered by, the claims of many in the field that the solutions to the problems of software lay in discipline, formality, and quantitative reasoning. My 30 years of experience in constructing software problem solutions, and my six years in the academic world ruminating over the relationship between software's literature and that experience, suggested the opposite—that the solutions to the problems of software lay in flexibility, creativity, and qualitative reasoning. Oh, of course, for huge, many-person projects, discipline was a necessary evil; but still, brilliant people, not brilliant process, were the way to progress, I felt.

However, as I began work on the book, looking to other fields for material to bolster the creativity theme, I also began a personal odyssey. There was a reason, I began to see, for considering the possibility of discipline, formality, and quantitative reasoning. No matter how deep the need for creativity in a field, there was also always a need for a more formal framework to nurture and support that creativity.

That thought crept up in many sometimes surprising places. In a book titled, meaningfully, *The Discipline of Curiosity* [Groen90], the author said, "Science is not just curiosity and creativity; it is a disciplined form of it . . . It is the seemingly odd couple of discipline and curiosity that makes for scientific progress. The curiosity of creative minds, asking continuously How? and Why?, and the discipline to realize that science is part of the world, that it is shaping it."

Once again, from a book on problem-solving [Judson80] in which the author reports on a conversation with Murray Gell-Man, the discoverer of quarks: "Any art that's worth the name has some kind of discipline associated with it. Some kind of rule—maybe it's not the rule of a sonnet, or a symphony, or a classical painting, but even the most liberated contemporary art . . . has some kind of rule. And the object is to get across what you're trying to get across, while sticking to the rules."

Yet again, in an interview with cellist Yo-Yo Ma [Shapiro91]: "Creativity, he says, is not a result of instinct. Rather it is an endless conflict between discipline and intuition. The discipline—the years of practice, the musical knowledge—informs the playing. But there is a point at which the musician must make a leap of faith . . ."

There it was, again and again. Science requires discipline as well as creativity. Art requires discipline as well as creativity. Music requires discipline as well as creativity. Obviously, and to my chagrin, software also requires both discipline and creativity!

My personal odyssey was nearly complete. I now understood why, in a world where creativity seemed essential to success, the notion of discipline kept being raised. But that brought about a new dilemma: Was there any point to writing this book at all?

I re-read the computing literature, seeking once again those portions that focused on discipline, formality, and quantitative reasoning. And once again, in spite of my odyssey, my anger rose. What I began to see is that the advocates of discipline and formality were making the same mistake that I had been making. They were assuming that formality was all that was needed, and that creativity was counterproductive, just as I had been assuming that creativity was all that was needed, and that formality was counterproductive.

Perhaps there was a reason for the book after all! Perhaps it would help those imbalanced as far to the right as I had been to the left to see that the truth in software problem-solving must lie somewhere between the extremes. Also, perhaps, for those not as biased as my "opponents" and I had been, it might help a little in structuring a vitally important topic in the field.

My powerfully felt personal perspective need not change. It did, however, need to expand to include that "odd couple," that "endless conflict," the interaction between that essential component, creativity, and that other essential, discipline. My odyssey was, at last, complete.

However, there still remained the matter of writing style. I had already decided that the book would be a collection of essays, framed by a set of polarities: discipline versus flexibility, formal methods versus heuristics, optimizing versus satisficing, quantitative versus qualitative reasoning, process versus product, intellectual versus clerical activity, theory versus practice, and industry versus academe. There were, however, essays that I had created at waystops along my odyssey. Should I rewrite them to conform to my new, hard-won wisdom?

I decided not to. I reasoned that the reader might be interested in sharing my odyssey, starting at my far-left starting point, seeing what happened as my own new awareness dawned.

I cannot decide if that was the right decision. Only you, the reader, can. My wish for you—my hope for you—is that you will share my odyssey through the pages of this book, and that you will be glad you made the trip.

Robert L. Glass

REFERENCES

GROEN90—*The Discipline of Curiosity*, Elsevier Science, 1990; Groen, Janny; Eefke Smit; Juurd Eijsvoogel

JUDSON80—*The Search for Solutions*, Holt, Rinehart and Winston, 1980; Judson, Horace Freeland

SHAPIRO91—"Yo-Yo and Manny," *World Monitor*, Aug. 1991; Michael Shapiro

1

WHY SOFTWARE CREATIVITY?

"Creative thinking requires an attitude that allows you to search for ideas and manipulate your knowledge and experience. With this outlook, you try various approaches . . . often not getting anywhere. You use crazy, foolish, and impractical ideas as stepping stones to practical new ideas. You break the rules occasionally, and explore for ideas in unusual outside places."

—Roger von Oech, *A Whack on the Side of the Head,*
Warner Books, 1990

There's a fundamental conflict in the software world, sometimes taking on the attributes of a war.

On one side, managers search for ways to impose more discipline and control on software builders, and researchers advocate and sometimes seek to mandate formal methods for the same purpose.

On the other side, software builders quietly continue to build software pretty much the way they always have, with freewheeling methods and creative solutions.

"Breakthrough" methods come, linger awhile, and go away, having made little impact on our ability to build software.

Methodologies fragment into variants, 4GLs give way to COBOL, CASE tools become shelfware, object orientation is forever "next year's goal." The attempts to simplify and routinize the construction of software largely fail, one by one.

What's wrong with this picture? Are we dealing with stubborn practitioners, so stuck in their ways that they are intolerant of all change? That seems to be the view of management and research.

Or are we dealing with ignorant managers and researchers, so caught

1

up in the new that they fail to understand the old? That seems to be the view of practitioners.

The key issue underlying this conflict, I believe, is creativity. If there is little or no need for creativity in building software, then those managers and researchers are right in what they advocate—we *can* simplify and routinize the work of software. If, on the other hand, creativity is and always will be an essential part of software construction, then those practitioners are right—we *will* continue to need freewheeling methods and creative solutions. It is this whole collection of issues, standing on this foundation of software creativity, that I hope to address, and perhaps to resolve, in this book. That's why the book is called *Software Creativity.*

We'll explore these polar views, and what might be done about them, beginning with Chapter 2 of this book. The view will be a disaggregated one. Rather than tackle creativity as a whole, we'll look at it one facet at a time, examining the roles of such aspects as discipline, formal methods, optimizing solutions, quantitative reasoning, process, theory, and fun. Each of those topics, and a few more, will be addressed by a series of informal essays. Along the way, we'll see a definition or two of creativity, and even the results of a study of how many of software's tasks really are creative (a study that has not previously appeared in the mainstream literature of the field).

Then, in Chapter 3, we'll move to a somewhat more formal view of creativity. We'll take two areas of the computing field in which creativity is particularly important—software design and the identification of potential strategic (competitive advantage) information systems—and examine the role of creativity in those areas in considerably more depth.

Then, in Chapter 4, under the assumption that the reader will by then believe that creativity plays at least *some* role in software construction, we'll look at ways of making creativity happen. There are a baker's dozen techniques for doing that, and they will be described and discussed.

Lest we be blinded by a narrow and constrained view of creativity from only software's point of view, Chapter 5 will examine some things we've learned about creativity in other fields. We'll see some surprising answers to the question "Can computers and software help (non-computing) people become more creative?", for example.

Then Chapter 6 will tat up the loose ends of the book.

That's the structured view of what lies ahead; but what about the emotional view? Where will the trip through this book take us?

My hope is that, as you read further into the book, you'll begin to see the role of creativity, and the conflict I spoke of at the beginning of this section, in an evolving light. I hope to drop an idea here, a clue there, that may prove useful to you as you move toward forming your own view of how important creativity is in software. Remember that my own travels through the source material for this book led me on an emotional and logical journey, one that left me in a far different place from where I started. Perhaps that will happen to you as well.

Along the way I'll call on a few colleagues to help out. For example, well-known software engineer P. J. Plauger shares with us his notion of "the falutin' index," a light-hearted way of measuring software projects far different from the more formal metrics we read about in the formal literature. Bruce Blum of Johns Hopkins' Applied Physics Lab explores the tension between fun and tedium on software projects. Dennis Galetta, a professor at Pitt, talks about creativity in strategic systems. Dan Couger of the University of Colorado (and director of its Center for Research in Creativity at Colorado Springs) contributes a couple of articles related to his own emerging book on software creativity. Penn State researcher Iris Vessey teams with me to conduct, and write about, studies of the nature of software tasks. It is something of a communal effort, this book.

However, let's return to the material at hand. Here, in Chapter 1, we will explore somewhat further the fundamental discipline vs. creativity conflict that led off this chapter, defining and clarifying it.

Many writers have written about, spoken about, and studied this polarity of positions. Among the most articulate have been Peter DeGrace who, with his co-author Leslie Hulet Stahl, has written a couple of books touching on this problem [DeGrace 1991, 1993]; and Stan Rifkin who, with Charles Cox, conducted an inside-industry study of the effects of the problem [Rifkin 1991].

Interestingly, both of these writers attached a name to the dichotomy they saw: DeGrace refers to it as the "Greece vs. Rome" dichotomy, while Rifkin calls it "management-driven vs. technology-driven." But no matter the nomenclature, I believe they are talking about the same thing.

Let's look at what these authors have to say, in their own words. How do they see the dichotomy? What do they see as the effects it causes? What is their own feeling about what ought to happen in the field of software?

As DeGrace and Rifkin set the stage, mull over your own beliefs on the subject. Where do you stand on the continuum from discipline to creativity, from management-driven to technology-driven, from Rome to Greece?

Then check your position after you read what DeGrace and Rifkin have to say.

REFERENCES

[DeGrace 1991] PETER DEGRACE and LESLIE STAHL, *Wicked Problems, Righteous Solutions*, Prentice-Hall, 1991.

[DeGrace 1993] PETER DEGRACE and LESLIE HULET STAHL, *The Olduvai Imperative*, Prentice-Hall, 1993.

[Rifkin 1991] STAN RIFKIN and CHARLES COX, "Measurement in Practice," CMU/ SEI-91-TR-16.

1.1   GREECE VS. ROME: TWO VERY DIFFERENT SOFTWARE CULTURES*

Roman philosophy was very different from Greek philosophy, but they both have their equivalents in today's society: particularly in the American workplace. These equivalents have serious influences on our work. We want to present highlights of these cultures in a distinctive and contrasting way, and then bend them to our purposes.

In ancient Greece, an individual would act as an agent in his own behalf, or combine with other people to act together as a team. In a Greek work environment, you bring your tools to work with you, you do your stuff, and then you pack up your tools and take them home. You are an individual . . . an independent contractor. You are not owned body and mind. You are merely providing a service for compensation.

In Rome, one's first duty was to the group, clan, class, or faction upon which one depended for status. Known as *gravitas*, this meant sacrificing oneself for the good of the organization, and giving up one's individuality and identifying closely with the group. In a Roman environment, you go to work, the company hands you your tools, and then it holds you and your mind hostage until you sever your relationship with the organization. You are not an individual: you are owned by the organization body and mind, twenty-four hours a day. There are substantial rewards for this, however. The organization provides you with security, money, and power.

This issue of Greece vs. Rome has not yet been entirely resolved in our society; but, we have found it over and over again in our research. It affects who chooses tools, who makes them, and who uses them. We offer Table 1.1, which lists the important contrasts between the Greek and Roman perspectives in software engineering.

We are not making any moral statements here; that is one reason we chose names that represent two very great civilizations. We are not suggesting that one group is superior or inferior to the other. However, we do stress the positive side of the Greek view in this book. That is because we see an imbalance in our field. This imbalance stresses the Roman view at the expense of the Greek view.

---

*Peter DeGrace/Leslie Hulet Stahl, *THE OLDUVAI IMPERATIVE: CASE and the State of Software ENGINEERING Practice*, ® 1993, pp. 17–22. Reprinted by permission of Prentice Hall, Englewood Cliffs, New Jersey.

TABLE 1.1   Greece vs Rome

Greece (or the Greek way)	Rome (or the Roman way)
Organizes things	Organizes people
Informal	Formal
Writes the programs	Manages the projects
Motivated by the problem at hand	Motivated by group goals
Uses structured stuff	Uses STRUCTURED STUFF
Minimum documentation	Maximum documentation
Works on a human scale	Works beyond human scale
Works alone or in small groups	Works in large organizations
Uses *things* as tools	Uses *people* as tools
Democratic	Imperial
Empirical/inductive	Analytical/deductive
Intuitive	Logical
Class based on merit	Class based on function
Engineer/scientist	Manager
Substance	Form
Does things	Plans things or goes to meetings

We accept the differences between the groups (at least, we think we do). And, we know that how well the tools and methods of our field are accepted varies according to where a person is on the Greek-Roman scale. For example, a Greek-type programmer will only reluctantly accept CASE tools (especially data-flow diagram editors) if he finds himself working in a group larger than he can handle. Conversely, a Roman-type developer expects always to be in such groups because he expects to work on very large projects and *expects* these kinds of tools to be available.

It seems to us that there is a negative aspect to the Roman view. It suggests that those who use informal methods (the Greeks) are somehow unfit to be programmers and must be expunged from programming groups. We know of software development projects where these so-called *eccentrics* were indeed expunged. The saying went: "We had the firing squad in the parking lot."

To let you know where we fit on the Greek-Roman scale, we both see ourselves as Greek in temperament, although we would both place the other closer to the Roman end of the scale. We favor the Greek temperament because it provides creative juice. Unless there is some creative juice present, programming is dull, boring, and uninteresting. We don't want to work in such environments.

Of course, we must give Cæsar his due; but, when Cæsar's method takes all the creativity, visualization, passion, and magic out of our work, then we will object. And, to us, that is what often seems to be happening using Cæsar's methods. We find that the system is analyzed down to the most minute detail, to the point where the actual writing of the software becomes automatic.

This might be where the future is leading us, and some observers believe it to be. But, if it is, then it will be an uninteresting future and the next book we write will be about how to switch careers. We hope these observers are wrong, or wrong to a large extent.

We have no problem with code generators producing COBOL at prodigious rates; we need them. It is a blessing to have some help there. But, we hope that no one mistakes the organizational power of the Roman method with the necessary creativity of the Greek one. When the balance between the Roman and Greek ways are overwhelmed by the Roman, the human interfaces are multiplied, the programmers are not able to form an integrated view of the problem they are solving, any shared vision of the solution disintegrates, costs go up, and quality goes down.

Along this line, here is a convention that will appear periodically throughout this book. When we are referring to the Roman view of some concept (for example, Structured Stuff, Structured analysis, design, and programming together with the Waterfall model), we will use all upper-case letters: STRUCTURED STUFF. When we refer to the Greek view, we will use all lowercase: structured stuff. When we refer to the balance we urge, which allows each side an appropriate role, we capitalize the first letters: Structured Stuff. In our opinion, the appropriate roles are that the Romans provide a working context in which the Greeks get to do their stuff and express their results in formal terms for the Romans.

Greece vs. Rome in Different Kinds of Shops

As an example of the Greek-Roman contrast we ran across repeatedly, we present the following descriptions of two kinds of software development shops. One is large and either has an internal customer, such as Payroll, or it has a very large external customer, such as the government. The other is small and usually deals with individual outside customers.

We have noticed that when we are dealing with a programming shop that has as its main customer either another part of its enterprise or the government, it has certain characteristics:

- It tends to be very formal
- It produces larger programs than otherwise would be the case
- It over-manages software projects

- It has a fairly strict hierarchy
- It loves CASE and methods such as STRUCTURED STUFF
- It produces a great deal of documentation of rather poor quality

When the customer is outside the enterprise (but not the government) the characteristics change:

- The organization tends to be less formal
- Programs seem to be smaller and have less functionality than otherwise would be the case
- Projects are, if anything, under-managed
- The hierarchy is not rigid
- CASE is a four-letter word and programmers use structured stuff
- Documentation is minimal, but may be of the highest quality

We know of an excellent teacher of Structured Analysis and Design who cannot produce software very well when he practices STRUCTURED STUFF in the workplace.

We know of another practitioner who does very well producing software, but he does not use STRUCTURED STUFF. Instead, he uses structured stuff. What we mean by this is that he holds the ideas of structured stuff in his mind and uses them informally in his work.

The first practitioner loves CASE and METHODS; the second sees no use for either one in the formal sense.

We know of an even better teacher who was first a successful practitioner. He gave up teaching structured stuff because the officials where he worked complained that he didn't teach STRUCTURED STUFF.

We have written about the parable of two programmers in our previous book. In the parable, two enterprises have exactly the same problem. The problem is given to two programmers to solve.

The first programmer sees the problem as an opportunity to use orthodox methods and create a team to produce the solution. He shows a great deal of activity: meetings, reports, etc. The other programmer sees the problem as an opportunity to apply his skills to solve the problem and spends his time thinking with little apparent outside activity.

The first programmer had an overblown solution and schedules for repair and testing. The other programmer produced a simple solution with no known problems.

The first programmer was rewarded (because, for example, his productivity rate in lines of code produced was higher), and the second was chastised. We cannot state categorically that this is the state of affairs in our field, but why were there so many knowing smiles when we showed the story around to our correspondents? Why did it seem to reflect the experience so many of us had? We believe that there was much truth in it. Some people depend on organization, thrive on formal processes, and use other people as tools. Other people depend on themselves, prefer informal processes, and use inanimate objects as tools.

1.2 CONTROL AND CORPORATE CULTURE

Companies seem to have a corporate culture that emphasizes either of the following:

- Management, with the goal being to control in order to improve
- Technologists, with the goal being to experiment in order to improve

Certainly, that is the message of the Greek vs. Roman material we have just seen. The deeply felt view of Peter DeGrace and Leslie Hulet Stahl is clear: there are Greek organizations focusing on the skills and talents of the technologist as the best way to good product, and there are Roman organizations focusing on the orchestration and control offered by management as the best way to good product.

Is *The Olduvai Imperative* the only place that dichotomous view is identified? As it turns out, the answer is no. Independently, and in a completely different part of the software forest, Stan Rifkin (then of the Software Engineering Institute—SEI) and Charles Cox came to the same conclusion at about the same time.

Whereas DeGrace and Stahl spent their formative years at an aerospace company, Boeing, participating in software projects of various kinds, Rifkin and Cox came to their similar cultural conclusions during an SEI-supported study.

The purpose of the study was to explore what made certain institutions better at generating and using software metrics than others. They visited one or more divisions of the following companies in pursuit of that question: Contel, Digital Equipment, Hewlett-Packard, Hughes Aircraft, IBM, McDonnell Douglas, NASA, NCR, and TRW. What did they learn there?

Interestingly, what they learned is what the lead sentences of this article say. That is, Rifkin and Cox came to the conclusion that some companies are management/control-driven and others technologist/experimentation-driven, and were saying that publicly and independently at about the same time that DeGrace and Stahl were putting the finishing touches on their book!

But Rifkin-Cox added one dimension beyond the experienced and educated opinions of DeGrace and Stahl. In their study, Rifkin and Cox clearly found that the companies which emphasized technology and experimentation were the leaders in the successful use of metrics. And the other companies, the ones that focused on management and control? Their metrics programs were not as successful.

Rifkin cited Digital Equipment and Hewlett-Packard as examples of engineering-focused companies. Most companies, he said, are of the other kind. They are characterized by a hierarchical organizational system with an emphasis on control.

What do the successful metrics companies do?

- They tend to have achieved an SEI process level of 4 or 5 (very good) without ever having passed through level 3. That is, they measure and use feedback to improve their software process without ever having invoked a defined process! (That is, of course, the epitome of technologist/experimentation vs. management/control.)

- They have "decriminalized" errors. People talk openly about what they have done wrong as a means of self-improvement. There is no need to hide failure; management is not allowed to, or simply does not, use it against you.

- Measurement is part of "how we do business." That is, there is no management mandate or policy that causes measurement to happen, but rather a common understanding that it is the only reasonable way to build product.

What we learn from Rifkin and Cox, then, is that not only is there support for the DeGrace/Stahl view of Greek and Roman software cultures, but there is some evidence—fairly narrowly focused, to be sure—that the Greek way (the technologist/experimentation way, in Rifkins/Cox's terms) can be shown to be the better way.

Neither Rifkin/Cox nor DeGrace/Stahl focus heavily on the word "creativity" in their discussions. However, it is not too much of a stretch of the imagination to say that the technologist/experimentation method would provide more opportunities for creativity than the management/control one. Perhaps Michael A. Cusumano best makes the linkage in his book *Japan's Software Factories* when, while discussing the benefits and problems of a software factory approach, he says:

"On the one hand, too much emphasis on individual creativity and independence might create problems in controlling development costs, quality, and long-term maintenance. On the other hand, too much structure and control might stifle creativity, innovation, and the ability to change—as well as prompt rebellion from managers, developers, and perhaps customers."

Certainly, our intuition would agree with Cusumano's words, that creativity and control are, to some extent, enemies. And that, in turn, supports the notion that the technologist/experimentation way is linked more closely than the management/control way to software creativity.

We will explore some further dimensions of these differences in the sections and chapters to come.

REFERENCES

STAN RIFKIN and CHARLES COX, "Measurement in Practice," CMU/SEI-91-TR-16, also published in *Proceedings of the Sixteenth Annual Software Engineering Workshop*, NASA Goddard Space Flight Center, December 1991.

MICHAEL A. CUSUMANO, *Japan's Software Factories*, Oxford University Press, 1991.

2

OF TWO MINDS:
AN INFORMAL LOOK
AT SOFTWARE CREATIVITY

> *"Our [Japanese] children are drilled and our school system is imbued with . . . uniformity . . . Deviation from the standard is [barely allowed]. Creativity is punished . . . The question 'why' is not interpreted as a healthy sign of curiosity—it is a personal offense toward the integrity of the teacher . . . Brain power in Japan is limited; the nation works hard, but it does not think hard."*

> —from "Breaking the Mould" by Hisao Yamada in *The Discipline of Curiosity*, Jenny Groen, Eefke Smit, and Juurd Eijsvoogel, eds. Elsevier Science, 1990

There are several ways to approach the creation of a book on software creativity:

- You could take a frothy swipe at the topic, the "whack on the side of the head" view of creativity, with a lot of good advice about how to be more creative and lots of anecdotes about people who used the advice successfully.
- You could take a fairly serious, academic view of the topic, doing a lot of library research and spelling out everything we've ever learned in any discipline on the subject.
- You could take an informal view of the topic from the point of view of whether creativity is important to software.

This book makes a gesture at all three of these approaches, but really puts its heart into the latter one. In this chapter we get to that heart of the matter. The essays that follow are largely an informal collection of thoughts about the importance of creativity in software.

Framing this issue, it seems to me, are several more well-known and already key issues in the software field:

- The role of discipline
- The role of formal methods
- The role of optimizing solutions
- The role of quantitative reasoning
- The role of process
- The role of theory
- The role of academe
- The role of fun

In my mind, every one of those issues is really an issue about creativity. To the extent that we are creative in building software, I believe:

- We break free of (at least some) discipline.
- We move from formal methods to less formal ones.
- We adapt to providing solutions that satisfy rather than optimize.
- We shift from quantitative to qualitative reasoning.
- We look at both process and product.
- We understand that sometimes good practice is ahead of good theory, and that industry knows some things that academe does not.
- And we have more fun in the doing!

It is in this spirit of dichotomy—that creativity means breaking free of traditional patterns—that I chose the words "of two minds" in the chapter title. Each of the titles that follow is expressed as a controversy: formal methods vs. heuristics, quantitative vs. qualitative reasoning, industry vs. academe. I believe we live in a world, as this book is written, that has placed heavy emphasis on the disciplined, formal approaches to building software. I want to express that there are not only alternatives to that contemporary conventional wisdom, but that there are good reasons for moving away from that wisdom and toward a more balanced view of the field.

There are as many questions as answers in this chapter. Is discipline always the right approach to use on software projects? Is computer science right in placing its emphasis so strongly on formal methods? Is it true that "you can't manage what you can't measure"? Is theory always ahead of practice? Must serious thinking replace fun in our field? While exploring answers to those questions, I encounter and raise others.

However, there are some definitive answers here as well. There are research findings from a study of the tasks of software: To what extent are they intellectual? Clerical? Creative? Some of these definitive answers may surprise you.

I noticed something interesting about myself as I put this material together. There are a few essays in what follows that I wrote some time ago. There is something present in those essays, I notice now, that is lacking in my more recent work. The recent work may be more thoughtful, better researched, with more substantiation of the points I want to make, but the earlier work makes better reading. The words chosen are more colorful. The word play is more artistic. The joy of authorship comes through more clearly. In short, those earlier essays are more creative.

There must be some way to retain that creative flair while evolving a more thoughtful technique. At least I hope there is. I think it is important for those of us who care about software to find a blend that works. That is what this chapter is really about.

"Science is not just curiosity and creativity; it is a disciplined form of it . . . It is the seemingly odd couple of discipline and curiosity that makes for scientific progress. The curiosity of creativite minds, asking continuously 'How?' and 'Why?' and the discipline to realize that science is part of the world, that it is shaping it."

—Janny Groen in *The Discipline of Curiosity,* Elsevier
Science, 1990; Janny Groen, Eefke Smit, Juurd Eijsvoogel

2.1   DISCIPLINE VERSUS FLEXIBILITY

Perhaps you could help me with something.

This section is about discipline and its opposite. It is about the relationship between an obedient, self-controlled way of building software and . . . its opposite.

What I want to say is that the opposite of a disciplined approach is a creative approach, but that's not really true. The two terms are solidly related, I believe, but they are not opposites.

The obvious opposite of disciplined, of course, is "undisciplined." But what a lot of baggage that word carries! Given that disciplined, in my dictionary, derives from discipline: "training that produces obedience, self-control, or a particular skill; controlled behavior produced by such training; punishment given to correct a person or enforce obedience; a branch of instruction or learning"; then undisciplined, although it is not listed in my dictionary, would surely have to mean "disobedient, not self-controlled, or skill-less behavior; out of control behavior."

That's not what I'm looking for at all!

The problem with creativity as an opposite to discipline is that it means a whole lot more than just that. Defining creative, my dictionary says "having the power or ability to create things; showing imagination and originality as well as routine skills."

Most of the rest of the sections of this chapter, in fact, explore various aspects of creativity and its collection of opposites. To bound creativity by calling it an opposite of discipline is too limiting, I think.

I've struggled with this dilemma of discipline and its opposite now throughout the creation of this book. Each time I return to the subject, hoping to have gained some new insight, my well comes up dry yet again. What I want to do is distinguish between behavior that is channeled and controlled (disciplined behavior), and behavior that is freewheeling yet focused (creative behavior).

While you've been reading this, have you had any good ideas?

What I have come up with is the word "flexibility." Focusing on the obedience and control aspects of discipline, I have chosen flexibility as its opposite. My dictionary defines flexible as "able to bend easily without breaking; adaptable, able to be changed to suit circumstances."

I like the definition, but I'm less sure that it's an appropriate opposite to discipline. So I'm not happy with the choice, but I guess it will have to do. If you have come up with a better word, mentally insert it into the title of this section!

Anyhow, enough of word play. Why is a section about discipline and (er) flexibility in a book on software creativity? Because one of the oldest dichotomies of our profession has been precisely this difference: Should software be built by teams that are disciplined and factory-like, or by teams that are flexible and highly self-motivated?

In fact, of course, the dichotomy precedes software. As the world moved out of the cottage-industry era into the smokestack era, it became very clear—at least back then—that disciplined approaches were the way of the future, and flexible approaches were not. The age of the automobile would not have been possible, of course, without Henry Ford's notion of a de-skilled, disciplined work force.

But that was then, and this is now. The smokestack era, most would agree, has given way to the information era. The society that used to depend on what we could make out of expensive raw materials by forging them in huge factories now finds that it depends on information enabled by literally cheap-as-dirt silicon. Knowledge workers are the key to the future, not factory workers. The question is, what is the best way to organize and optimize teams of knowledge workers?

Surely software developers are the ultimate knowledge workers. If you even slightly believe the claims of David Parnas and Fred Brooks that "software is hard" to build, that it is "the most complex activity ever undertaken by human beings," then it is easy to imagine that old models for organizing factory people simply would not work in the information era.

It is interesting to note that today's successful software houses fund their software development activities under the financial heading "research and development." That is, these companies see the building of software not as some sort of manufacturing activity, but as something more analogous to the mental explorations of a researcher.

Now think for a moment about research and development. Is it about "obedience" and "controlled behavior"? Of course not. Discipline may play a role in research and development (we will explore this theme further in the essays to follow), but flexibility—or whatever your choice for that word is—is far more important.

The relative roles of discipline and flexibility in software, then, should be determined by a model right at the heart of our understanding of the field of software development. Is the correct model destined to be factory-like, where assembly-line workers stamp out and install software parts all day long, or is it craft- and research-and-development-like, where developers puzzle over intellectual challenges during their workday?

That is the issue we explore in this section. To illustrate that the question is not a new one, I include ("reuse" sounds like a far better word in our field!) an essay first published 20 years ago (note its reference to keypunch operators, listings, and programmers in suits!) That first essay, "Will the Real Henry Ford of Software Please Stand Up?", still frames the issue nicely, I think. And the final essay, "The 'Odd Couple' of Discipline and Creativity," represents my personal choice for a resolution of the dichotomy.

Read on! And think about your own answer to the "Discipline versus Flexibility" dichotomy as you do.

Will the Real Henry Ford of Software Please Stand Up?

The corporate headquarters of Alchemy Chemical and Softli Paper are no more than a mile apart on the Straightarrow Turnpike in Open Spaces, Massachusetts.

But their computing shops might as well be on Mars and Mercury.

They are light-years apart in organizational philosophy. And the extremes in which they find themselves are characteristic of the dilemmas of modern computing.

Over at Alchemy, Stan Sorcerer runs a tight ship. His employees have a dress code, fixed working hours, specified coffee breaks and a strict behavior program. The standards defined for his programmers are profuse and rigid. Both documentation and listings are subject to periodic inspection and surprise review. Fortran and COBOL are required languages for all applications, and precompilers are used to both encourage and enforce structured programming standards. Management of tasks is by schedule, and if a programmer gets behind in his work he is expected to put in voluntary overtime to make it up. The atmosphere in Alchemy is tense, businesslike and productive. Stan is fond of quoting data which shows his programmers produce at 3 times the national average. From all outside appearances, Stan Sorcerer has built himself a software factory, and he runs his shop like an assembly line.

But at Softli Paper, Herb Bond sees things differently. Herb's programmers' dress could best be described as neo-hippy. They come and go through the swinging doors of Softli at all hours of the day or night. Their standards manual would fit within the index of that used at Alchemy, and it uses words like "can" and occasionally "should" instead of "shall" and "will." Herb uses peer code reviews but never conducts management code inspections. Fortran and COBOL are the predominant languages, but one of his ace programmers is coding a report generator program in PASCAL now, and loving it. Management of tasks is by progress reporting, with emphasis on product quality rather than schedule. The atmosphere at Softli is laid back, unbusinesslike, and resembles a graduate school seminar. Herb never quotes statistics about programmer productivity, but he has been heard to say that he doesn't believe anyone who does—he's seen how they got their numbers. From all outside appearances, Herb Bond is herding a group of untamed software craftsmen in the general direction of product completion.

Now it is patently obvious that Stan Sorcerer and Herb Bond can't both be right about how to run a computing shop. Either programmers should function like an assembly line, or as craftsmen, right? But which?

Well, the question just isn't that easy to answer. Ten years ago, the assembly line philosophy appeared to be the only way to go. Software was characteristically overly complex, too expensive, and behind schedule. Software modules were hand-fabricated and fitted together by craftsmen. It seemed obvious that software's characteristic problems were caused by its craftsman approach.

Acting on that presumption, management poured a great deal of money into finding ways of assembly-lining software construction. COBOL was the first hope—an English language by means of which you talked to computers. Managers could read it, and grocery clerks could code it.

It didn't work out that way, though. No matter how you sliced it, programs were still programs. They had a level of nitty-gritty detail that managers simply didn't care to read, and grocery clerks couldn't fathom. And COBOL didn't change that.

Management kept trying, though. Techniques which promised standardization were encouraged. Individuality was played down, and teamwork stressed. The term "ego-less programming" was invented. Configuration control and quality assurance were formalized. And when structured programming came along promising miracles, management bought it with alacrity. The promised land of assembly-line programming seemed on the horizon at last.

But there was a giant irony in this quest for the ultimate automation. While researchers poured their energy into assembly line techniques, hardly anyone was paying attention to the technologist's state of the art. In spite of all the assembly line action, it was still craftsmen who were producing software. And no one was developing and promoting better tools for those craftsmen. Oh, actually, that's not quite true. There were technologists whose efforts were directed toward creating better tools. But hardly anyone cared. If a new technique didn't promise a dramatic shift toward the assembly line, few managers cared to look further into it. And without management support, new tools never made it into the production programmer's hands.

Let me make one thing perfectly clear. I don't mean to be saying that assembly line programming won't happen, some day. Like, the Henry Ford of software may be designing the ultimate fabrication method somewhere right now. But while researchers and funders continue that search, someone needs to be concentrating on the nearer term needs. It is foolish to move the field impetuously into an assembly line posture when no one knows how to design an assembly line. And it is foolish to suspend tool development and usage because someday we won't need them any more.

That's enough of a soapbox presentation, though. Perhaps I digress too far from the world of Straightarrow Turnpike, and Stan Sorcerer, and Herb Bond.

Or perhaps I don't. Stan Sorcerer's shop is the culmination of today's state of the art in assembly line techniques. And Herb Bond's shop is the culmination of the craftsmen-at-work approach. And that soapbox oratory was an attempt to explain why no one can really say that Stan and his productivity figures are right, and Herb is wrong. Or vice versa.

But, to get back to the realm of Alchemy and Softli . . . the dichotomy between the two companies obviously did not go unnoticed by the programmers in the two shops. In fact, Friday evenings at the Straightarrow Tavern sometimes got fairly exciting if a few of the crew from Alchemy and Softli showed up at the same time. And it was one of those Friday evenings which led to the point of this story.

Picture the scene. Promptly at 4:43, a couple of car pools of Alchemy programmers drop by the Straightarrow on their way home from work. Properly dressed in their code-compatible dark grey suits and ties, they look with some disdain on a couple of bearded Softli folk nursing drinks in a corner, clad as they are in faded Wranglers and less than new Adidas. The look does not go unnoticed, and one of the Softli pair, who has been at the Straightarrow longer than is wise considering that he is scheduled for a 6 p.m. block of computer time, makes a derogatory comment about the coding skills and ancestry of Alchemy programmers in general, and about this group in particular.

Now if the Straightarrow drew a factory crowd, fisticuffs and other physical symptoms might have erupted on the spot. But in the think-tank-type atmosphere of this particular tav, skilled and polished verbal violence broke out instead. Fine phrases formed and flew forcefully about the room. Before the battle was half warmed-up, Alchemy's dress code had been characterized as Hitlerian, and Softli's standards as vacuous; Alchemy's working hours as beancounter-inspired, and Softli's productivity as high but negative; and Alchemy's structured programming as proceduralized nits, with Softli's working habits as kindergartenish. And the verbal fireworks were still escalating.

I'm not sure who it was who first suggested the code-off. I'm not even sure it was a good idea, in the long term. But as a battle stopper, it was a winner. The idea clanged like a bell in the forensic uproar, and silence followed by enthusiastic negotiation over terms quickly subdued the crowd. The idea was amazingly simple—it was one of those "my father is bigger than your father" numbers. It was a put up or shut up topper to all the other verbiage. It was "if you think you're such a good group of programmers, let's see if you can beat us."

The idea spread like wildfire. By the time the assorted group left the Straightarrow in their various directions that night, the groundrules had been set.

The code-off was simple enough. Two programs were to be designed and coded by two teams, one from each company. The first program was a report generator, relatively straightforward and unsophisticated. The second was a small precompiler for a language with a couple of complex data types and tricky semantics. Entities to be measured in the study were time to complete the program, cost to complete the program, and quality of the finished program. Quality was subjective, of course, but the group negotiated a matrix of quality attributes to help introduce some objectivity into the scoring, and selected a team of scorers from each company. Four successive Saturday mornings at the Straightarrow were set aside for the competition.

The Rose Bowl had nothing on the Straightarrow that series of Saturdays. Crowds from both companies packed the place, as word spread rapidly through both computing departments. Some of the keypunch girls from Alchemy formed a somewhat impromptu cheerleading team, clad in matching and properly modest skirts and sweaters; and a group of staff analysts from Softli used a portable CRT terminal to track the competition in real time. By the time the third Saturday had rolled around, the local ACM chapter had turned out en masse, and on the fourth Saturday reporters from the Open Spaces Clarion Call and the Straightarrow Post were there taking notes and pictures. It was the biggest thing to hit Open Spaces since Hurricane Giselda.

The results of the codeoff, in case you're waiting with baited breath, were an anti-climax. Scoring anomalies aside, it was a standoff. The Alchemy Assembly Liners had an easier time with the report generator, and scored well in time and cost factors. But the Softli Craftsmen did better with the precompiler, and their quality scores were higher. Which was perhaps a best-of-all-possible-worlds resolution, given the nature of the competition—nobody lost, and nobody felt bad as the crowd filed out of the Straightarrow that last Saturday, many of them three coding sheets to the wind.

Sometimes, though, I wonder what would've happened if someone had really won. I mean, suppose you could really prove that assembly lining was better than craftsmanship. Or vice versa.

Can you imagine Stan Sorcerer being wrong, and letting his programmers come to work in sports shirts? Or Herb Bond being wrong, and demanding that his programmers work an 8–4:30 shift? Somehow, I'm glad the Henry Ford of software hasn't come forth yet. But maybe he'll show up at the Straightarrow next year—just in time for the second annual Open Spaces code-off!

Software Automation: Fact or Fraud?

"A no muss, no fuss software factory." That's the alluring picture painted in [Moad90] and a thousand other popularized articles on the future of software development. But is it really achievable?

The claims are well-known. "We produced more than 400 new programs with no failures and helped reduce maintenance by 70–90%," claims one enthusiastic manager who employed some new technology. "We can deliver [an application] as fast as they [the users] can take it," he goes on to gush [Moad90].

However, there is an opposite side to that picture. A lot of software people are less than enthusiastic about the same kinds of new technology. Is it stubbornness, or is there something missing in those glowing reports of success? Will advanced technology—some call it "software automation"—be able to fulfill the claims now made for it?

In the same article with those positive reports comes a sober warning: "The reason so many are cautious is that we've had so many dead ends," says another software manager. And: "Right now, very few [IS] people can go on record as saying that the high-level analysis and design tools don't work. Who wants to be the bringer of bad news?" says yet another.

The battle lines are clearcut. But who is right here?

There is certainly plenty at stake. We all know those numbers that say the cost of building software in the world is very large. So, we've all been exposed to the data that says software productivity has increased comparatively little over the last few decades. Certainly we in software all wish there were some magic solution to that data and those numbers. But can wishing—coupled with a little perspiration—make it so?

Some say yes. They tend to be the people selling solutions and the people seeking research grants to find new solutions. There is no shortage of promised breakthroughs in our ability to build software.

Some say no. They tend to be the people who have built software for a living for a long time and have seen similar claims rise and fall. There is also no shortage of naysayers to those promised breakthroughs.

Unfortunately, there is no data to support either position. There is, of course, wonderful and profuse anecdotal evidence. The gentleman above who built software so fast that his customers couldn't use it all is one case in point. So are the managers who trained all their people in some new "breakthrough" methodology, forgot they did it, and then tried to impose a competing and incompatible methodology a few years later because of the claims made for *it*. One can attempt to prove *any* point of view with anecdotes.

Slowly but surely, however, there are an increasing number of key people who are dubious about these claims. Among the first to go on record was noted computer scientist David L. Parnas, who expressed his doubts about the potential for automated software development in his article, "Software Aspects of Strategic Defense Systems" [Parnas85]. Then came another software guru, Fred Brooks, who expressed similar doubts and many more [Brooks87]. Two specialists doing research in the field of software automation expressed their concerns over exaggerated claims (they went so far as to call them myths!) [Rich88].

More recently, the chorus has grown. Carma McClure, known in the past for being in the super-enthusiast's camp, has characterized the CASE movement as one in which "the emperor has no clothes"—CASE, she says, has yielded little in productivity gains [SD90]. In my own analysis, also reported in [SD90], the decade of the '80s, born in the hope that it would be the decade of productivity improvements, had its belief in that buzzword go bust. Wonderment was expressed by Mark Duncan, also in [SD90], who found himself "amused and perplexed at MIS's frenzied preoccupation with productivity."

Could these (admittedly very personal) beliefs be valid? Is there, in fact, no breakthrough to be had here? Is the only thing "to be had" the people who believe that breakthroughs are possible?

What we need here is some good, old-fashioned, scientific-method research. Propose a hypothesis about some particular "breakthrough" in software productivity. Design some research to explore the truth or falsehood of that hypothesis. Perhaps set up an experimental study, conduct a survey, or do protocol analysis on people actively using the new idea and its older counterparts. There are many legitimate choices of research approach. What is lacking is not the knowledge of what ought to be done, but the commitment—and, unfortunately, the funding (this kind of research is not cheap)—to do it.

In short, what is needed here is to strip away the advocacy, the locked-in posturing, that characterizes much of what we know about "software automation" in 1995 (and, for that matter, in 1985, and 1975, and 1965!) and replace it with some objectivity, some truth-for-truth's-sake exploration.

There *are* a few examples of this kind of work, fortunately. A lot of it is being done at NASA-Goddard's Software Engineering Laboratory and being reported at its annual Software Engineering Workshop. Some is being done in the community that explores programmers at work to evolve theory: the Empirical Studies of Programmers people, who are trying to reinstate their annual conference that suspended activity for awhile in the late 1980s.

There is also a scattering of good work done by individual researchers who are more concerned with truth than with advocacy. As one tiny example, [Davis88] contains a particularly insightful and specific analysis of what is good—and what is not—about modern CASE tools.

If enough people—researchers in both the academic and industrial worlds, and at institutions like the Software Engineering Institute—get caught up in this kind of exploration, perhaps we will come to better understand the underlying issue here.

Some say that software production is or should be a science. Lots of rigor. Lots of theory. Some mathematics sprinkled on to facilitate the work. There is a feeling that with enough science, enough discipline, software automation is possible.

Some say that it is more like an art. Lots of creativity. Lots of free thinking. Some techniques sprinkled on to facilitate *that* work. There is a feeling that discipline and automation simply won't work.

Yet another manager quoted in [Moad90] expressed it best. "What we've been trying to do is make software development more of a science, but what we have found is that some people are scientists and some people are artists. Many of our most creative people come from the artists, so we don't want to lose that."

With appropriate research findings, perhaps we can learn how and when best to use those scientists and artists among us. As with most issues where the opposing sides have become entrenched, the truth probably lies in some middle ground.

REFERENCES

BROOKS, FRED—"No Silver Bullet," *IEEE Computer*, April 1987.

DAVIS, GORDON B.—"Commentary," *Accounting Horizons*, June 1988.

MOAD, JEFF—"The Software Revolution," *Datamation*, February 15, 1990.

PARNAS, DAVID—"Software Aspects of Strategic Defense Systems," *American Scientist*, September 1985.

RICH, CHARLES, RICHARD C. WATERS—"Automatic Programming: Myths and Prospects," *IEEE Computer*, August 1988.

SD90—"Report on the System Development Conference," *System Development*, April 1990.

Are Programmers Really "Out of Control"?

A famous computer scientist often says that, when he first joined a software-producing group in industry, his observation was, "These programmers are out of control."

It is certainly possible to build a case for this control problem in software development. The traditional stereotype of a programmer is an unkempt person clad in torn jeans and sandals working strange hours and eating enormous quantities of unhealthy food. And that stereotype applies not just to the programmer of yesteryear, but to the hacker of today. With people such as that, anarchistic in appearance, is it any wonder that control leaps to a potential manager's mind as an issue to be dealt with?

The issue of control is, of course, intimately connected to the issue of programmer discipline. Control is the vehicle for instilling discipline. If discipline is vital to the ability to produce software, control is an essential part of the software manager's repertoire.

Certainly it is easy to find those who cry out for more control and more discipline. For example, we frequently see statements to this effect: " . . . the introduction of strict discipline and mechanization through the application of advanced software engineering . . . offers a practical solution . . . The time for such introduction is ripe . . . " [Lehman89].

However, there is a vital underlying issue here. Does control really result in more effective software development? Are there any studies, any data, to support or refute the need for control? Is it really true in general that programmers are out of control?

The answer, unfortunately, is that there are few such studies. However, there are some odd findings, clinging to the fringes of research directed at other issues, which suggest that control and discipline may not be the solutions to the problems of software that some claim them to be.

One such odd finding is presented in [DeMarco87]. The result comes from an earlier study [Jeffery83] of the relationship between software estimation practices and the ability to achieve those estimates. In that study, these situations were set up:

1. Software was built to a schedule established by management.
2. Software was built to a schedule established by the technologists.
3. Software was built with no schedule imposed at all.

The study evaluated the productivity of the people who did the building. The findings were in some ways predictable, but in some ways quite a surprise:

1. Software productivity was higher when the developers set their own schedule as opposed to when they tried to meet one set by management. (This, of course, is not a surprise.)
2. Software productivity was highest when there was no schedule for them to keep to at all. (This, of course, is quite a surprise.)

These findings can be interpreted in a variety of ways. One interpretation hard to ignore is that, when left to their own devices (and thus "out of control"), software people are at their most effective! It is as if software people have an innate sense of responsibility, perhaps coupled with love of doing a good job, that is a more effective motivator than any amount of management pressure and control!

There is another similar finding, from an even older source. In an article exploring management technique, Lehman the author found that the tighter the control imposed on programmers, the less they produced [Lehman79]!

Granted that two pieces of data do not a finding make, this information should still make one pause. The trend since the very origins of software as a profession has been to seek more effective ways of controlling and disciplining programmers. The assumption here has been that in this spectrum of choice:

Theory X Management—Workers are unmotivated and must be coerced by management into doing a good job.

Theory Y Management—Workers are heavily motivated, and management need only facilitate them to obtain a good job.

Theory Z Management—A mix of facilitation and control is the best way to get workers to do a good job.

Somewhere between Theory X and Theory Z lay the proper method of managing software development. These findings suggest instead that proper management of software should be between Theory Y and Theory Z.

It is interesting to note that in more traditional scientific fields, the required mix is better understood. In the quotations below, for example, both speak of the need for a combination of creativity and discipline; but notice that the discipline they discuss must be largely *self*-imposed rather than imposed from without:

"Science is not just curiosity and creativity; it is a disciplined form of it . . . self-discipline . . . to follow up the brilliant new ideas with down-to-earth applications . . . It is this seemingly odd couple of discipline and curiosity that makes for scientific progress. The curiosity of creative minds, asking continuously How? and Why?, and the discipline to realize that science is part of the world, that it is shaping it" [Groen90].

"Any art that's worth its name has some kind of discipline associated with it. Some kind of rule—maybe it's not the rule of a sonnet, or a symphony, or a classical painting, but even the most limited contemporary art . . . has some kind of rule. The object is to get across what you're trying to get across, while sticking to the rules" [Judson80].

It is time to think more deeply about what we really mean when we speak of the need for more discipline and control in software. If it is self-discipline that we are discussing, control is not the way to achieve it. If it is the more traditional form of discipline, that imposed by control from without, we need to understand why these strange findings from the world of research do not mesh with that view.

Such fundamental questions as these may seem out of place 40 years downstream in our field. But 40 years is a very short time, after all, when compared to the history of other fields. It is not too late for software management to reconsider the questions "How?" and "Why?"

REFERENCES

DeMarco, Tom, Tim Lister—*Peopleware*, Dorset House, 1987.

Groen, Janny, Eefke Smit, Juurd Eijsvoogel—*The Discipline of Curiosity*, Elsevier Science, 1990.

Jeffery, Ross, and Lawrence, M. J.—"Managing Programmer Productivity," *Journal of Systems and Software*, January 1985.

Judson, Horace Freeland, quoting from a conversation with Murray Gell-Mann, the inventor of quarks, in *The Search for Solutions*, Holt, Rinehart and Winston, 1980.

Lehman, M. M.—"Uncertainty in Computer Application and Its Control Through the Engineering of Software," *Journal of Software Maintenance*, September *1989*.

Lehman, M. M.—"How Software Projects Are Really Managed," *Datamation*, January 1979.

Discipline Is a Dirty Word: A Story About the Software Life Cycle

Once upon a time there was a neat and tidy software life cycle. We studied the requirements of the problem to be solved. We designed a solution to fulfill those requirements. We coded that design. We tested that code. And we released the resulting software solution to the user for use and to the maintainers for maintenance.

Management became so enthusiastic about the software life cycle that they decided to manage to it. Literally. First you analyze the requirements, they would say. Then—and only then—should you start the design. And only when the design was complete could you start writing code. And of course testing could not begin until the code was complete, and users could not get the product until the tests had all been run.

In the world of intangibles that is software construction, it was so nice to have an ordering, a sequence of events that you could count on. And, in fact, you could do even more.

You could invent a "document-driven" version of this life cycle. After each phase was completed, there would be a document produced that would serve as the basis for the next phase. The requirements specification was needed to start design. The design document was needed to start coding. The unit development folder was essential to testing. The test report was a precursor of production and maintenance.

And—beauty of all beauties—suddenly the intangible became tangible. Management could now check project progress by examining those documents. And they could almost understand them! Instead of a few scraps of paper and an incomprehensible listing, there were now artifacts produced as part of the software process that management could read—even if it couldn't (or wouldn't) read the final product, the code itself.

But slowly, people began to realize, some bad things were happening.

First of all, software developers began spending enormous amounts of time on those documents. That wasn't all bad, of course, because the documents WERE important in the handoff to the next life-cycle phase. But if you know that a particular facet of your work is being judged by management, of course you spend quite a bit of time getting that right. And getting it pretty. The documents, realized the programmers, were more important than the program itself. After all, management didn't ever look at THAT! Those documents produced at the end of each life-cycle phase became the most important products of the software development process!

And then something else went wrong. As standards emerged for the content of the various phase-ending documents, software developers began to see that some documents that they had thought were important in the past simply were not. Or at least they were not high on the management check list, or in the standards definitions. For example, the standards for producing a user manual were cursory at best. And the standards for building maintenance documentation were sometimes non-existent. In the U.S. Department of Defense's standards, for example, little was said about either of these documents. And the result was, of course, that work on the user manual and the maintenance manual—hard to motivate in the past because many software developers hate to write—became afterthoughts, worth little more than cursory attention. After all, the phase-ending documents were clearly more important.

Maintainers were especially troubled here. Software documentation, from their point of view, has a short shelf-life. As the inevitable changes are made to the software product, most of the documents become out of date and worthless quite quickly. And the most worthless, from the maintainer's point of view, were those phase-ending documents. Who cared about the original Unit Development Folder, for example, when there was little or no information on how the software product was supposed to be used, or how it could be maintained? Everything seemed topsy-turvy. The maintainer got beautiful and polished documents that were mostly put on a shelf to gather dust, and didn't get the documents they needed to do their job. Did anyone really believe the data that said maintenance was 80% of the cost of software? If so, where was the emphasis on documentation that the maintainer could use?

Time passed, and slowly so did the emphasis on this rigid, document-driven life cycle. There were several forces at work to change the status quo. Most of those forces sprang in various ways from people who knew that this was not the right way to build software. Some people began discussing "rapid prototyping" and noted that its early cycle of design/code/test simply didn't fit with rigid phase endings and big, polished phase-ending documents. Other people began exploring alternative life-cycle definitions, like spirals and circles. Still others—primarily those who built software for a living who wanted to do the best job they knew how—quietly ignored the management direction and went ahead to do what they knew was right.

Let us stop and ponder, for a moment, that last group of people. These were the folks who might be characterized as "out of control." These were the folks who were using far from "disciplined" approaches. And yet, these were the folks who were doing the job right. What was going on here? And how prevalent was this situation?

The answer to the second question came, interestingly enough, from a research study. Marvin Zelkowitz, working at the University of Maryland, investigated the practices of a group of software developers, what they were doing and when they were doing it [Zelkowitz88]. He had them record what life-cycle phase they were nominally in (that is, what phase did management think they were in?) and what their activities actually were. He found that, in fact, almost no one was following the rigid life cycle. Developers nominally studying requirements may actually have been doing a little prototype coding and testing. Developers nominally doing design may have created design experiments, writing and testing sample code to check the feasibility of their design solution. Developers nominally doing coding might be going back over, and perhaps even revising, the requirements (occasionally) and the design (surprisingly often).

And developers nominally doing testing were doing almost all of the above.

In fact, Zelkowitz found, the rigid software life cycle was (although he didn't put it that way) a developer's joke. They told management what management wanted to hear, and did what they needed to do.

The answer to the first question above ("What was going on here?") was, in fact, that these unruly, undisciplined, out-of-control software developers were doing a good job of work *in spite of* management.

More time has passed since then, and of course the rigid view of the software life cycle has long since gone out of favor. Perhaps, then, software developers and management are in synchronization at last, and discipline and control have again been imposed on the software workplace.

However, I suspect that's not really true. My suspicion is that there is some other management-caused insanity happening out there now, and the programmers—as they have always done—are programming around it, doing things the right way, ignoring the foolish management direction, "out of control" as always. After all, nearly every study we see about the major problems of software says that it is management, not the technologists or the technology, that is the problem.

Some people have been saying for years that, in software, "discipline is a dirty word." That is probably going too far. And yet here, in this once upon a time story, it certainly was!

REFERENCE

ZELKOWITZ, MARVIN R.—"Resource Utilization During Software Development," *Journal of Systems and Software*, September 1988.

The Faking of Software Design

It's not often that someone is brilliant enough to solve a problem before the rest of us can even see that there is one.

But this is a story about just such an event.

Once upon a time, more than a decade ago, all of us in software learned that top-down, requirements-driven approaches were the best way to build software. We take the top-level requirements, and use hierarchic decomposition techniques to chop up a big, unsolvable problem into a bunch of smaller solvable ones in an orderly fashion, so that when we are done there is this nice tree-structure-like definition of our problem and our solution.

Then something strange happened. One of the best-known computer scientists, David Parnas (who gained perhaps his greatest fame via his paper on the decomposition of software into modules), wrote an odd paper that essentially told us how to fake top-down design when we wrote our design documentation—the words "fake it" were even in the title of the paper!

Fake top-down design? Why should we do that?

Time passed. Parnas's paper seemed an anomaly, something out of synch with the rest of the brilliant work he had done. Fake top-down design indeed!

And then, from another part of the computing forest, came another rather strange finding. Bill Curtis, leading a group of computing researchers at the Microelectronics and Computing Consortium (MCC), began to do empirical studies of the process of design as conducted by skilled designers. In Curtis' early papers, he contrasted two design approaches; "controlled" design and "opportunistic" design. Controlled design proceeded the way we all knew it should, top-down and at least somewhat hierarchically. Opportunistic design proceeded in ways totally dependent on the individual designer, sometimes appearing almost random. At this early stage in these findings, we all wondered at those disorganized, opportunistic designers. Why would they behave in such an obviously incorrect way?

However, as more time went by, the findings of the Curtis people changed. Controlled design, they began to see more and more often, was not what good designers really did. Opportunistic design became more and more what they observed in their studies. The designer's mind, engaged in solving one problem, would dart off to another, usually more complex, problem. If one thought of the overall and emerging design as the tree structure we all thought it should be, these opportunistic diversions went to places on the tree that were remote and relatively unconnected to the place where the mind was nominally functioning.

What was going on here? Whatever it was, the finding became so prevalent that Curtis began saying, publicly, things like "The undisturbed design process is opportunistic." People simply don't do what we were all sure they were doing.

Were we observing here a fundamental flaw in how practitioners design software? Or were we observing a fundamental flaw in our model of how they *should* design software?

It is time now to reintroduce Parnas' "fake it" into our story. Remember that, for some odd reason, he told us how to fake a top-down design in our documentation even if we hadn't done our design in that way.

In Curtis's findings lies the explanation. Those opportunistic designs produced by good designers simply aren't going to be top-down. Yet it would be impossible for the non-designer to follow the opportunistic trail of the creative process of building such a design. So we "fake" a top-down description of the design, because that is the only way readers of the design will be capable of understanding it.

With the Parnas piece of the puzzle clicking into place with the Curtis pieces, we begin to see that the problem lies not with design practice, but with design theory. Theory was idealized and, as it turned out, inaccurate. Our fundamental flaw lay in the model of the design process, not in its practice.

So where does this leave us? With our theoretical model of design serving us well as a representation schema, even if we have to fake it; and with our empirical model of design, called "opportunistic" by Curtis, serving us well as the real way we perform our design activities.

Because "opportunistic" still has a strange, perhaps random, perhaps even negative connotation, I like to think of this process in another way. When the mind reaches off in its opportunistic way, most often what it is doing is making sure that it solves the hard problems before it solves the dependent easier ones. We could almost define a new kind of tree structure here, not driven from the top by its overall requirements, but by some ordering of difficulty blended with coupling.

However, there is a problem with that view. What is a hard problem to one person may not be to another; problems tend to be hard if we have not solved them before, and each of us brings a different set of experiences to the act of design. Therefore, each person's hard-problem tree structure will be different from each other person's. How can a sensible model of design be built from that?

I prefer to think that the act of design is and should be what I call "hard-part-first design." I believe that covers, at least to some extent, what Curtis's empirical studies have discovered; and "hard-part-first" has a more organized image (whether it should or not!) than "opportunistic."

Be that as it may, it is not the terminology that counts here, so much as the understanding. Design is and ought to be opportunistic. Design representation ought to be, and usually is, top-down. And David Parnas gave us the answer even before most of us understood the question!

The Strange Case of the Proofreader's Pencil

Sometimes the battle between discipline and freedom narrows down to absurdly small details. The case of the pencil behind the ear is just such a story.

It happened when I was in college, eking out a living—as do most college students—with a summer job unrelated to my eventual professional interests. I was a proofreader, one of those people who read the newspaper galley proofs before they become the newspaper delivered to your door, looking for errors (it was the first paid debugging experience of my career!). The newspaper was the Quincy Illinois Herald-Whig, a small-city, middle-America newspaper with all the conservative stability that the paper's name implies.

There were two of us proofreaders on the evening shift of the paper. Our job was to proof the galleys for the morning edition, which was delivered to the rural subscribers of the paper by overnight mail. The paper was, at heart, an evening paper, and *that* edition had been delivered to the residents of Quincy by delivery people before we evening shifters even showed up to go to work. The point of all of this is that the evening shift was not a prestige time to work—we summer temporaries, and our boss, were not on the Herald Whig's advancement fast track!

One evening, as I had almost every other evening, I was sitting at my proofreader's desk, a bright light shining down on proof copy spread out in front of me, looking alertly for the inevitable typos. The typesetters were pretty good at their job, so the error incidence was well under one per paragraph of copy. My proofreader's marking pencil rested, as it always did, behind my right ear, ready to be grabbed to mark an error whenever I found one.

My boss, who had a peculiar mix of management styles that included gruff command-barking and slouching around, was making the rounds of his tiny evening fiefdom. As he approached me, I could see a scowl on his face. That was not unusual; what *was* unusual was that this particular scowl seemed directed at me. I began to feel a bit apprehensive.

My apprehension was confirmed moments later when he fixed a direct gaze on me and barked, "Get that pencil out from behind your ear, and put it in your hand poised over the copy like it should be!"

My mind whirled. My first reaction was to tell him where *he* could place my pencil, but I quickly realized that such a suggestion would be no help in this particular confrontation. Next I thought about ignoring the command . . . but that, of course, was totally impossible. Finally, I considered refusing to do as he bid. However, the absurdity of making a serious issue out of where my proofreader's pencil was during my job finally made me realize that doing what he commanded was the intelligent response.

The pencil moved from my ear to my hand; but, seething inwardly, I scowled outwardly back at him to make sure that he knew how I felt about his command. Even then, in those young college years so long ago, I knew that what he asked of me was an absurdity, and that it would simply compound the absurdity if I made it into a fight.

Over the years, I have thought a lot about that incident, and what I have thought goes something like this: There is a thin line between appropriate and inappropriate management styles. Certainly, management must take responsibility for the product its employees produce, and therefore to some extent the process by which they produce it.

However, management must also take responsibility for the productivity of its employees in performing the processes and producing the product. Productivity stems from a lot of different things, but high among them is the employee's knowledge that he or she, and his or her opinion, is valued by management. That feeling of well-being and contribution goes a lot further toward raising productivity than large heaps of process improvement, particularly when the process improvement is mandated from above rather than grown from below.

That manager was simply wrong in micro-managing my pencil, but he was not the last manager in the world to make that kind of mistake. As the computing world has been overwhelmed by calls for discipline—more methodologies, more attempts at process automation, more structured whatevers—more and more often, the managers involved are trying to solve computing's problems by changing the location of the proofreader's pencil. And it just doesn't work that way.

Discipline is a necessary part of the process of large-scale software development, of course, but there is discipline, and then there is discipline. Discipline is *not* one of those areas where if a little is good, a lot more is better. Like seasoning, it must be applied with care. And the manager who micro-managed my pencil—like the manager who forces his employees to use dubious "silver bullet" software "solutions"—was really pouring an excess of salt onto a wound of his own creation.

Structured Research? (A Partly Tongue-in-Cheek Look)

There is a problem hardly anyone wants to talk about, but I think it's time to bring it out into the open. It's what I'd like to call the "software research crisis."

The software research crisis? What *is* this crisis? I hear you saying.

It's the tendency of research to be over budget, behind schedule, and unreliable. And it's a real crisis. When did *you* last hear of a research project that worked to a tightly controlled budget, came through on a predictable schedule, and was reliable enough to be put to immediate productive use?

I am not here just to bemoan this crisis. I have positive suggestions as to what we should do about it.

First of all, I think it is time we structure our research. In fact, I would like to propose a structured revolution for research.

What do I mean by structured research? First, we need a disciplined, rigorous, orderly, straightforward process for doing research. None of those random opportunistic "goto's." None of that slovenly, uncontrolled, freedom-loving serendipitous stuff out of the past. We will have a research life cycle, carefully controlled milestones for monitoring research accomplishments, and a set of research documents to be produced along the way so that management can get visibility into research progress.

And research metrics. We need ways of measuring both the productivity and the success of research projects. (Perhaps we could measure person-hours per Source Line Of Published research Paper (SLOP). In order to compare future research under this new paradigm with the undisciplined research of the past, we'd better begin collecting these metric data now. Contemporary research metrics data collection is perhaps the most urgent need of the research crisis.

Ah, and then we need to define research process. Perhaps we could even define a research process model, and invent a process language in which we could define the activities of research and monitor a specific project against that model.

What would be in the process model? First of all we would have all the elements of the research life cycle. We would define the requirements for the research in a formal, rigorous, mathematical language so that we could clearly convey them to our funding sources. In fact, with a rigorous enough language, perhaps we could look forward in the future to the automatic generation of research findings from these rigorous requirements languages.

And then we would have research design. Perhaps we could have a research design methodology, the Gane-Sarson or the Yourdon of research, a set of orderly steps and processes for doing design. And when we finished the design, we could represent that design in a collection of structured languages: idea flow diagrams (IFDs), in which the flow of ideas and the processes that manipulate them could be shown; research structure charts (RSCs), in which a hierarchic view of the research functions could be represented; and research design languages (RDLs), in which we could represent in a rigorous way the many minuscule details of the design. In fact, even without automatic generation of research from requirements specifications, we could probably, with the help of rigorous and thorough design representations, use technicians to finish the research once thorough designs were written.

And then research implementation. With all the formalization of the preceding processes, research implementation should be straightforward.

We will have research design folders (RDFs), a sort of repository in which we put everything pertaining to the research implementation for the future use of whomever looks at RDFs, and we will hold research structured walkthroughs (RSWs), in which research peers will examine and critique research implementation findings. And we will get ready for the research testing process.

There are two possible approaches to structured research testing. The traditional approach, of course, is via the use of sample inputs, either structured or random (statistical), where test cases are run against the implemented research in order to seek flaws in its implementation. Or there is formal verification of the research, in which mathematical proof processes are used on the research findings to both seek errors and to prove the correctness of the results. Either way, these testing processes will be performed to structured test plans and be reported in structured test reports.

And maintenance? Well, of course, there is no maintenance problem in research (or if there is, it is the same as the research development process) and so we will not define a separate research maintenance process. (Note that here alone we have saved 40 to 80 percent of the research budget.)

Now, with this rigorous approach to research, we can finally get control of these researchers. We can estimate the time it will take to do research from estimates of the lines of published papers that will result. And with appropriate estimates based on these structured and rigorous approaches, we can then more tightly control and monitor research, eventually solving the research crisis.

There is one more facet of contemporary research approaches to be dealt with. Current research is heavily ego based, with both institutional and self-belief intimately tied to the work and its publication. Research must be freed from its ego dependence. To do this, regular reviews will be held, matching the phases of the research life cycle, to monitor progress in front of both managers/customers and research peers. Then there will be aperiodic audits performed, to check troubled research projects for inherent flaws, and of course to enforce the structuring process on those projects that are trying to avoid its use. The result will be a team-based, egoless approach to research.

And there it is. With a well-defined research process program, appropriate discipline applied to researchers, a research life cycle with milestones by which we can measure research progress, reviews and audits for getting visibility into the process, and metrics to evaluate how well we did when the research ends, we can begin to control this elusive area.

Researchers of the world, rejoice! The structured revolution is at hand, the enforced discipline of rigorous and formal methods is coming, and the research crisis will soon be solved!

(This research was funded by the International Theological Society for Research and Other uncontrolled Things (ITSROT), and the author wishes to thank them for making this work possible. In particular, it is important that the sponsors did not insist that *this* research be subject to the proposals contained herein. These ideas, of course, are for *other* researchers and for software engineers, not for elite people such as myself.)

The Falutin' Index*

P.J. Plauger

What kind of programmer are you? Are you the kind who likes to curl up in a corner and bang out code? Do you prefer working in small groups? Or do you believe that all good software requires project plans, weekly progress reports, and CASE tools?

The interesting thing about our business is that we have room enough for all these working styles. Even in the narrow field of embedded programming, projects come in all sizes. You can usually gravitate to the kind of work environment you find most comfortable—but not always. We're in the midst of a recession, in case you hadn't noticed, which can often limit your choice of projects to work on. It also limits your ability to hop to another job that's more to your liking. And even if you're happily and stably employed, life is seldom simple. Problems come in all shapes and sizes. Try as you might, you can never make them all look exactly alike.

You probably try harder than you think to make your problems look alike. Most people do. It seems to be a major problem in our business. People repeatedly fail to accurately gauge the problems they face. Instead, they look for the size problem they *want* to solve and go solve that one. It's a recipe for wasted effort, at least. In extreme cases, it's a recipe for disaster.

The mismatch applies recursively as well. You attack a large project by dividing it into smaller chunks. Each of these chunks offers further opportunity to guess wrong. In an organization that doesn't work hard to improve its estimating skills, disasters pop up at all levels of complexity.

I find embedded systems programming to be particularly vulnerable to misjudgments about problem size. I think it's because the hardware and software are more closely intertwined than in other branches of the software business. You're more likely to have hardware-trained managers

*From *Embedded Systems Programming*, May 1992, pp. 89–92; used with permission

guessing about software complexity or the converse. We all know about the greater demands for high performance and reliable operation. Both goals up the stakes considerably.

The name of the game is congruence. The effort you bear had better be consistent with the intrinsic complexity of the problem. Don't try hard enough, and you don't meet your deadlines—not by a long shot. The classic disasters in our business involve gross underestimates of a problem's complexity. Or, they reveal a wholly inadequate management style for the problem being tackled. (A large enough project is primarily an exercise in management. The programming technology has only a minor effect on the outcome, or the total cost.)

So what happens if you try too hard? Well, you certainly waste money and time. You end up so preoccupied with specifying and reporting that you fail to notice whether the job gets done right. Here is the origin of those notorious $500 toilet seats that the Pentagon occasionally purchases. Most of the cost lies in proving that the trivial hardware meets the nontrivial specifications.

I'm still oversimplifying. More is involved in developing software-based technology than just problems and programmers. In fact, I can identify at least half a dozen aspects of the business. Each has an intrinsic complexity. Your goal is to keep all the aspects of a project at a comparable complexity.

Measuring Complexity

How do you measure complexity? If we could quantify that question reliably, we'd all be better at our jobs. However, a certain type of qualitative measure is widely used. I refer, of course, to the well-known "falutin'" index. A high-falutin' problem has a high degree of intrinsic complexity. A low-falutin' problem is relatively trivial. For the sake of subsequent discussion, I will talk in terms of this qualitative scale.

The first aspect to consider is the problem. Yes, each problem we face has an intrinsic complexity. In principle, it is the job of the systems analyst to capture this complexity in a readable specification. The analyst interviews the "customer" to capture the essence of the system to be modeled. A good analyst may recommend one or more possible implementations, but should resist the urge to dictate the one right way to do things.

In practice, of course, systems analysts only work on high-falutin' problems. For a middle-falutin' problem, you may put on your analyst hat long enough to write a page or two of specifications. You have every right to intermix analysis and design to your heart's content. After all, that's the hat you get to put on next.

For a low-falutin' problem, you probably won't even speak the "A" word. Analysis consists of a sentence that begins with the words, "What we need is . . . " Complete the sentence and you're done. No need to apologize. Just get on with solving the problem.

In all cases, your primary concern is guessing right about the degree of complexity (sorry—the falutin' index). Yes, I said "guess." In the software biz, you never do exactly the same thing twice. If the current problem looks very much like one you've solved before, you can guess pretty accurately that it has the same degree of complexity. The more new issues it raises, the more trouble you're in.

That's why divide-and-conquer is such an important approach to partitioning analysis problems. The sum of several wrong guesses about a small problems is almost always less disastrously wrong than a wrong guess about the whole problem. (Isn't it reassuring to know that much of our success lies in limiting how wrong we are?)

The second aspect is the solution you design for the problem. Don't confuse it with the problem itself. The problem is real. The solution is an abstract model of the problem. It is the job of the system designer to form an abstract model that manages the problem's complexity. If the analysis has been done right, the designer knows how falutin' the problem is and will act accordingly. A good designer will plan an implementation that is as complex as it has to be, but no more.

A high-falutin' design for a low-falutin' problem is tremendously expensive. We are in the business of controlling complexity, so excess complexity means excess cost. It is not just a development cost but an ongoing burden to maintainers. Consider how rapidly complexity grows with apparent size. You soon learn that minimizing complexity is much more than an aesthetic goal. It lies at the heart of our business.

I once saw an embedded system that essentially ran a glorified vending machine. It did the moral equivalent of counting coins, dispensing goods, and making change. The analysis consisted (rightly) of a page of data-flow diagrams and another page of constraints written in English. The proposed design modelled the data transforms as half a dozen processes running under a commercial real-time operating system. I'm sure the designer enjoyed using what he had learned, but he overdid it. The final system used a simple polling loop, and it ran on an 8-bit processor instead of a 16-bitter, with much less RAM.

An equal danger lies in oversimplification. Beware of a low-falutin' design for a high-falutin' problem. A naive design causes expensive problems, because you often don't see the subtle cases that are mishandled until later in the development cycle. We now have ample data about the cost of finding and fixing design flaws. The price goes up dramatically with time.

It's considerably cheaper to find and fix shortcomings in a design review than by responding to bug reports from the field.

Design and Implementation

I check for two things every time I review a design for an embedded system. First, I look for synchronization points. If shared data is not protected from dual access, problems are inevitable. (Often, however, they only appear when the system is loaded.) Next, I check each module that must make decisions. If data that might affect the decision isn't available to the module, it will surely be ignored by the implementors. When the need is discovered later, the data will probably be smuggled to the right place by some undesirable channel.

The actual implementation is yet another aspect. Don't confuse implementation with design. The designers come up with a blueprint for solving the problem. The implementors make the solution work. Designers like to think that they dictate all the important details of an implementation. They are wrong.

A high-falutin' program for a low-falutin' design can mask a lot of simplicity. Here is one place where hotshot assembly-language programmers cause a lot of trouble. They like to turn five pages of C code into 30 pages of unreadable text, just to shave bytes and microseconds in a few "critical" places (they usually guess wrong about which places are critical, by the way).

You get the same problem at the other extreme. The latest fad is object-oriented programming (in case you've been in Antarctica for the past two years). You can do many good things with OOP, but you can also obscure problems. Between polymorphism and operator overloading, you can make a C++ program that actively misleads. It may look like C, but it acts like APL—with performance to match. As I've said repeatedly, save the big guns for the big problems.

A low-falutin' program for a high-falutin' design is even worse. The disease is common in large programming shops that are managed "top down." Management embraces the comfortable notion that programmers are a commodity. They hire undertrained programmers (so-called "Mongolian hordes") then train them only superficially, if at all.

Most competent programmers soon learn to command higher salaries as analysts and designers. Management tries to control the process by frequent progress reports, code reviews, and a form of quality assurance (QA). But the QA usually consists of still more undertrained programmers writing low-falutin' test cases to beat against the low-falutin' deliverable code. You don't have to guess the outcome. You've either experienced this sort of fiasco personally, had a friend who did, or read about the financial fallout.

Now we get to the programmer. Simply put, you can't expect low-falutin' programmers to pull off high-falutin' programming jobs. It's just not in the cards. Please understand—I'm not talking native intelligence here. The smartest people in the world with only a year of experience are going to be low-falutin' programmers. They simply lack the skills and experience. Give them a few years of training, guidance, and on-the-job successes, however, and their falutin' index will rise.

Should high-falutin' programmers be given low-falutin' jobs? Of course. A good programmer should be prepared to tackle anything. A really good programmer will know not to use a sledge hammer when a nutcracker will suffice. A good manager will know when to team a low-falutin' programmer with a high-falutin' one on a medium-falutin' job. Programming is a craft, and apprenticeship is a proven method for passing along craft knowledge.

Here is an important opportunity for self-examination. You should have a good sense of your falutin' index as a programmer. Some people have a natural ability to deal with lots of complexity (Ken Thompson and Dennis Ritchie, the designers of UNIX and C, are two notable examples). The rest of us must struggle with complexity in smaller chunks. Not to worry. The more techniques you learn for crafting programs, the more complexity you can manage. You may take smaller bites than others, but you learn to chew faster, as it were.

If you know your limits, you are less likely to get in over your head. You also have a better notion as to where you must stretch yourself to grow. And you are more aware of the bias I spoke of earlier—you know what size problems you want to solve.

How Falutin'?

I began this article with several questions. They were not rhetorical. They concern yet another aspect of the program development business—the kind of organization you like to work in. Just as you can have a mismatch between design and implementation, you can be a person in the wrong kind of organization (for you, that is).

Organizationally speaking, a low-falutin' programmer is a loner. That's not necessarily bad. Give a low-falutin' type a low-falutin' job, and it will get done quickly. I have worked with many competent people of this description with success. In fact, I favor the low-falutin' style myself, at least organizationally (I like to work on low-to-medium-falutin' problems).

Organizationally, a medium-falutin' programmer is one who can work in a group. You need these folks to tackle the medium-to-high-falutin' problems. Once a job gets too big to be handled by one person, communication skills become important. Programming skills are also important, but less so. Unless the pieces fit together, it doesn't make a bit of difference how good each piece is separately.

A high-falutin' programmer is one who can work on projects that require multiple groups. Here is where the management becomes more important than the technology, as I indicated earlier. You need folks who know the technology well enough but don't have to actually write code to feel fulfilled. These types sublimate their technical urges by helping others get the job done. I have never seen a large project succeed without a serious complement of good technical managers. Never mind what the business schools say, an M.B.A. can't cut it alone in our trade.

Low-falutin' programmers in high-falutin' organizations are literally in over their heads. They don't know how to behave in committee meetings. They don't understand the need for all those Mickey Mouse reports. They are, in short, accidents waiting to happen. Bear that in mind the next time you get a tempting job offer. Is the organization much more structured than the ones you've worked in so far? In your effort to get ahead, make sure you don't walk off the end of the pier.

You also have to be wary if you're accustomed to a high-falutin' organization. That neat consulting opportunity may not be what you expect. Don't give up your data repository and QA department until you know you can work comfortably without them.

The falutin' index applies to other aspects. You have low-falutin' customers who are unsophisticated and high-falutin' ones who demand lots of deliverables. You may have a low-falutin' work environment in a high-falutin' organization (upper management may be cheapskates).

Given all these aspects, the number of falutin' profiles are practically endless. Think about the projects you have worked on. Were they successful? How consistent was the complexity profile? My experience is that these two answers tend to be highly correlated (you may know of a few exceptions). Successful projects are congruent, or they aren't successful.

The "Odd Couple" of Discipline and Creativity

Some have called discipline and creativity an odd couple.

They call them that because each word conjures up a totally different image in our minds. How can we consider both of them together?

Discipline causes us to think of identical marchers, moving in lockstep toward a common goal in a common way.

Creativity causes us to think of colorful and individualistic seekers, moving to a different drummer, choosing their own path. What can these two have in common?

Yet our lives are constantly made up of blendings of the two. If we play or enjoy music, we love both the disciplined playing of a carefully crafted musical work and the creative improvisations of a master performer. If we appreciate science, we understand that the discipline imposed by the scientific method forms a frame for the opportunistic, even serendipitous, and certainly creative discoveries that constitute an amazing portion of what science has given us.

If we dabble in the writing of poetry, we know that the cadence of a poetic form guides, rather than constrains, our creative choices. Certainly in the search for rhymes, for example, we intermix the discipline of rhyming search (i.e., in seeking a rhyme for a particular word, we may pass through the alphabet prefixing our rhyme ending with the letters of the alphabet in order, hoping to find an appropriate rhyming word) with the creative flair of idea presentation.

The construction of software is no different; it requires that same odd couple. The creativity of design, for example, is interspersed with the discipline of coding. Design methodologies attempt to convert design into a disciplined activity, but they will never completely succeed in doing that as long as there are new problems to be solved. There is creativity in the writing of code, in solving the detail-level problems left unsolved in an inevitably incomplete design, and in the midst of the enormous disciplinary requirement to write code that tells a dumb computer in infinitesmal detail how to provide a desired solution.

We especially find this odd couple in software maintenance. The existing software, the program undergoing maintenance, imposes enormous disciplinary constraints on the creative maintainer. The current functionality of the existing software must be kept intact in the midst of adding new capability. Probably, this heavily constrained creativity is the most difficult kind; and in that difficulty lies the real reason that most programmers try to avoid doing maintenance. In the complex world of software construction, probably nothing is more complex than trying to be creative within inviolable disciplinary constraints.

There is a temptation, especially in the world of software, to see discipline and creativity as enemies. Those in the discipline camp say that more of it will lead to more effective software development. Those in the creativity camp say that less discipline is the key to more effective software development! A battleground is established; people choose up sides; and advocates lose sight of the fact that neither camp can be right by itself.

Finding an effective way of blending the odd couple of discipline and creativity is essential to further progress in our field, and achieving that progress requires that both camps lay down their arms and find ways of working together.

"There are still enormous amounts of trial and error . . . You go back and forth from observation to theory. You don't know what to look for without a theory, and you can't check the theory without looking at the fact . . . I believe that the movement back and forth occurs thousands, even millions of times in the course of a single investigation."

—Joshua Lederberg, Nobel prize winner (genes), as quoted in *The Search for Solutions*, Holt Rinehart and Winston, 1980; Horace Freeland Judson (Reprinted by permission of Henry Holt and Company Inc.)

2.2 FORMAL METHODS VERSUS HEURISTICS

I hope you'll forgive my penchant for word play.

This section, as you can see from the title above, is about formal methods and heuristics. It is about the relative role in the construction of software of an approach advocated by most of the computer scientists of our day—formal methods—and about another, alternative, almost opposite approach.

So what do these words mean?

My dictionary defines "formal" to mean "conforming to accepted rules or customs; regular or geometrical in design," and it defines "heuristic" to mean "encouraging students to discover information themselves; proceeding by trial and error."

Now, the dictionary definition of "formal" doesn't get very close to the computer science term "formal methods," but it certainly gives a hint of the intent of those methods. The essence of formal approaches is that they are rule-based and regular. (Although computer science definitions of formal methods vary somewhat, they generally include as a nucleus two notions: "formal specification," the use of mathematically rigorous languages to express problem requirements, and "formal verification," the use of mathematical approaches to "prove" a program to be consistent with its specification.)

The essence of heuristic approaches is that they are exploration-based and irregular. Unlike the dilemma I faced in the previous section, where I struggled to match "discipline" with an opposite, here I think we have a fairly nice case of an obvious opposite.

What makes this pair of words particularly important in a book on software creativity is that, as we saw in the previous section, there are factions backing each word—and its underlying concepts—as the best way to build software. Not only are there advocates for each word, but in fact major emotional explosions have occurred in the literature over the years as the backers of each faction jockeyed for position!

What explosions? There was the "social processes" explosion in the late 1970s. Three respected authors—Richard A. DeMillo, Richard J. Lipton, and Alan J. Perlis—wrote a paper and published it in a couple of key computer science journals that took the position that formal mathematical—and therefore computer science—proofs were not the absolute we have always taken them to be, but rather that proofs require elaborate social processes before they can be relied upon. The reactions and explosions were almost immediate. Noted computer scientist (and formalist) Edsger Dijkstra took up the cudgel, saying in a published response that the authors had written "A Political Pamphlet from the Middle Ages," referred to the paper as "very ugly," and said that the authors had "gone much further than the usual practitioners' backlash."

Supporters of the original paper soon rallied. In the November 1979 issue of *Communications of the ACM*, frustrated pragmatists hailed the anti-proof paper as "the best I have read in a computer publication," and "marvelous, marvelous." One even said "It was time somebody said it—loud and clear—the formal approach to software verification does not work and probably never will . . . "

(A more complete account of these incidents, including references to the papers in question, may be found in [Glass 1981].)

There was another major explosion to come. About 10 years after the previous anti-proof, anti-formal-methods paper, another was published, this time by James H. Fetzer. Once again, the reaction was swift and forceful. Ten respected formal methods supporters accused Fetzer, in a letter to the editor of *Communications of the ACM*, of "distortion," "gross misunderstanding," and being "irresponsible and dangerous." Fetzer responded in kind: his detractors, he said, exhibited a "complete failure to understand the issues," "intellectual deficiencies," and called their behavior that of "religious zealots and ideological fanatics."

(A more complete account of these incidents, including references, may be found in [Glass 1991]).

Why is there such heavy emotional overload on formal methods? Because it is a radically different approach to building software. Because it is largely unevaluated and unproven. Because, over the years, it has not attracted much support or use in the practitioner community. Because it is unabashedly advocated, and sometimes even enforced, by those who believe in its powers. And because those who advocate formal approaches tend to put down those who oppose them.

Above, I mentioned jockeying for position over formal approaches. The clear winners in this position-jockeying, as this book is being written (and in spite of the fiery opposition mentioned above), are the supporters of formal methods. Elementary computer science textbooks are more and more often including material on formal methods as a basic part of the framework for novices. The force of government and law has been invoked to support formal methods, such as the action of the British government requiring the use of formal approaches to build certain kinds of software. Most computer science professors teach and advocate formal methods, and (as we will see later in this book) are unwilling to listen to arguments that the value of the methods are unevaluated and unproven. Most conferences on computing subjects, at least those catering to academic audiences, contain mainstream tracks on formal approaches. There is little doubt, as the new millennium approaches, that formal methods have achieved a significant level of positional power.

Is there any support for the notion of heuristic approaches at all? Is the battle really over?

Off in another part of the computing forest, adjacent to a larger forest populated by more traditional disciplines, there is a subject area called "problem-solving"; and in problem-solving, we see that the belief is quite the opposite of that in computer science. Problem-solving academics believe that, as the complexity of a problem increases, formal approaches become less and less valuable. In spite of the fact that heuristic (i.e., trial and error) approaches are conceptually inferior, the fact of the matter is—according to these specialists—they are the only ones that work for problems of significance. Herbert Simon, he of the Nobel and Turing awards, is one of the chief advocates of this point of view.

That, of course, brings us to the question, "Are problems solved in computer software complex and significant?" The truthful answer is, of course, "It varies." But here, the findings documented in [Dekleva91] become significant. The problems solved by software maintainers in 1990, he discovered in a survey, were 50 times larger than those of 1980! From these findings, it is fair to say that even the not very complicated problems solved by software are far more complicated than they were a decade ago.

In this section, I search for a truth or two in this emotionally charged morass. Whether you agree with the truths I discover, I suppose, will depend on your initial position on the line between formal methods and heuristics (this issue has moved well beyond intellectual analysis into the realm of advocacy and warfare, I'm afraid). Nevertheless, as you read, try to think as openly as you can about this vitally important issue. The future of computer science may well depend on it.

REFERENCES

[DEKLEVA1991] "Real Maintenance Statistics," *Software Maintenance News*, February 1991.

GLASS 1981—"A Look at Other Upstream Paddlers," *Software Soliloquies*, Computing Trends, 1981; Robert L. Glass

GLASS 1991—Preface of *Software Conflict*, Yourdon Press, 1991; Robert L. Glass

FORMAL METHODS VERSUS HEURISTICS: CLARIFYING A CONTROVERSY

There is a controversy smoldering in the computer science world at the intersection of two important topics: formal methods and heuristics. The controversy, though it may sound esoteric and theoretic, is actually at the heart of our understanding of the future practice of software engineering.

What is meant by formal methods? Techniques, based on a mathematical foundation, which provide for systematic approaches to problem solution. What is meant by heuristics? Techniques that involve trial-and-error approaches to problem solution.*

There are some who see no controversy here. Many in the computer science community strongly advocate formal approaches and tend to look at heuristic ones as inferior. This viewpoint was reflected in the recent orchestrated theme issues of three leading IEEE software journals [Computer90, Software90, Transactions90], which said that the result of using formal methods would be "virtuoso software."

In addition, formal methods often form the substance of recommendations by computer science advisory groups about how to proceed toward software's future. In a report of the Computer Science Technology Board of the National Research Council (CSTB90), under the heading "Strengthen the Foundations," this statement is made:

*Dictionary and popular usage definitions are often strangely at odds. Whereas the dictionary defines formal as "conforming to accepted rules or customs," and formalism as "strict observance of form, excessive regularity or symmetry," here we use the more commonly accepted computing definition. Whereas popular usage sometimes defines heuristics as "rules of thumb," here we use the dictionary definition.

"In the absence of a stronger scientific and engineering foundation, complex software systems are often produced by brute force, with managers assigning more and more people to the development effort and taking more and more time. As software engineers begin to envision systems that require many thousands of person-years, current pragmatic or heuristic approaches begin to appear less adequate to meet application needs. In this environment, software engineering leaders are beginning to call for more systematic approaches: more mathematics, science, and engineering are needed."

It is hard to disagree with such a statement. Somehow we all know that subtle force is better than brute force, rifle shots are better than shotgun blasts, and systematic is better than heuristic.

But there is an opposing viewpoint. We see it articulated increasingly often in the literature. Typically, its expression is subtle, appearing in the midst of a paper on some other subject. Consider these examples:

In a paper on software design [Rombach90], H. Dieter Rombach says, "The creative nature of the design process means that many aspects cannot be formalized . . . at all. While formalization . . . is a solution for more mechanical processes . . . it is not feasible for design processes."

In a book on the history of medical informatics [Blum90], Bruce Blum says it even more strongly: "For well understood domains . . . formulas and statistical inference as the best knowledge representations; for other tasks, heuristics and cognitive models provide the greatest power."

Even in the special formal methods theme issues mentioned above, there are niggling doubts expressed:

"Most formal methods have not yet been applied to specifying large-scale software or hardware systems; most are still inadequate to specify many important behavioral constraints beyond functionality, for example fault tolerance and real-time performance" (Jeanette Wing, [Computer90]).

" . . . less formal methods apply better to the more upstream problems [systems analysis and design]" [Software90, Gerhart].

These contemporary expressions of the value of heuristics and the limitations of formal methods have firm theoretic, historic roots. In *The Sciences of the Artificial* [Simon81], Nobel prize and Turing award winner Herbert A. Simon focuses on this very issue in a chapter titled "The Architecture of Complexity":

"The more difficult and novel the problem, the greater is likely to be the amount of trial and error required to find a solution . . . selectivity derives from various rules of thumb, or heuristics, that suggest which paths should be tried first and which leads are promising."

Perhaps surprisingly, then, there *is* an argument to be made for heuristic approaches. In fact, as problems become more complex, some suggest that *only* heuristic methods are capable of providing solutions.

Examples

Because this discussion has been somewhat intellectual and abstract, an example may help clarify things. Let me recount a homespun anecdote from my own experience to illustrate what happens to formal, mathematical approaches when problems become complex. The problem is, in fact, a largely non-computing one—it is the problem of determining the feasibility of loading a large object into the back of a station wagon.

Considered at its simplest, the cross-sectional shape of the interior of a station wagon is largely trapezoidal, and the feasibility question can be settled simply by measuring the trapezoid, measuring the object, and checking the dimensions to see if fit is possible.

But the problem becomes complex when we discover that station wagon interiors are not simple trapezoids. For one thing, there is a narrowed and lowered tailgate mouth to the trapezoid that restricts entry. For another, most of the trapezoid surfaces are actually curved. For a third, there are things that protrude into the trapezoid—wheel wells, door openings, clothing hooks, etc. The result is that, if the object fit in the trapezoid is marginal, the mathematics become exceedingly complex. Surfaces must have curves fit to them. Exception conditions must be dealt with repeatedly. The problem of determining fit becomes one of intersecting complicated surfaces in three dimensions. Even for a former mathematician with professional experience in Master Dimensions (the use of mathematics to determine aircraft geometry), this was a problem too difficult for me to want to tackle.

Confronted with dimensions that suggested fit was marginal, I rejected the complicated mathematical approach, and resorted to heuristics. I took the object to the station wagon, inserted it lengthwise through the narrowed tailgate opening, twisted and pulled and tugged it to the front end of the space, and finally found that (only) by opening the back doors to provide additional temporary interior space could I rotate the object into a position that would work.

Here, then, we see an example of a heuristic approach to a complicated problem. Perhaps mathematics and formal approaches could have solved the problem eventually (although I am doubtful that, immersed in the mathematics of the problem, I would have noticed the wisdom of opening the doors to increase interior space!); however, those approaches would have

- required complicated additional skills
- required algorithms not immediately available
- probably required a computer program implementing those algorithms
- taken significantly longer to achieve
- been error-prone

In the world of pragmatics, it is important to note, time to do a task may often be as important as the quality of the result, and reliability is probably the most important result characteristic. Given that, I would assert, in this [prototypical] complex situation, heuristic methods did work and formal methods simply would not.

Some of the problems in the above bulleted list can be illustrated in another example, this one out of the computing literature. The Naval Research Laboratory funded, several years ago, a project that has been known variously as the A-7 project and the Software Cost Reduction Project (there is irony to the latter name, as we will see). Its outcome has been a series of frequently-referenced papers on formal approaches to stating the requirements of complicated systems, and in that sense it has been a dramatic success. But there is another sense in which the project was a failure. It was originally conceived as one in which a formal approach to software development would be contrasted with an ad hoc one by redeveloping software for the A-7 aircraft using formal approaches, then comparing the maintainability of the formally developed code with the maintainability of the original (ad-hoc) code (by installing the same changes in both). This aspect of the project had to be aborted, because the formal approach simply took too long. With the schedule and budget more than consumed, it was not possible to conduct the experiment that would have evaluated the benefits of the formal approach. The conclusion of one of the key players in this project was that "Software is hard"—that is, developing complex software is far more difficult than those who have developed only simple software might ever imagine. (A more complete version of this story appears later in this book.)

"Smoldering"

At the outset of this essay, the word "smoldering" was used to describe the state of the controversy. The word was deliberately chosen.

Twice in our time [DeMillo79, Fetzer88], the subject of formal verification of programs ("proof of correctness") has exploded into controversy in the literature. Opponents published papers suggesting fundamental flaws in the concept, proponents lashed the opponents with emotional and personal arguments, and more opponents leaped into the fray, making a verbal free-for-all. Arguments took on the characteristics of religious wars.

More recently, Edsger Dijkstra [Dijkstra89] was encouraged to engage in a public debate on a variety of topics focusing on the wisdom of teaching formal methods to computer science entry-level students. This (planned) exchange was more temperate than the previous ones, but the result was the same: strong emotional and sometimes personal reaction among the debaters and those who followed up with letters to the editor.

These incidents show that the drive toward formal methods is currently immersed in zealous fervor and reactionary resistance. Neither side of the controversy seems able to see any value in the beliefs of the other. Clearly, the issue of solving complex problems is central to the future of software engineering. Just as clearly, any controversies that stand between us and the solution of that problem must be addressed and resolved.

Conclusion

It is the position of this paper that there is conflict between those who advocate formal methods and those who advocate heuristic ones; that the controversy spawned by the conflict is legitimate, with "right thinking" on both sides; and that the controversy needs to be aired in a nonemotional setting. Because discussions of formalism have tended to be forceful "pro" advocacy presentations countered by "con" rebuttals, this paper has attempted to summarize the positive aspects of the opposing position by reference, example, and anecdote.

It should be noted that careful reading will disclose a potential middle ground. Formal methods, perhaps, are appropriate for solving mechanistic and well understood problems or parts of problems; heuristics are necessary for more complicated and creative ones. Perhaps formal methods could help to steer the process of "selective trial and error" that Simon describes (by, for example, giving us rules and methods for seeking choices and making selections). As is true in most significant controversies, the eventual "true" position will probably amalgamate considerations from both extremes.

REFERENCES

[Blum90] BRUCE I. BLUM, "Medical Informatics in the United States, 1950–1975," *A History of Medical Informatics*, ACM Press, 1990.

[Computer90] Special issue of *IEEE Computer*, on "Formal Methods—Prelude to Virtuoso Software", September 1990.

[CSTB90] "Scaling Up: A Research Agenda for Software Engineering," a report of the Computer Science Technology Board of the National Research Council, *Communications of the ACM*, March 1990.

[DeMillo79] RICHARD A. DEMILLO, RICHARD J. LIPTON, AND ALAN J. PERLIS, "Social Processes and Proofs of Theorems and Programs," *Communications of the ACM*, May 1979.

[Dijkstra89] EDSGER W. DIJKSTRA, "On the Cruelty of Really Teaching Computing Science," *Communications of the ACM*, December 1989.

[Fetzer88] JAMES H. FETZER, "Program Verification: The Very Idea," *Communications of the ACM*, September 1988.

[Rombach90] H. DIETER ROMBACH, "Design Measurement: Some Lessons Learned," *IEEE Software*, March 1990.

[Simon81] HERBERT A. SIMON, *The Sciences of the Artificial*, MIT Press, 1981.

[Software90] Special issue of *IEEE Software*, on "Formal Methods—Developing Virtuoso Software," September 1990.

[Transactions90] Special issue of *IEEE Transactions on Software Engineering* on "Formal Methods," September 1990.

A GUILT-FREE APPROACH TO SOFTWARE CONSTRUCTION

Does your approach to building software involve a lot of trial and error? Does that feel like a poor way to go about things? Do you think you ought to be mastering all those computer science formal approaches that some people are talking about?

Well, one possible answer to all of those questions is "Yes." Yes, you do a lot of trial and error. Yes, it seems like a poor way to go. And yes, perhaps you ought to try formal methods.

However, that is only one possible answer. There is another possible answer, it may surprise you to know, that is largely the opposite of "yes." With this answer, it is all right to use trial and error. Successful people do it all the time. In fact, the more you try and fail, the more likely it is that you will succeed!

I like to think of this as the "guilt-free answer" to building software. That guilt you may have been feeling about trial-and-error approaches is largely unnecessary and, in fact, uncalled-for.

So let's take a look at trial-and-error approaches to building software for a minute, especially from the point of view of the importance of failure in achieving success.

One of the finest ironies I know is that people who are successful tend to fail more often that those who are not!

That peculiar finding shows up in a lot of different places in a lot of different ways. For example, in software we see it arising in analyzing the work of good people versus those who are not so good: in [Vitalari83] we see that good systems analysts try, and reject, more hypotheses than do bad analysts. In [Curtis87] we see that good designers use a trial-and-error process to create mental models of a design solution, running mental simulations on them to see if they are correct—and that poor designers tend to seize on a solution with fewer trials and errors than good designers. In [Soloway88] we see that good maintainers conduct repeated "inquiry episodes," in which they read a section of code with some particular question in mind, conjecture an answer, search the documentation and/or code for information about the answer, and then reject or accept the answer based on the information found—and if the answer is rejected, they begin the iterative process again.

Good systems analysts, designers, and maintainers may have several traits that distinguish them from their less-good colleagues, but we see here that one of those traits is the ability to fail and recover. That kind of trial and error is what we call a "heuristic" process, and we could express this finding in another way: good people in software are those who have mastered heuristic processes.

That is not, of course, just true for software people. In fact, there is a whole book about the importance of failure—[Petroski85] finds, over and over again, that one cannot succeed without failing first. In the book, he hammers home that thought with chapter after chapter:

"Falling Down Is Part of Growing Up"
"Success Is Foreseeing Failure"
"When Cracks Become Breakthroughs"

and with quote after quote:

"The engineer no less than the poet sees the faults in his creations, and he learns more from his mistakes and those of others than he does from all the masterpieces created by himself and his peers."

(quoting T. H. Huxley, *On Medical Education*) "There is the greatest practical benefit to making a few mistakes early in life."

and even with wonderful stories:

"Pencils tipped with erasers were originally condemned by some educators because 'the easier errors are to correct, the more errors will be made'" (this quote is from Petroski's *The Pencil*).

Not only is failure important, but it is frequent. Nobel prize winner Joshua Lederberg (genes), quoted in [Judson80] and talking about the scientific method, says, "There are still enormous amounts of trial and error . . . You go back and forth from observation to theory. You don't know what to look for without a theory, and you can't check the theory without looking at the fact . . . I believe that that movement back and forth occurs thousands, even millions of times in the course of a single investigation."

It is even possible to point to some of the better successes of our century—people like President Harry S. Truman, or phenomenal candy maker Milton Snavely Hershey, and see that they failed for years, even decades, even with failures as severe as bankruptcy, before eventually becoming the successes that made them famous.

There are a couple of risks in advocating these failure approaches to success, of course. One is that the material here verges on the sickeningly sweet. It would be all too easy to lapse into a chorus of "if at first you don't succeed, try, try again," with "The Bluebird of Happiness" playing softly in the background; and that, of course, falls into the category of "trite and true."

The other risk is that all of this should not be an excuse to allow creeping errorism into your work. There is a time to fail in pursuit of success, and there is a time to fail out of laziness. The former is fine; the latter is a cop-out.

Still, the next time you feel guilty about the amount of error that trial-and-error solutions require, remember that without that error—and sometimes plenty of it—there's hardly any success.

Welcome, then, to the guilt-free approach to softward construction!

REFERENCES

[Curtis87] CURTIS, BILL, RAYMONDE GUINDON, HERB KRASNER, DIANE WALZ, JOYCE ELAM, and NEIL ISCOE, "Empirical Studies of the Design Process: Papers for the Second Workshop on Empirical Studies of Programmers," MCC Technical Report Number STP-260–87, September 1987.

[Judson80] JUDSON, HORACE FREELAND, *The Search for Solutions*, Holt, Rinehart, and Winston, 1980.

[Petroski85] PETROSKI, HENRY, *To Engineer Is Human—The Role of Failure in Successful Design*, St. Martin's Press, 1985.

SOLOWAY, ELLIOT—"Designing Documentation to Compensate for Delocalized Plans," *Communications of the ACM*, November 1988

VITALARI and DICKSON—"Problem Solving for Effective Systems Analysis: An Experimental Exploration," *Communications of the ACM*, November 1983

Formal Methods: A Dramatic (Success, Failure) Story

One of the best-known software projects of all time actually has the strangest history of any software project I know. This is the story of that project.

The strangeness of this project begins with the project name. It is called two different things, depending on how you look back on its history. (That is not so unusual . . . The Civil War was known for years in the South as the "War Between the States," and the British fought over the "Falkland Islands" while Argentina was fighting over the "Malvinas.") Those who see the project as a success call it the "Software Cost Reduction project." Those who see it in a different light simply call it the "A-7 project."

But whatever it was called, the project started out with Noble Hopes that ended as either a Roaring Success or a Dramatic Failure, depending on what your expectations were about those Noble Hopes. Let me explain.

This was no ordinary project, whatever else you may say about it. As our story begins, the Navy has some real-time avionics software for one of their aircraft, the A-7. It is not very maintainable, poorly documented, and shoehorned into a computer too slow and too small to do the job for which it was intended. In short, it is a fairly typical embedded computer system!

What made the project extraordinary had nothing to do with the problem being solved. What made it extraordinary was that the Navy was willing to use this project as a guinea pig to see if there were better ways to build such software.

Enter noted computed scientist David Parnas and a group of supporting researchers. Enter some funding from the Naval Research Laboratory. Enter the idea that the A-7 software would be redone, from scratch, with new and modern software approaches. Enter the idea that this whole project would be a giant experiment, with the effectiveness of the new approaches versus the old being measured at the end. Here's the way it was to go:

Parnas and his team were to retrieve the requirements for the A-7 software and start it all over again, using none of what had been done before. As they proceeded to develop a new version of the software, the old version, of course, would continue to be used and undergo maintenance. A record would be kept of all the changes to the old software, as well as the schedule and time cost of making the changes. When the new version of the software was up to the capability of the old software at the beginning of the experiment, the changes made to the old version would be made to the new. Once again, resource costs would be tracked. A comparison would then be made of the resource cost of the changes to the two versions.

In short, this was to be the biggest and most comprehensive experimental software research project ever done. There was little doubt about what the findings would be—most people assumed that the new version would be enormously easier and cheaper to change than the old—the only real question in most people's minds was "how much cheaper?"

However, trouble arose almost immediately. That simple phrase in the previous paragraph, "retrieve the requirements," turned out to be an immensely difficult problem. The requirements were embedded in the as-built code, of course, but that did not mean they were easy to comprehend. The original sources of the requirements—the responsible engineers and the project documentation—were either missing or unavailable, or the understanding they *did* provide was obsolete due to changes in the software that had taken place since the original requirements. The A-7 software had, in fact, taken on a life of its own, beyond documentation and human knowledge.

(As time goes by, we in the software business are beginning to realize that that problem is not that unusual. Many in the information systems field, for example, have experienced the dilemma of starting over on old software, only to realize to their astonishment and perhaps even horror that it is effectively impossible to glean the underlying problem from its software solution. No matter how sensible that approach may seem at first thought, it is now all too often impossible to reconstruct existing software from scratch [Glass91]!)

Parnas and his people struggled on, however. They did the best job they could of retrieving the old requirements, using whatever means necessary. They also began inventing techniques to record and later be able to reference the requirements. Here, in fact, is where the success of the "Software Cost Reduction" project is found. The formal approaches for stating and referencing requirements have probably been mentioned as frequently as any other work in the requirements field in recent years [Heninger80].

But time was passing; and with the passage of time, the original goal of the project was fading. There was an assumption, it is important to remember, that the new software project would in some sense "catch up" with the old, allowing the maintenance-focused part of the experiment to begin. The old project was instead pulling away from the old. No matter how spiffy the new formal methods for recording requirements were, the goals of the original experiment were slipping out of reach. If the new software couldn't catch up with the old, it was simply impossible to begin the experiment.

More time passed. The successes of the "Software Cost Reduction" phase began to pale. From an "A-7 project" point of view, the whole thing began to resemble a government boondoggle. Even David Parnas, in discussing the work, said he wasn't sure, at the end, whether this would be seen as a wonderful research effort or a candidate for a "Golden Fleece" award (a hypothetical award given by a U.S. Congressman to someone who has wasted a large sum of government money in some foolish way).

Eventually, the financial plug was pulled on the project. The experiment, the original goal of the project, was never really begun.

Some could "point with pride" at the work done in requirements analysis and representation. From a practical point of view, it was a truly impressive attempt to create and/or restore order in a project that in some sense had gotten out of control. From a research point of view, a foundation was laid for follow-up work in requirements-in-the-large analysis.

However, some found it easy to instead "view with alarm" the inability to achieve closure on the original goals of the project. There were no experimental findings whatsoever. Nothing quantitative was learned about maintainability. The old A-7 software continued to be used, and the new was not.

There was even disagreement about the usefulness of what *was* accomplished. David Parnas says things like "The Navy Quality Assurance people [used the new requirements statement] to go through their tests to see if they were checking every case . . . The Air Force took our A-7 document and rewrote it so that it covered their software . . . They now use it for contracting [to] give them a quick way of writing a watertight request to contract for changes" [Zvegintzov88].

But then there are other reports. One key player in the original A-7 work took me aside at a luncheon one day and said, "We couldn't use the Naval Research Lab approach in industry; we had to give up on it."

So there you have it. The formal approaches used on the Software Cost Reduction project did a wonderful, useful job of attempting to extract order from chaos. Or, from another point of view, those A-7 project approaches took so long to accomplish that the work surrounding them was scrapped, and the methods were simply unusable in future work.

Success or failure? The answer probably depends on whether you think like a researcher or a practitioner. But however you view the ending here, this story of a project with an ambiguous name and an unhappy ending does a nice job of characterizing the dilemma of using formal approaches or their pragmatic alternatives.

The rigor of formality, we can see here, is sometimes something you can't afford to do without, and at other times something you simply can't afford. The trick is in knowing which instance *you* are involved with!

REFERENCES

[Glass91] GLASS, ROBERT L. "The Re-Engineering Decision: Lessons from the Best of Practice," *The Software Practitioner*, May 1991.

[Heninger80] HENINGER, K. L. "Specifying Software Requirements for Complex Systems: New Techniques and Their Applications," *IEEE Transactions on Software Engineering*, January 1980.

[Zvegintzov88] ZVEGINTZOV, NICHOLAS "Parnas Interviewed at ESP-2," *Software Maintenance News*, March 1988.

BEYOND FORMAL METHODS

Some years ago two books appeared on the computing scene. One was called *The Science of Programming.* The other was *The Art of Programming.* They came out within months of each other. And, probably accidentally, they each constituted a challenge to the other. Which one was right? Is programming science or art?

Years pass, and the scene is played out again. Same theme, different chorus. Two keynoters address the annual International Conference on Software Engineering. One stresses the need for formal approaches to building software. The other stresses the need for approaches based on the needs of the application. Once again, the question arises: Who is right here? Should software development proceed along formal mathematical lines, or along lines dictated by the application in question?

A few more months pass. Buried deeply in a paper on an apparently unrelated topic, the issue surfaces again. In [Grudin89], we find, "There is an easily overlooked conflict between the search for formal properties of [user] interfaces and the call for 'user-centered' design and task analysis . . . the more closely one looks [for formal, consistent interfaces], the less substance one finds."

Meanwhile, the issue surfaces in other forms. Most often, someone sees formal methods as the solution to the software problems caused by "undisciplined, heuristic approaches." "Heuristic," especially, begins to feel like evil incarnate . . . or a straw man to attack on behalf of formalism.

Then a surprising new voice is heard from. Peter Denning, a long-time academic computer scientist and activist, in an editorial [Denning91], advocates some surprising heresy. "There is nothing wrong with formality," he begins, innocently enough. "It has demonstrated remarkable technological power." And then comes the surprise: "I am saying it limits what we can accomplish. We need to go beyond formality and learn about communication in our organizations and in our software designs . . . The time has come to pay more attention to the murky, imprecise, unformalizable domains of everyday practice."

The roots of computer science, at many academic institutions, lie firmly wrapped around the roots of the disciplinary tree called "pure mathematics"; and in the world of pure mathematics, where something called "applied mathematics" has been treated as an unwanted stepchild, analytic and formal approaches have been at the heart of the discipline. That same focus has, for historic reasons, become a strong part of the flavor of computer science.

However, off in the wings is a new cousin to that stepchild, called "software engineering," having the same applied relationship to computer science as applied math has had to pure math. And for that new cousin, what is good is what works, whether it is formal or not. As the complexity of problems solved in software engineering has magnified over the years—some say by a factor of 50 in 10 years!—we find, for example, problems being solved by simulation techniques (and thus heuristic approaches) that are simply too complicated to be solved by analytic (and thus formal) approaches. It seems possible that, with the power of the computer to move us forward, we are beginning to bump into problems subject to the limitations of formal approaches.

Contrarily, with the increase in complexity of problems to be solved, we are beginning to run into problems where formality is the only solution, and only the powerful computers available make those formal methods applicable!

The debate is clear. Some say that complex problems can only be addressed by formal approaches. Others say that formal approaches simply fail to scale up to complex problems.

Yet a third group—the ones I suspect will be seen to be correct when the smoke clears—say that "beyond formal methods" lies the answer to complexity. It's now time to begin exploring what "beyond formal methods" really means.

REFERENCES

[Denning91] DENNING, PETER J. "Editorial," *Communications of the ACM,* March 1991.

[Grudin89] GRUDIN, JONATHAN "The Case Against User Interface Consistency," *Communications of the ACM,* October 1989.

MY READERS WRITE: SOME THOUGHTS
ON FORMAL METHODS

Once people know that you have a contrarian view of a popular topic, you tend to become a magnet for those who share your view. My opinion of formal approaches, expressed in various forums over the years, has attracted some interesting responses.

A couple of years ago I wrote to Jeff Offutt, then a professor at Clemson University (and more recently at George Mason University) regarding my concern that tight coupling (characterized by, among other things, the avoidance of the use of global or common data access) was advocated by most computer scientists but used by few of them when the time came for them to actually build software. I chose to write to Offutt because he had presented some material on coupling at a conference that year. It turned out, however, that I had gotten the subject wrong—coupling, as used in the testing community that Offutt had addressed, was about something very different from what I was concerned about.

In spite of my mistake, Offutt took up the challenge of the topic that I had presented, with some surprising thoughts:

"The question you raise about advocacy of tight coupling by people who actually use loose coupling is a very thought-provoking problem. This could even be raised to a higher arena to ask why we, as software engineers, constantly teach students and practitioners to develop software in carefully measured, structured ways, but then we go back to our laboratories, close the doors, and implement programs in C that multiply pointers and the like. I myself am guilty of not always following my own advice; as a graduate student I implemented large portions of the Mothra mutation [testing] system and never once wrote down a requirement or specification and my designs were largely scribblings on sheets of scratch paper. There is obviously something fundamentally wrong with our formal approaches to building software*—and I think this coupling contradiction is one symptom of this."

Another correspondent, this time practitioner Douglas King of Hughes, also chose to share some thoughts with me. He was primarily concerned about the relative importance of people and process in the construction of software. However, regarding formal approaches, he said:

"Some of Herbert Simon's works refer to 'Gresham's Law of Planning':

---

*The underlining in quotations in this article are my own, not those of the quoted source.

"'[Gresham's Law] states that programmed activity tends to drive out nonprogrammed activity. If an executive has a job that involves a mixture of programmed and nonprogrammed decision-making responsibility, the former will come to be emphasized at the expense of the latter' [Simon65].

"When Simon talks about 'programmed' activities, he's talking about solving well understood problems via some systematic, structured procedure such as a formal method. When he talks about 'unprogrammed' activities, he's talking about solving ill-understood problems, using a weakly structured approach such as a heuristic. To me, Gresham's Law of Planning suggests that *the tension between formal and informal methods is rooted in human nature and will therefore never be permanently resolved.* Having a method in our madness is always more attractive than madness by itself, but sometimes there is no alternative. Methods, after all, are just rational, postmortem generalizations of madness. The interesting thing is that even though systematic procedures enable us to solve more and more problems, we never seem to run out of new problems that defeat them. It's a bit like medicine: as soon as researchers devise a vaccine to cure a particular flu, a new strain appears . . . The real fun of engineering is tackling the new strains!"

From Offutt we see that the tension between formal and informal approaches is very real, and that we do not always practice what we preach (which, of course, suggests that something is wrong with what we preach).

From King we can see that this tension is ages old, not only unresolved but perhaps unresolvable. (That thought probably can be applied, in fact, to any of the dichotomies presented in this book!) But we can also see that the choice may be dependent on the nature of the problem being solved—for well-understood problems, formality is apparently appropriate. For new problems (such as Offutt's work behind the closed doors of his office!), it is apparently not.

I thank both of them, and anyone else who chooses to write to me about these matters (that is a non-subtle hint!), for helping reshape my thoughts in some new and worthwhile directions.

REFERENCE

[Simon65] HERBERT SIMON, *The Shape of Automation for Men and Management*, Harper and Row, 1965.

"Uncertainty is present in most situations we face. It is a part of the human condition. We must learn to accept this fact and deal with uncertainty in two fundamental ways: develop tools to reduce it when we can, and learn to tolerate it when we cannot . . . the predisposition to tolerating uncertainty is a crucial attitude for creative human thinking and problem-solving."

—Moshe F. Rubinstein, in *Tools for Thinking and Problem-Solving*, Prentice-Hall, 1986

2.3 OPTIMIZING VERSUS SATISFICING

In the title of this section, I stretch the English language a bit. Optimizing, of course, is a pretty legitimate word, derived from optimum: "best, most favorable."

Satisficing, however, is a bit more questionable. It's based on a perfectly legitimate word, satisfy: "to give a person what he wants or demands or needs; to demand no more than this, to consider that this is enough."

But satisficing itself, I suspect, you will have difficulty finding in any dictionary. Certainly it's not in mine.

It is, however, a perfectly legitimate word in some circles. In fact, to the best of my knowledge, it was invented in those circles.

What circles? In the previous section introduction, I discussed the discipline of problem-solving and its belief that heuristics were the most appropriate solution to complex problems. It is the problem-solving community, I believe, that invented this word, probably because there was a serious problem it needed to solve.

The problem was this: If you use rigorous, formal methods to solve a problem, you can probably arrive at a correct, perhaps even optimal, solution. Remember, from above, that optimal solutions are ones that are "best and most favorable." Nice solutions to have, optimal ones.

However, the problem confronted by problem-solvers was that, in the nasty world of heuristic problem-solving, it was never quite so clear that a problem solution was indeed a best one. According to the definition, a satisficing solution might be "good enough," but it would be difficult to call it "best."

There's a figure in one of the papers in this section which illustrates that dilemma fairly nicely. Suffice it to say, at this point, that complex problems often have multiple solutions, and because of the complexity of the problem it is often not possible to identify a clearly best solution.

What is a problem-solver to do? The invented answer, according to the best and brightest problem-solvers, is the invented word "satisfice." If you can't find an optimum solution, then find one that satisfices.

What does that mean? Find a solution that, from the best heuristic efforts you have employed, seems to be a best solution.

But that's not good enough, I hear you saying. And, of course, you are right. Here are all these formal approaches parading their optimal solutions, and there are those poor heuristics not having the faintest idea whether their solutions are really very good or not.

What, then, should a problem-solver do? The answer is that satisficing solutions must be "supportable." (To justify one invented word we have to invent another?!) A solution is said to be a satisficing one by problem-solvers if it is supportable; that is, if there is a solid rationale for why it *could* be optimal.

One of the nice things about complicated problems is that it is difficult for anyone to say that your satisficing solution is, in fact, non-optimal. The very fact that your problem is complex means that few, if any, will be prepared to challenge your "optimal" (really, "satisficing") answer. And if they do successfully challenge your answer, of course, you simply adopt their new answer as a satisficing one—it is unlikely that theirs is truly optimal either—and wait for another, better but still satisficing answer to come along!

What do optimizing and satisficing have to do with software creativity? In the realm of problems where software creativity is most needed, I say in this section, the software developer will quite likely have to give up on the goal of optimizing and (reluctantly) move on to the goal of satisficing. And, if that happens, the creative software developer must understand the role of supportability in the world of satisficing.

Under the guise of this title, we wander a bit. We define and explore one of those cutesy acronyms that we computer people love so much ("BIEGE"); we engage in a little word play, making the discovery along the way that computer scientists, for some bizarre reason, have been misusing the phrase *ad hoc*. In the midst of all that, we pay a visit to pre-Yeltsin Russia and come to understand a bit more about that respected but now deposed leader, Mikhail Gorbachev, in a psychological investigation of "ambiguity." Can all of this diversity really relate to optimizing and satisficing?

Obviously, I think the answer is yes. A clearer understanding of things *ad hoc* and things "ambiguous," I believe, leads us to a clearer understanding of when we must transition from optimizing to satisficing solutions. However, at best that's a satisficing, not an optimizing, call. Read on, and make your own decision!

THE BIEGE PRINCIPLE OF PROBLEM SOLUTION

How hard should we work to design the software solution to a problem?

That sounds like a fairly simple question, and you would think it would have a fairly simple answer. It's sort of like the old conundrum about writing an essay or giving a speech: it should reflect the man's viewpoint on a woman's skirt, that is, it should be long enough to cover the subject but short enough to be interesting.

So the design solution to a problem should be good enough to completely solve it, and no more. Sounds simple, right?

Except that it's not that simple. There are solutions, and then there are solutions. Some solutions are overly elaborate and complex (practitioners know these by the name "goldplating"). Some solutions are simplistic and trivial (practitioners know these by the name "inadequate" or even "wrong"). And some solutions, the ones we all wish we could provide, are elegant and beautiful and creative because they are simple solutions to terribly complex problems. The trick is first to strive for that elegance, and then, if we can't achieve it with an appropriate expenditure of resources, to make sure that, if we are forced to a complex solution, it's because the problem is complex, not just our solution.

However, all of that discussion suggests that there are a lot of different solutions to a problem, and that it's hard to know when you've got a good one. Well, surprise! That describes the software world, and the difficulty of providing software solutions, in a nutshell. Even for fairly simple problems, there is not—at least in this (waning) century—one clearly best solution approach (or one clearly best solution) when designing software solutions (or coding software solutions, for that matter). Most problems addressed by software fall into the category that problem-solvers call "unstructured"; and for that class of problem solution, knowing how hard to work to solve the problem is a serious (er) problem!

(I remember the speaker at a recent computing conference who postulated a reuse-finding mechanism that depended on today's designer posing a design solution in the same form as that of the designer of the reusable component being sought. That sort of thing is simply unlikely to happen in the real world of software design solutions.)

For most complex problems, in fact, there are a lot of different levels of possible design solution. There's the ultimate, best-of-all-possible-worlds, solution. There's the acceptable, it-works-but-wouldn't-it-have-been-nice-to-do-it-better solution. There's the totally inadequate, this-won't-do-at-all non-solution. And there are lots of stops in between. Figure 2.1 gives a nice example of how one might arrive at such a diversity of solutions from the problem of trying to find the maximum point on the curve in the figure.

Now this whole issue is getting complicated. If there are many different levels of solutions, then, once again, "How hard should we work to solve a problem?"

Fortunately, there are some answers in the literature on problem-

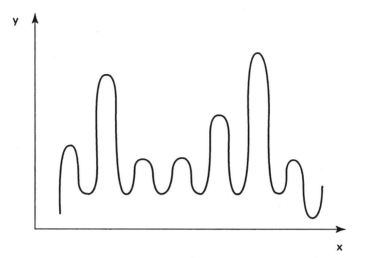

Figure 2.1 Optimizing versus satisficing. Think about a trial-and-error non-visual search technique for finding the maximum *y*-coordinate on this curve. (Assume that there is no analytic approach; for such a curve, that is probably an accurate assumption.) Unless the granularity of the search is exceedingly fine (and thus expensive), a less-than-optimal solution is likely to be chosen.

solving. Interestingly, the field of problem-solving is, as you might imagine, as old as humankind, but it encountered a resurgence about a third of a century ago with the advent of the computer as a new problem-solving tool. And there's one book on problem-solving that, I would assert, rises head and shoulders above the rest.

It's *The Sciences of the Artificial*, a masterpiece of a book by Nobel and Turing award winner Herbert Simon. There's so much in that book that it dwarfs this simple essay, but one of the more fascinating ideas in that book is the notion of "optimizing" and "satisficing." Optimizing is what we do when we try to find the best possible solution to a problem. However, Simon says, for difficult problems there often is no obvious way to find an optimizing solution. For that class of problem, Simon concludes, it is necessary for us to settle for a satisficing solution.

What does he mean, "satisficing"? He means a solution that works, one that is "good enough," one that stops short of being an optimizing solution but will do the job in question.

How do you know when you have one of those? The answer, according to Simon, is when you can provide an adequate rationale for your solution. That is, the satisficing solution is "supportable."

Is this just semantic armwaving? Well, look back at that curve in

Figure 2.1 and try to figure out an approach by means of which you could guarantee that you would discover the true maximum. Be realistic, now. You do not have infinite resources to find a solution. Assume there's a boss breathing down your neck for a solution a week ago yesterday, which is the situation that most software folks are in; and assume that he or she has put severe cost constraints on what you could spend along the way.

This notion of a satisficing solution is an important one, but it also adds a new complication to the problem-solving process. It's not enough to begin the search for a solution. It is necessary, beforehand, to know what an acceptable level of solution is. Is this one of those rare problems where nothing short of an optimizing solution will do? Or is it one that is time-constrained and cost-constrained, and what is needed is simply something that works? Both kinds of problems exist in the real world, and it is important to know which kind you have before you begin to try to find a solution.

There's a nice saying that fits the message here. It's called the BIEGE principle. BIEGE is an acronym, and the principle goes like this: the Better Is the Enemy of the Good Enough.

It means, simply, that if you have a problem for which a satisficing solution will do, don't keep working the problem trying to find the optimizing one.

IN DEFENSE OF AD-HOCRACY

What is the worst dirty word in the computer scientist's vocabulary?

Based on what I've observed over the years, I'd say it's *ad hoc*. Computer scientists use it to refer to anything evil in the way people build software. They use it to mean "unrigorous" and "without planning" and even "chaotic." If your way of working has been branded *ad hoc* by a computer scientist, you know that he or she doesn't think much of how you do business.

Now let me make a confession. When I first heard computer scientists label something as *ad hoc* years ago, I didn't know what they meant. So I quietly looked it up in the dictionary, and what I found there didn't seem all that bad. That early dictionary of mine said this:

> *ad hoc:* for a special purpose, as an *ad hoc* committee (*Oxford American Dictionary*)

I was puzzled. There was nothing in the dictionary that forced *ad hoc* to carry all the baggage that computer scientists had heaped on it. Certainly, just because I do something for a special purpose doesn't mean that I'm doing it badly. What was going on here?

Time passed. I continued to keep the puzzle on a low-priority burner in the back of my mind. As that time passed, computer scientists continued to use the word in the same way. If anything, the synonymizing of *ad hoc* with "badness" intensified. Even reports to the federal government about the future of software said that we had to move from these old *ad hoc* and chaotic ways of doing business to some newer, and apparently better, ones.

Recently I found myself in the presence of one of those library wonders, the dictionary so heavy that it takes a crane to lift it! "Perhaps," I said to myself, rummaging around in the back of my mind to find that burner on which I had filed the definition of *ad hoc*, "perhaps this dictionary will solve the puzzle." With great physical strength, I opened the cover of this huge dictionary and found the definition of *ad hoc* once again:

> ad hoc: for this (special purpose); with respect to this (subject or thing) *(Webster's Encyclopedic Unabridged Dictionary)*

The puzzle, far from being solved, was growing deeper. Computer scientists, it was now becoming clear, had been misusing the word!

Since replacing the cover on that second dictionary and recovering from the physical exertion it entailed (!), I have begun to think a little more about this semantic curiosity. What would cause a whole generation of computer scientists to follow each other, lemming-like, to the wrong use of a word?

Here's what I've come up with. I think there are two things going on here. The first is about the history of computing, and the second is about the origins of computer science. Let's do the first one first.

From the early days of commercial computing in the 1950s, weird and wonderful people have been struggling with the issue of how to build this artifact called software. In the beginning, it was difficult but not impossible to focus in on the particular problem at hand, devise a solution, and code it. The solution was typically some machine or assembler code that ran on a relatively bare machine, one with little or no operating system, and solved the problem at hand efficiently (inefficiency in those days was intolerable) and simply (machines were too small to allow complicated solutions).

The problem was that each problem solution got us only a little closer to being able to solve the next one. What we needed was to generalize the software problem-solving process. In those early days, a small but growing effort was put into producing generalized solution approaches. Generalized programming languages were invented, generalized computers were manufactured, generalized tools and parts were made available, and the beginnings of a repeatable process to be used from one project to the next were put in place.

Most software people in those early days were pleased to move from old technology to new. After all, you weren't involved in software in those days if you weren't an innovator, and besides, technology was changing so rapidly—every year or two, dramatically—that if you didn't change you were almost immediately out of date. Moving from specific to general solution approaches was clearly the way to stay even with the rapidly changing times.

Now let's return to that pseudo dirty word, *ad hoc*. Back in those early days, if you stayed with solutions only relevant to a specific problem and didn't stay abreast of the rapidly encroaching generalizing technologies, you truly were a "bad" software developer. There was a time, I am saying, when it may have made sense to equate *ad hoc* with all the worst ways of building software.

What about that second reason for the misuse of *ad hoc*, the one having to do with the origins of computer science? Most academic computer science programs have emerged from a mathematics heritage, and many computer scientists are still tightly tied to that heritage. There are lots of both good and bad facets to that heritage, but one of the bad ones is that mathematicians, over the years, have divided into two professional camps: those who deal in "pure" mathematics, and those who deal in "applied" mathematics. Neither camp thinks much of the other. There are turf wars in mathematics departments that you wouldn't believe unless you'd been there to see them yourself.

How does this heritage effect computer science? Well, most computer scientists, I would assert, are closer to the pure math camp than the applied math camp. What this means is that they would much rather work with intellectual challenges close to the computer, rather than those close to the application problem. It is easy for people caught in that trap to view application/specific things as beneath them. *Ad hoc* things, those concerned with the solution of a particular application problem, are of no interest. Carrying that a little further, those people who use problem-specific solution approaches, seen through this knothole, could be using inadequate, chaotic approaches.

This has been a lot of words to discuss the definition of just one term. Is there any point to what I'm saying here? Obviously, I think there is.

I think the computer science community, over the years, has done a relatively good job of defining and advocating generalized solutions to the problems tackled by software folks. The representations and devices and methods and tools which that approach has produced have been, in aggregate, remarkable. However, I think that these same computer scientists have gone about as far as they can go with these generalized approaches.

Further progress in computer science, I would assert, must take into account the notion of application.

We are already beginning to see that happening. "Domain analysis" is a term computer scientists have invented for exploring application-focused reuse approaches. We have programming languages that focus on a particular application domain, methods that are better for some than for others, and we've even played with computer hardware that is problem-specific, such as the database machine.

In addition, over the years there have always been some parts of the software job that simply had to be *ad hoc*, focused on the problem at hand:

- Systems analysis, where the analyst defines the problem to be solved.
- Top-down design, where the design is focused on the problem as defined by the requirements.
- Top-down implementation, where a skeletal total solution is produced, focusing on the problem in overview, before the lower-level parts are screwed in.
- Various kinds of testing. For example, "boundary value testing" is about inventing test cases to check application-specific boundary situations, and "statistical testing," part of the Cleanroom methodology, is about focusing test cases on a "usage profile" specific to the problem of interest.

I think the use of such *ad hoc* approaches is increasing. And I think that is something to be viewed with applause, not with concern.

There is an interesting distinction in the problem-solving literature between "strong approaches," those focused on the problem at hand, and "weak ones," those more general in nature. A strong method, like a specific size of wrench, is defined to fit and do an optimal job on one kind of problem; a weak method, like a monkey wrench, is designed to adjust to a multiplicity of problems, but solve none of them optimally.

The misuse of the term *ad hoc* by computer scientists has, for too long, steered us away from strong approaches and toward weak ones. It is time to turn that around. The first move in doing so is to remove the overload that burdens the perfectly respectable term, *ad hoc*.

Mikhail Gorbachev and Software Productivity (!?)

I read something awhile back that seemed to have nothing to do with software productivity; and yet buried within it was some insight that makes it worth sharing with you, I think.

It was a piece called "Psyching Out Gorbachev" from the Insight section of the *Washington Post*, December 17, 1989. It consisted of an analysis of Russia's Mikhail Gorbachev by three prominent psychologists who specialize in studying political leaders and their thoughts (as expressed in their speeches and writings). One of those psychologists, Philip E. Tetlock has developed a scheme that measures the complexity of thinking and the ability to deal with ambiguity that he believes characterizes a significant leader.

Gorbachev, Tetlock finds, scores near the top of his seven-point scale. (Certain American politicians, he said, rank at one, citing Senator Jesse Helms as an example.) A person getting a seven would be able to see alternative approaches, balance judgement about them, and either act to resolve the dichotomy or tolerate the ambiguity if action is not warranted. It is interesting to note, Tetlock points out, that some view those who deal well in complexity and ambiguity to be weak (in Russia, he said, some perceive Gorbachev that way), while someone who sees things in more black-and-white terms is perceived as strong. That is, of course, the opposite of Tetlock's own position.

Now, what does all of this have to do with software productivity?

I want to take two positions here. The first position is that, in a field as complex and young as computing and data processing, there is massive ignorance and therefore massive ambiguity in doing our job. We really don't know a *best* way to build software; it is unlikely we are going to find such a way in the near future.

The second position I want to take is that, given our level of ignorance, the best thing we can do is to expose and explore differences of opinion as openly and as honestly and with as much tolerance as we can.

For example, I would assert that the general topic of software productivity is probably more open to ignorance and ambiguity than any other subject in the software business. It has only been a little over a quarter of a century since our profession began. How could we expect the state of the field to be anything else?

Now, in the face of that ignorance and ambiguity, we seem to have two schools of thought. On the one hand, we have those who proclaim each new idea that comes along as *the* solution to software productivity. First it was structured methods, then it was 4GLs, then it was CASE tools, and next it will be object orientation. These people, I would assert, are the level one thinkers. Some perceive them as strong, because they see a solution clearly and move swiftly toward it. Others see them as simplistic, for they ignore the complexity in the problem and seem unable to accept the ambiguity.

On the other hand, we have people like Fred Brooks in his "No Silver Bullet" paper, and David Parnas in his "Star Wars" papers, who see no breakthroughs on the horizon and are willing to say things like "Constructing software is simply hard work."

Let us go back to Tetlock and Gorbachev for a moment. It is unusual, Tetlock says, to find tolerance of complexity in politicians. "Usually," he says, "stress pushes them toward simple, rigid dichotomies."

I would like to assert that it is also unusual to find that tolerance of complexity in software managers, software entrepreneurs, and software academics. The search for simple solutions, and the image of strength, is too strong a lure for many to resist.

However, we in the software field are the poorer for it. As each new productivity proposal dissolves into mild success rather than the breakthrough originally claimed for it, we move swiftly to the next one. It is as if we are saying, "Somewhere out there is a breakthrough, if we only believe hard enough."

And perhaps there is. But breakthroughs cannot be scheduled, and they arise when we least expect them. Believing and proclaiming will not make them come.

For those of us in software who see our business as making change as well as solving problems, we could do worse than study Mikhail Gorbachev, probably the most profound changemaker of our time.

Complexity and ambiguity. They certainly characterize a lot of what our software field is all about. It is time we began accepting them, rather than trying to wish them away.

Where are the level seven leaders of our field who will be courageous enough to take that position?

"One of the deepest traditions in science is that of according respectability to what is quantitative, precise, rigorous, and categorically true. It is a fact, however, that we live in a world which is pervasively imprecise, uncertain, and hard to be categorical about. It is also a fact that precision and certainty carry a cost. Driven by our quest for respectability, we tend to close our eyes to these facts and thereby lose sight of the steep price that we have to pay for high precision and low uncertainty. Another visible concomitant of the quest for respectability is that in much of the scientific literature elegance takes precedence over relevance."

—Lotfi A. Zadeh, in "Soft Computing and Fuzzy Logic,"
IEEE Software, Nov. 1994 (© 1994 IEEE)

2.4   QUANTITATIVE VERSUS QUALITATIVE REASONING

The Q-word part of the dictionary is pretty short, and populated almost entirely with words starting "qu." However, lying among those few pages are two towers of intellectual strength—the words quantitative and qualitative.

Quantitative is about numbers: "an amount or number of things; ability to be measured through having size or weight or amount or number."

Qualitative is not: "of or concerned with quality"; where quality is defined as "a degree or level of excellence."

As I mulled over these two definitions, a spurt of indecision ran through me. We have traditionally made a sharp distinction, in our society, between quantitative and qualitative methods. Some things can be discussed in terms of numbers, and some cannot. My assumption, based on this tradition, was that the two words held a nice, crisp distinction between them.

But what's this? Qualitative is about quality? Does that mean that, if quant and qual are two very different concepts, that we cannot talk about quality in terms of numbers? Note that if we can quantify quality, the two concepts are not all that separable.

Quality, of course, is an elusive concept. It drove the main character of Pirsig's *Zen and the Art of Motorcycle Maintenance* over the wall mentally. It is the subject of more contention among definitionists in the computing world than any other word I can think of. (To pursue that train of thought, take the track leading to my book *Building Quality Software*, Prentice-Hall, 1992.) If we have trouble defining it and the very search for its meaning drives people crazy, can it ever be quantified?

The answer is, "we do it all the time" or at least "we try to do it all the time." We measure the quality of racers by timing them as they run. We measure the quality of jumpers by measuring the distance they jump. And when all else fails, we measure the quality of divers and skaters by panels of judges who hold up numbers giving them a score for their performance. Either we have real quantitative measures of quality, or we invent them.

In software, too, we try to measure quality all the time. We track errors per something or other (lines of code or function points) and say we're measuring reliability. We count operators and operands (or lots of other things) and say we're measuring complexity. We clock running time and say we're measuring performance. We count instructions and data and say we're measuring space efficiency. All of those things that we say we're measuring are part of that elusive thing called quality.

But let us not go too far down this particular path. In spite of all the quantitative aspects of qualitative things we have just discussed, there is still a fundamental difference between the two things. Some things can be readily understood in terms of numbers. Some things cannot. It is that fundamental difference, and its importance in the software world, that I discuss in this section.

What do quantitative approaches, qualitative approaches, and creativity have in common? My belief is this: As we enter more and more into the world of flexible, heuristic, satisficing approaches to solving problems—that is, as we enter those portions of the world of software creativity that we have explored in previous sections—we are moving from a nicely measurable world toward one that is not dealt with so simply. Just as we wish the world were addressable with appropriate applications of discipline, formal methods, and optimizing approaches, we would like a world that is easily measurable.

However, our world, the complex cultural, intellectual, and, yes, creative world in which we live, is not that simple. For example, compare this book with some of the other software engineering essay books you might have read. How would you go about comparing it with the latest book by Weinberg, or Yourdon, or DeMarco? What we would like—what we would all like, even I who might be embarrassed by the findings—is to be able to give some kind of neat, quantitative score to each book and thus place an ordering on them. DeMarco gets a 9.723 on a scale of 10, due to his clever mind, contrarian views, and humor. Yourdon gets a 9.683 due to his comprehensive outlook, his enormous circle of contacts, and his world-girdling search for information. Weinberg gets a 9.706 due to his clever intertwining of psychological and technical concepts, his wonderful anecdotes, and his enormous productivity. Glass? He gets a 1.738 for trying.

But, of course, there's a problem with all of that (aside from the fact that I have come in dead last!). Few among us would have much confidence in any aspect of those numbers. For one thing, their authenticity lies in the eye of the beholder. (I would like to believe that my mother, for example, would score the authors Glass 9.999, DeMarco 1.111, Yourdon 1.111, and Weinberg 1.111). For another thing, it is difficult to support the meaning of any of the digits in those numbers, and certainly the value of the digits goes down drastically as we move in a general rightward direction through the decimal point. In other words, we have created a quantitative scheme here for something for which it is largely inappropriate. Something for which qualitative approaches would, in fact, have been better. Aha! There is a valid difference between the two Q-words.

Where do we go in this section? First we explore one of those dangerous things, a computing truism: "You can't manage what you can't measure." Like most old wives' (or husbands') tales, this one contains a lot less than meets the eye.

Then we explore a few more relationships between quantitative methods and computing, always ending up with the notion that qualitative methods, although probably less desirable than their alternative, may be all we have sometimes. And finally, like a carpenter finishing a cabinet he is particularly proud of, we hammer that point home with one last essay. On a scale of 1 to 10, what kind of score would you give a section like that?!

"YOU CAN'T MANAGE WHAT YOU CAN'T MEASURE"—
OH, REALLY?

"You can't manage what you can't measure." That is one of the truisms of computing and software in the '90s.

But is it really true? Is it really impossible to manage unmeasurable things?

My answer is, "Of course not. We do it all the time." Let me suggest a few fairly generic examples.

For openers, we have been managing software projects for several decades now, and we have had few if any metrics. Of course, some would say that we have been doing it rather badly, but it is unarguably true that, even with "bad" management, we are well into a successful "age of computing," one that will go down in history as one of the most significant transitions humankind has ever undertaken. Could that have happened if it were impossible to manage what we weren't measuring?

We manage research and development, a virtually unmeasurable activity; and the results of that work have changed the face of the world.

We manage managers. In the hierarchically driven world of enterprise management, the higher up you go the less measurable is the work of people under you. And yet, even though you may debate how successfully we do that, we nevertheless do it.

In fact, probably the most generic statement you can make on this subject is that whenever you manage knowledge workers, the chances are that you are managing in a world of diminished quantitative techniques.

So I think it is fair to say that the truism is untrue. We do, in fact, manage what we can't measure, and it is being done by thousands of managers around the world even as you read these words.

We would, of course, like to manage quantitatively and to have appropriate measures for doing it. However, even in the absence of appropriate metrics, we can still manage to manage.

That is, of course, fortunate. Software management has persisted for decades without any good measures to rely on. Those products that successfully implemented the age of computing emerged from a world where there were neither good measures nor good advice on how to use them.

That is not to say that no one tried. In the late 1950s, I worked for a supervisor who tried to implement some fairly potent, for the time, measuring techniques for evaluating software development. I was his staff person defining and implementing the metrics. It got fairly detailed and specific, as I recall, moving far beyond the simple defining and achieving of milestones, to include measuring such things as the extent to which the declaration of all data items in a program was done with commentary, including the units in which the item was measured (a metric about a metric, I suppose you might say).

It was an interesting, very early attempt to manage by measurement, but it died aborning. Most of this manager's peers had no interest in managing to that level of detail, so no one else adopted it. The technical people resented what appeared, at the time, to be management intrusion into the details of their work, and they avoided it. When that manager moved up the management ladder another rung, his metric approaches atrophied in his absence.

The academic community tried as well, about a decade later. Murray Halstead, famous for his work in compiler-writing, embarked on a noteworthy attempt to add science and measurement to the software discipline, inventing something he called "software science." (It is interesting to note that "software engineering" and something called "software physics" were invented about the same time. Some of those notions survived, and some did not.) Software science, as most of us know by now, was about measuring the complexity of software through its operators and operands.

Enormous controversy has surrounded the work of Halstead and the others who followed in his wake. Both academics and practitioners have criticized the validity of the software science measures, academics via the soundness of Halstead's research, and practitioners via the usefulness of his findings. Tempers have even been known to rise when the subject is brought up; at one computing conference, a well-known figure in the software engineering field accused another of presenting "astrology" (implying an invalid science) when discussing software science. Although most spokespeople in the field now find the subject of dubious value, there is still an enormous quantity of publication on the topic in the academic literature, and there are now (ironically!) fairly successful commercial tools that calculate those metrics.

Those who measure the state of the practice find that the use of metrics to manage software projects has not even reached a state of infancy. At the annual "Applications of Software Metrics" conference, Bill Hetzel of the sponsoring organization has regularly reported on the spread of metrics in practice and found it abysmal.

However, interestingly enough, there is no shortage of candidate metrics. In fact, there is a bifurcation in the metrics field. Academic metrics, including those of Halstead and the many who have gone beyond (Zuse has produced a nearly encyclopedic compendium of this field), have progressed in one direction. Practitioner metrics, even though they are admittedly not being used, have progressed quite successfully in another (the work of Grady of Hewlett-Packard in this area has been exemplary).

(There is irony, of course, in the use of the word "successful" in the previous paragraph. How can something be "successful" if it is little used in the field?! However, it is fair to say that if a software organization of the '90s is interested in beginning a metrics program, there are plenty of both practical and theoretic metrics to base it on.)

The problem in the use of "You can't manage what you can't measure" is one of zealotry. Those who deeply believe in the usefulness of metrics are frustrated at the lack of progress in the field. To get the attention of funding sources and implementors, they use catchy phrases; but it is important to think through those phrases before they are given too much credence.

Can we manage what we can't measure? Of course.

Given a choice, would we prefer to measure the things we manage? The answer, once again, is of course.

The world is far more complicated than most of the catch phrases we use to describe it would imply. And the absurdity of a catch phrase like "you can't manage what you can't measure," far from motivating change, may become an excuse for the current state of the practice—not measuring at all.

MATHEMATICS AND THE COMPUTER SCIENTIST

Computer science grew up in the mathematics departments of the world. It cut its teeth there, it moved to prominence there, and it continues to have strong ties to its mathematical heritage. In many colleges and universities, mathematics and computer science continue to cohabit in the same organizational structure.

But is that mathematical heritage important to computer science? Especially its software part?

Many would take that question to be heresy. "Of course," such people would answer. "The logic and rigor that mathematics represents are a vital part of what computer science is, was, and will strive for." And it is hard to find fault with such an answer.

However, there is another point of view. It is a little more complex, a little more unusual, and therefore it needs careful articulating, but it goes something like this.

There was a time that computers did nothing but compute. Back in those days, in fact, computers had no capability for doing anything else. They could not represent any characters other than digits, and therefore it was unthinkable that these marvelous new devices could be useful for much else.

That was the era of computing as applied mathematics. Computers performed wonderful tricks with numbers that either humankind had previously thought undoable or required rooms full of arithmeticians to accomplish over staggeringly long periods of time. The original productivity improvement that computers provided, in fact, was to the mathematician of that time.

But that era passed over 35 years ago. From the moment that computers expanded their character sets to encompass more than the ten digits, I would assert, they became "information processors." From the limited early days, when the six-bit byte limited alphabetic characters to upper case, to the present day, when we strive to incorporate into the "computer" every character used in every language in the world, the predominant work of computers has ceased to be numbers and has become digitized information.

Other academic disciplines have arisen that have chosen to focus their look at computing and software on information rather than mathematics. However, for better or for worse, the disciplinary powerhouse of the field continues to be computer science; and computer science continues to see mathematics to be the heart of the field. Government reports that study the future of the software field, for example, frequently call for "more mathematics" as part of the still-fledgling software theory and practice.

Meanwhile, the nature of computing practices has shifted over the decades. In the beginning, math- and information-focused computing were split into two rather different and non-communicating disciplines. The computing people had grown up with mechanical calculators, and saw the computer as a marvelously faster and more reliable calculator. The information people had grown up with punch-card equipment, and saw the computer as a marvelously faster and more reliable punch-card processor. Mathematical computers spoke in binary words, each consisting of a fixed number of bits, and—in the beginning—rarely thought in terms of any kind of "character," even the digit. Information processors, on the other hand, spoke in digits and characters, and the notion of "word" was dynamic—executing programs set a "word mark" to indicate how many characters were in the present version of a particular information field.

Gradually, the hardware separation between computing people and information people eroded. It was discovered in the early 1960s that binary computers, with character and perhaps decimal as well as binary arithmetic capability, were faster and cheaper than the traditional character-digit-oriented information machines of the prior era. With the advent of the IBM 360, which appeared on the scene in the mid/late 1960s, the hardware separation between the fields essentially disappeared. The same computers could perform both functions economically, and there was no longer any need for a hardware separation between the disciplines. Oh, the information processor continued to have decimal arithmetic capability in addition to binary, but that was a minor difference compared to the rest of the computer, most of which dealt with more essential things than mere arithmetic.

Today's computers, even the most mathematical die-hard would have to admit, are used for many more things than arithmetic and mathematics. There are word processors and simulators and games and software tools of various kinds, such as compilers, all of which do virtually no mathematics whatsoever. Oh, there are spreadsheet programs that do considerable arithmetic, and there are still scientific/engineering application programs that focus strongly on mathematical services, but the fact of the matter is that math applications of all kinds have become relatively minor in terms of the practice of the computing field.

With that slice of history, let us return to the original question. Is the mathematical heritage of computer science important to it? We can see, emerging from a quick look at the history of the field, that its importance as a function to be performed has diminished enormously.

But what about its underlying value? That is, are the concepts and skills of mathematics important to the computer scientist, even if the application of its techniques is not? Many computer scientists take this point of view.

Interestingly, there appears to be a hardware/software dichotomy in the answer to this question. The answer to the hardware specialist seems to be a clear "Yes." But computer scientists broaden this importance to the world of software as well.

I call this the "Latin Syndrome." Years ago, as the teaching of the language Latin began to slowly atrophy in the school systems of the world, there was a powerful argument that the skills one learned in acquiring competency in Latin were important to all other learning experiences. Latin lingered as a pedagogical topic far longer than its importance in the world might have argued simply because of this line of reasoning. And mathematics, I am saying, may be to computer science as Latin was to the rest of the disciplinary world of its day.

Now this analogy to Latin can be badly misused, of course. Mathematics is not now, and never will be, a dying discipline. Its contributions to the sciences, and to our lives in general, are potent and significant; and the underlying skills of logic and rigor that are a necessary part of doing mathematics are, indeed, a vital part of software's work. Software systems, in fact, are almost the personification of logic and the essence of rigor. A non-logical or non-rigorous piece of software is worthless and even dangerous.

However, that begs a question. Is mathematics the best way of teaching the logic and rigor that software specialists need? The opening answer to that question is that, to my knowledge, no one has ever investigated it.

Mathematicians-become-computer-scientists are not motivated to; and the rest of us, awed by the beauty and value of mathematics, are loathe to raise—or investigate—such a controversial question. As I said before, it feels a bit like heresy.

Let me make a confession here. I am an ancient mathematician. I took my advanced degree at one of the citadels of mathematical learning several decades ago. And although my degree is ancient and my knowledge terribly rusty, I think I have at least entry-level qualifications to criticize my mother discipline.

From the very beginning of my movement from the world of academe to the world of software practice, I found little relevance in what I had learned in school to what I did in practice. My mathematics background had been in "pure" mathematics, among a group of academics who, like many of their "pure" colleagues, looked down on my application of the field. And my job, now that I was wearing an industry hat, was applying mathematics. Almost nothing in the courses I had taken, except for the two computing courses, was useful to me in my new environment.

All of that, as I have already confessed, is ancient history. Of course, it is easy to see that the mathematics of several decades ago might have had little relevance to the software specialist of today. Which brings us to the next obvious question: Is today's mathematics more useful to software practice?

I have browsed most of the books recommended by my mathematician/computing colleagues to see what they contain, and to analyze the relevance of that material to what I have now been practicing for over four decades, and I find very little, if any. If these mathematics-based books that are required reading for computer scientists of today are truly important to the field, then it is in some branch or some application of software that I have not yet encountered. And I (unlike most of my academic colleagues) have encountered most of them!

That, I suppose, is why I have invented the notion of the "Latin Syndrome." I have come to believe that we continue to go through the motions of linking mathematics to software long past the point where it is truly necessary. I am not saying, it is important to note, that mathematics is unhelpful to the software specialist. I am simply saying that the help it provides, for the vast majority of software people, is marginal at best. Perhaps, in fact, Latin would be at least as useful in terms of the logic and rigor it offers.

It has become popular in recent years to link mathematical thinking with new software concepts. The whole idea of structured programming, for example, was founded on a mathematical theory that all language forms could be represented by a significant few. The newer idea of formal approaches, for another example, is founded on the notion that mathematical representations and mathematical proofs are—or should be—an essential part of the practice of computing. There is a "power by association" trip going on here, one almost the opposite of "guilt by association." We have heard so many times that computing ideas with a mathematical foundation are somehow superior to those without it that we have come to accept such statements uncritically. I tend to think of this as the "Virgin Birth Syndrome." Some religious folk, over the years, have taken the position that a virgin birth is somehow more satisfying than its other, perhaps less immaculate, alternative. Certainly, there is enormous satisfaction to believing that mathematical computing is somehow purer and better than its less immaculate alternative.

But is immaculateness really important? In the messy and complicated world of software reality, the ground rule is more closely akin to "pretty is as pretty does." An idea must stand on its own merits, not the mathematical foundation from which it was spawned. If structured programming is useful, it is because it results in good programming products, not because it is mathematical. If formal methods are to become useful—and to date they have not shown themselves to be—it must be because, once again, they lead us to good programming products, not because they are grounded in the purity and beauty of mathematics. Mathematics must not be allowed to become a crutch that props up unevaluated ideas.

Is this issue worth this much space? That is, is there really any harm to all this mathematical mischief in the computing world, or is it more like Latin—there is value there, why should we worry about what form it takes? I believe there is a problem.

Our mathematical brethren, in their research approaches and research thinking, have found that analysis and proof are the ultimate research tools. A proven theory is a correct theory. There is no more powerful statement that can be made, mathematically speaking.

Computer science research has emulated that same approach. Much of the research in the field, I would assert, consists of a strong analysis of a new idea, some sort of attempt to prove that the idea is correct, and then a conclusion in which the idea is advocated. Proofs, in this newer field, are of course more complicated than in the world of mathematics. The real world tends to intrude into computing ideas, and proofs cannot exist in an environment separated from the ugliness of that reality. As a result, most computing research proofs are, in fact, simply arguments favoring the findings of the analysis. What we have, then, is poor mathematical research masquerading as good computer science research.

I would assert here that mathematical research is simply not a good model for computer science. I think a better model to consider is that of science. The scientific method, we all know, consists of formulating a hypothesis, evaluating that hypothesis, and reporting on the evaluative findings. Any advocacy must be dependent on fairly strong findings.

Computer scientists rarely use the scientific method. There is a modicum of hypothesis formulation, very little evaluation, and far too much advocacy in computing research. The result is a computer science theory world that tends to believe things that may not be true and places value on ignoring the real world and concentrating on brilliant thinking. There is nothing wrong, of course, with brilliant thinking but there are many serious things wrong with ignoring the real world in a field whose products interact with, and in fact are rapidly changing, that world.

There is irony in where I believe we have come in our search for an answer to our original question. Is the mathematical heritage important to computer science? I would assert that this heritage has led computer science into research that is neither good mathematics nor good science. Given that, as I suggested in the beginning of this essay, computing is no longer about "computing"; if it is also bad mathematics and bad science, then the name of the field is a hollow shell, and the content that underlies the field is something of a sham.

It is time for computer science to begin to understand what it is really about. If it is to be true to its mathematical roots, it must find new ways to express that heritage. If it is to continue to call itself a science, it must behave like one. And if it is to say it is about "computing," it should at least acknowledge that the name is retained for historical purposes, not because it is descriptive of the field.

Meanwhile, back to the original issue. Is its mathematical heritage important to computer science? The correct answer, I am afraid, is "far too much so."

THE ROLE OF INTUITION IN DECISION-MAKING

Our society tends to put down intuition as a decision-making method. Given our choice of decision-making techniques, most of us would use quantitative approaches first, rational ones second, and intuition would come at or near the bottom of the list.

Truth to tell, we don't understand intuition very well. We attribute it to women, and in our institutionally sexist way treat it derisively. We see it as wisdom that emerges from some unknown fount, a wisdom not necessarily to be trusted.

But the funny thing is, when it comes time for real decision-making in complex topic areas, the other methods tend to fail us. Quantitative methods desert us first. They are beautiful and pure for fairly clear or mathematically inclined problems, but in the rough-edged everyday world, they simply won't often work. Simplifications to the real world to enable their use tend to give us good-looking, untrustworthy results. Whether we call our quantitative decision-making mathematics, statistics, or management science, or simply base it on numeric results obtained in some other fashion, applications of these approaches are only occasionally useful.

Rational methods stay with us a lot longer. We gather together the underlying information, we abstract out of that our decision factors, we apply decision criteria to those factors, and we come up with a decision. It all sounds plausible, crisp, and clear. And, in fact, if we do it well enough, it can look very quantitative. Numbers derived rationally can look just like numbers derived quantitatively! (There is a danger in that, of course, which is why numbers should always be questioned just as regularly as other forms of answers.) But even rational methods fail us, more often than we would think—or like. We tend to move beyond rational methods when politics or extreme complexity enter into the picture.

For example, take the topic of software estimation. If you look in the textbooks or in most practitioner standards manuals, you'll find some very rational suggestions for how to do estimation. Whether that rationality is based on expert judgment or historical data or algorithm, there is a nice, procedural, intellectualized definition of how to produce a project estimate.

However, in the world of reality, that rational approach seldom survives. The real estimates, the ones that go to upper management and to customers and up on those schedule charts, are derived politically. There is a negotiation process, in which those who need the results of the project tell the producers when they need it, and the producers respond with rationality, whereupon (in the majority of cases) the schedule is somewhat adjusted and then edicted based on need. Not on rationality based on production time, but on need—independent of production time. This conclusion has been documented in a study by Lederer [Lederer90], reinforced by findings of a CASE tool survey [HCS90], and experienced by most practitioners over and over again.

Now, of course, those political, need-based schedules could be rational in their own way. That is, the marketing organization could be determined to release the software product at the next COMDEX, for example, and that alone establishes the schedule delivery date.

But how does marketing conclude that the next COMDEX is the required date for product availability? After all, COMDEXes come along with great regularity, two a year the last I heard. What is it that tells the marketing people that the product must be out by COMDEX next?

The answer, I would assert, is intuition. Based on their experiences with the marketplace over a long period of time, marketing believes that a product announced at this very next premier computer show will have the maximum chance of penetrating its desired market. Oh, they may have numbers and rationale to support that position, but if really challenged they will have to fall back on, "I *know* that we must release by the next COMDEX."

The problem we have seen above in estimation is, in fact, ubiquitous. Most people who have done staff work in industry have had an experience similar to the following one:

Your boss asks you for an answer to a question, one requiring some amount of research and analysis. You go away, do the research and the analysis, and come back with an answer. "That's the wrong answer," says the boss. "Go away and do it again." You repeat the process a few times, until you begin to realize that what is happening is that the boss knows what he wants the answer to be; your job is not really to find an answer, but to find a rationale to support the boss's answer. (Of course, the boss doesn't put it that way because that sounds contrived and suspicious.) At that point, you deal one way or another with the ethical issue you have stumbled into, and either (a) give the boss the answer he is obviously looking for, with a rationale to support it; or (b) find a way out of your awkward position, such as insisting the boss take a really rational answer (this approach seldom works!), withdrawing from the assignment, or finding another job.

Once again, where did the boss get his "correct" answer? Out of his intuition. All that time spent bossing in his business has convinced the boss that he knows his field better than the quant jocks and the analysts who are now his hirelings.

Now it's time for two key issues:

1. Is this approach a valid one?
2. What, really, is intuition?

It is easy for most of us to be suspicious of the boss's approach. It doesn't fall into any of the patterns that we have been taught. It violates both what we learned in textbooks and what we learned in ethics. In private, we joke about these assignments and marvel at our intransigent, old-fashioned boss. How can he ever have gotten to be boss with this kind of approach?

But the fact of the matter is, in a surprising number of cases, the boss turns out to be right. That off-the-wall, irrational decision-making he uses seems to lead to some kind of success: a clean process, a crisp product, or good financial results. What is going on here?

The answer to *that* question is also the answer to our second question, above. Intuition, I would assert, is a function of our mind that allows it to access a rich fund of historically gleaned information we are not necessarily aware we possess, by a method we do not understand.

Notice that this definition allows us to say some further, more interesting things. For example, since intuition is a function of the mind, perhaps we can say that it is, in fact, also a rational approach. The fact that we do not understand how it works simply means that we can't explain it, not that it isn't rational. The reason the boss feels so confident of his apparently irrational decision is that, at some strange level, it may be rational after all.

Actually, this kind of decision-making has been treated more positively. We invent other names for it, cloaking its apparent irrationality in socially acceptable terms. For example, we speak of "gut" decision-making—decisions coming from some deeply felt belief that goes against the grain of the environment surrounding the decisions. In all likelihood, the origin of these gut decisions is our old friend intuition. And given that, "gut" decision-making—usually attributed to men as a positive trait—is also little different from "women's intuition," the process that we have found faintly suspicious!

This phenomenon is well known in the world of practice, but less well in the world of theory. Quantitative and rational decision-making are teachable, testable topics; intuitive decision-making just doesn't fit into our academic scheme of things. So it was especially interesting to me when an academic presenter at the annual International Conference on Information Systems, a few years ago, suggested recognizing the existence of at least political (and non-rational) decision-making by building decision support systems that would not quantize and analyze and rationalize, but rather accept as input an answer, and produce as output the rationale to support the answer! Whether one could ever build such a system could be the basis for hours of intellectual debate and exploration. However, in the final analysis, given that it might have to involve computerizing intuition, a process that we don't even understand in human beings, it seems a dubious goal. But a fascinating one, nonetheless!

Where have we been in this essay? What is the point I am trying to make? There are several points, and they are these:

1. Quantitative decision-making, when it really works, is usually preferable to its alternatives, but it doesn't work as often as we would like.

2. Rational decision-making is a good second choice, but it often gets overridden in practice by something else.

3. That something else is intuition, and even though we don't understand it, it is an acceptable and commonly used decision-making approach.

Isn't it nice to know that, when all else fails us, we have an innate decision-making tool to fall back on?

REFERENCES

[HCS90] 1990 CASE/CASM Survey, HCS, Inc., Portland, OR.

[Lederer90] ALBERT L. LEDERER *et al.*, "Information System Cost Estimating: A Management Perspective," *MIS Quarterly*, June 1990.

PLENTY OF PITFALLS: THERE ARE NUMBERS AND THEN THERE ARE NUMBERS

There are two opposing views of the importance of numbers in decision-making.

There's the "you can't manage what you can't measure" school of thought, which says that quantitative decision-making is better than its opposite.

There's the "lies, damn lies, and statistics" school of thought, which says that quantitative decision-making is no better than its opposite, and in fact is sometimes worse.

Which is right?

Ironically, the correct answer is probably "both." Certainly, quantitative decision-making using honestly obtained, relevant numbers is better than not doing it. But just as certainly, quantitative decision-making using dishonestly or ignorantly obtained or irrelevant numbers is not only no better, it is probably worse.

The problem is, it is all too easy to use the wrong kind of numbers unknowingly. What makes bad quantitative decision-making *really* bad is that bad numbers look just as good as good numbers. If I see 25.623 as a measure of something, I figure that it must be a pretty accurate representation of whatever it is measuring (e.g., average lines of code per module). However, if I think a bit about what has been measured, I see several things:

1. Is it really worth having a measure of this entity? For example, does "average lines of code per module" really tell me anything?

2. Has the measure been done accurately? For example, how many modules were taken into account to obtain this number? How were lines of code counted? Were these good modules or bad? Should these be both good and bad?

3. Is the measure meaningful? For example, does the .623 in 25.623 tell us anything more than 25 alone? Or does it lend a note of credibility that the number doesn't deserve?

Looking at 25.623 in this light, and considering the example of average lines of code per module, it is possible to say these things:

1. Until we identify a goal for the measurement, the number 25.623 is at best simply a number.

2. Until we identify the validity of the measurement, the number 25.623 may be no better than a random number.

3. Until we identify the correctness and relevance of all of the digits, the number 25.623 may be no better than the number 25. In fact, in this example, 3/5 of the digits are worthless. (The ".623" adds only a confusion factor to the "25".)

In other words, there are numbers and then there are numbers. Somehow, it is important to be able to distinguish between good ones and bad ones.

To complicate matters, advocates of quantitative decision-making have opened up a barrage of sloganeering designed to pressure the unwary software manager into accepting the approach:

"To measure is to know," James Clark Maxwell.

"You cannot control what you can't measure," Tom DeMarco.

"Invisible targets are usually hard to hit," Tom Gilb.

But sloganeering cuts both ways. Consider these, excerpted from [Leveson93]:

"Risk assessment data can be like the captured spy: if you torture it long enough, it will tell you anything you want to know," William Ruckelshaus, two-time head of the U.S. Environmental Protection Agency.

The numbers game in risk assessment "should only be played in private between consenting adults, as it is too easily misinterpreted," E. A. Ryder, of the British Health and Safety Executive.

"In our enthusiasm to provide measurements, we should not attempt to measure the unmeasurable," Nancy G. Leveson and Clark S. Turner.

As is usually true, sloganism and religious advocacy are poor bases for any kind of decision-making, quantitative or not.

None of this should be taken to discourage quantitative decision-making. There is a sufficient number of excellent books on software metrics now, by such authors as Robert Grady and Bill Hetzel and Norm Fenton, that there is no excuse for a software organization not beginning to seriously consider the question, "Should I develop a metrics approach to make my software decision-making more quantitative?"

But beware. There are plenty of pitfalls along the way.

REFERENCE

[Leveson93] NANCY G. LEVESON and CLARK S. TURNER, "An Investigation of the Therac-25 Accidents," *IEEE Computer*, July 1993.

"Process innovation merely streamlines an established system of belief . . . and does not call for any radically different patterns. But revolutionary science starkly calls into question the established system of belief and eventually replaces it with a new one."

—Noah Kennedy in *The Industrialization of Intelligence*,
Unwin Hyman, 1989

2.5 PROCESS VERSUS PRODUCT

Ah, now, here's a hot topic!

When the next-to-final decade of this millennium got yanked off our calendars, and the digits "199X" came up for the first time, what was the biggest, most hot-button topic in software?

Software process. Thanks to the Software Engineering Institute's (SEI) Capability Maturity Model work, we have studied, evaluated, and rated software process like we never had before.

Companies have pursued strange slogans: "Capability 3 by '93," or "4 by '94." And what those companies meant by those slogans was, "We want to achieve process maturity level X by the year 199X." They cared a lot, those companies. There was talk that the level of process maturity might determine how many contracts those companies would get. Survival and process suddenly got linked in the minds of a lot of people at a lot of computing companies.

Well, hold on thar, folks! I have a feeling we've pushed a little too hard down this particular trail too fast. We're roughly halfway through the decade, we're deeply committed to process as a measure of software success, and yet we still haven't evaluated the fundamental, underlying consideration: "Does good process lead to good product?"

That question ought to raise a lot of thoughts in our minds, almost simultaneously. One question is, "Is process our goal, or is it product?" (Most practitioners would answer that question immediately and forcefully—product is certainly our goal, without doubt. Some academics are not so sure.)

Let's assume that product is in fact the goal. Then another immediate question is this: "What other ways besides process are there to good product?" Or, "How do we know that this particular SEI process is the one that gives the best results?" And, of course, there's the important question underlying the overriding question that ended the previous paragraph: "How can we tell whether good process leads to good product?"

With all those questions dangling, let's do one thing before tackling them. In all the previous section introductions of this chapter, we defined the two key terms that identified the material. Let's do it again.

Process is "a series of actions or operations used in making or manufacturing or achieving something; a series of changes, a natural operation; a course of events or time."

Product is "something produced by a natural process or by agriculture or by manufacture or as a result."

(As an aside, notice how often manufacturing gets into the act in our 20th century definitions. Our dictionaries, at least, do not seem to have absorbed the transition from smokestack America to knowledge-worker America.)

Be that as it may, how about those questions?

Does good process indeed lead to good product? Truth to tell, we really don't know. Our intuition suggests that it ought to. However, there are few if any studies that have tried to answer this question for the software world. Not even the SEI has tried. We'll provide a variety of answers to this question in the sections to follow.

Is process our goal, or is it product? We've already seen the typical practitioner answer. Product is it; it is nearly all that matters. I suspect that answer goes for most of us. I have a friend who's into genealogy. He deeply enjoys the hours he spends in libraries, pouring over dusty old record books, trying to put the pieces of a family history together like a jigsaw puzzle. But no matter how much pleasure he gets from the act of pursuing those records, the thing he's really seeking out is product. He wants to trace that family back farther than anyone else has done. And when he hits a genealogical dead end, where he can't find the ancestor of a character at the head of his evolving family tree, the look on his face says it all. He'd trade all the good process in the world for one good product at that point.

What other ways besides process are there to good product? That was another of the questions we asked above. And here, there are plenty of answers.

Good people are a way to good product. (Many say that good people are, in fact, more important than good process. The cover of Barry Boehm's book *Software Engineering Economics* shows very clearly that people, far more than process, are the key to software productivity. Bill Curtis, who succeeded Watts Humphrey [the originator of the SEI process work], tried to add a maturity model based on people to that based on process.)

Good technology is a way to good product. (The Capability Maturity Model is about management process rather than technical process.)

Good contracting and negotiating are a way to good product.

If product is a table, there are many legs that hold it up—and process is clearly only one of them.

How do we know that the SEI definition of good process is the one that gives the best results? That's another of our questions from above. The truthful answer is, "We don't." There have been no significant studies doing an evaluation of the SEI model against others. (Although in Capers Jones' latest book, he takes the position that he has done such studies, and they show his way is better than the SEI's!) But what we do know is this: The SEI's approach is probably the best scrubbed, most analyzed, best evolved process model around. Visiting researchers have been invited from all over the world to pour over the model. Suggestions from those visitors have been incorporated. Here, perhaps, is the time to employ one of the key thoughts of this book: There will probably never be an optimizing definition of software process, and therefore (as we saw a couple of sections back) it is necessary to employ a satisficing one. And remember the key test of a satisficing answer . . . Is the SEI model supportable? The answer here is certainly "yes."

Our final question above was something of a clone of our first one: How can we tell if good process leads to good product? That, of course, is the key to all of this chapter; and it is, in fact, the subject of many of the essays that follow.

Read on. You will find multiple, conflicting answers to that key question in this section; but maybe, out of that confusion, some clarifying thoughts will emerge as well. The final essay, for example, takes a fairly straightforward view of when process focus must (unfortunately, in my view) replace product focus.

Here's an interesting point for you to ponder. Is it the point of reading this book to enjoy the trip between its covers? (That's process.) Or is it to learn something? (That's product.) Either way, I hope you achieve your goal!

DOES GOOD PROCESS LEAD TO IMPROVED PRODUCT?

We live in an era where process (the approach by which we build product) is considered to be more important than product itself.

Academic computer scientists focus on better process, with the underlying—and sometimes overtly stated—assumption that improving process will certainly improve product. For example, the high-visibility SEI Capability Maturity Model is based on that assumption. Companies throughout the U.S.—and, to some extent, worldwide—are spending a great deal of money on studying and improving their software development processes. They may be doing it because a better rating on the SEI 5-level scale will result in more business and more income, or they may be doing it because they truly believe that better process leads to better product—but either way, they are doing it.

But does process really improve product? Are there any studies on the subject? It would be nice to say, at this point in this essay, that there is the following collection of definitive studies, all published in the literature, that give us the answer to the matter beyond a shadow of a doubt. However, the fact of the matter is that I am not aware of any such studies. There are studies that tell us something about fringe issues related to the central topic, but I know of none (in fact, it is difficult to envision how such a study would be conducted) that clarify the central issue once and for all. Certainly the SEI, though aware that some kind of validation of the CMM is needed, has been unable to produce one to date.

Given that, let's focus on the studies that attack the periphery of the issue. My favorite, probably because its results are so wonderfully intuitive and counterintuitive all at the same time, is a paper by Sasa Dekleva [Dekleva92] based on a survey of information systems professionals. The issue Dekleva sought to address in his study was this: What is the effect on the maintainability of software if the developers use advanced, improved software engineering approaches? That comes fairly close to the central issue, after all—does better development process lead to a more maintainable product?

Intuition—mine, and I suspect yours as well—cries out that the answer is obvious. In spite of all the palaver up above about the relative importance of process vs. product, somehow we know that improved development approaches will lead to a better product. The feeling is so strong, I would assert, that you might even wonder—as I did—if it is worth the bother to conduct the study at all.

But what Dekleva learned from his study, conducted by surveying software managers, surprised even Dekleva. Let's set the stage for what he learned.

First of all, Dekleva surveyed the existing literature for studies about the effect of improved development processes on productivity. What he found there was his first surprise. There were very few evaluative studies at all (Vessey and Weber [Vessey84] had found the same thing a few years earlier when they sought to identify studies quantizing the benefits of structured programming). Lots of people are proposing and advocating new software development processes, but hardly anyone is evaluating them. (The same finding was stated more generally in a paper published more recently [Fenton93].) The only things Dekleva *did* find suggested to him that the productivity benefits simply didn't show up. (One author [Banker91] said, "Many of the presumed benefits of using a detailed methodology that requires a lot of documentation are not observed until the follow-on projects, when enhancements or repairs need to be made to the system." On which Dekleva wryly commented, "In other words, if development productivity does not benefit from the use of modern IS development methods, perhaps maintenance will.")

With that input as stimulus, Dekleva surveyed 112 managers of information systems at Fortune 500 companies regarding what effect these development processes *did* have on maintenance. He defined the improved development processes fairly specifically, identifying them as (1) the use of software engineering concepts, (2) the use of information engineering, (3) the use of prototyping approaches, and (4) the use of CASE tools. He sent off the survey instrument and waited for the results to come in.

The results, when they did come in, were in general not surprising. In most cases, what those managers told Dekleva matches pretty well with what our intuition tells us. Software developed with better methods was more reliable, with fewer repairs needed.

However, there was, as I previously mentioned, a surprise. When Dekleva measured the total time spent on maintenance vs. the use of improved development approaches, he found that the better approaches led to an *increase* in total maintenance cost. The pattern was clear. The cost dropped during the first year or so of system usage, as he had imagined it would, but then it moved sharply upward. What could explain this counterintuitive trend? And did this in fact demonstrate, as it seemed to, that better process led to a less maintainable, and therefore poorer, product?

Dekleva massaged his data a bit more, and a clearer picture began to emerge. It was not error correction that caused the cost of maintenance to rise; it was the cost of enhancements. Apparently, the customers and users of the well-developed system, far from needing fewer changes, were flocking to take advantage of the increased modifiability of the systems and asking for more changes. And that, in turn, meant that the implication of the data was that the product was in fact better, not worse, for the improved development efforts, even with this counterintuitive factor of total maintenance cost factored in.

So let's pause here and go back to the original issue. What does all of this say about process vs. product? Did better process in fact lead us to better product?

The answer, if you think about it a little bit, is in fact a resounding YES. With respect to error incidence, the yes answer was straightforward and obvious. With respect to enhancement, the yes answer was indirect and counterintuitive. And yet it was a YES answer. A system that is so maintainable that its customers and users wish to change it frequently is clearly a better product than one they are reluctant to change because, for example, the cost of doing so is too high.

This study, then, which aims—I would assert—at some point around the periphery of the central question of process vs. product, still presents us with a positive answer to the question at hand. The results may surprise us, as they did the researcher himself, but they nevertheless provide some support to the notion that good process leads to good product.

We will explore this issue further in the pages to come.

REFERENCES

[Banker91] R. D. BANKER, S. M. DATER, and C. F. KEMERER, "A Model to Evaluate Variables Impacting the Productivity of Software Maintenance Projects," *Management Science*, January 1991.

[Dekleva92] SASA M. DEKLEVA, "The Influence of the Information Systems Development Approach on Maintenance," *MIS Quarterly*, September 1992.

[Fenton93] NORMAN FENTON, "How Effective Are Software Engineering Methods?" *Journal of Systems and Software*, August 1993.

[Vessey84] I. VESSEY and R. WEBER, "Research on Structured Programming: An Empiricist's Evaluation," *IEEE Transactions of Software Engineering*, July 1984.

DOES GOOD PROCESS LEAD TO IMPROVED PRODUCT (II)? GETTING A SECOND OPINION

In the previous essay (with roughly the same title as this one), we explored the title question and came up with a positive, yet surprising, answer.

But let's take another look at this question. As we said before, it would be nice to come up with a series of experimental findings that demonstrate the truth of the viewpoint that good process leads to good product, but there is little such evidence around. Note, once again, that asking the question does not imply that good process does *not* lead to good product; it simply suggests that here is an issue worth pursuing.

Given the lack of evidence on the matter, another alternative in pursuing the issue is to examine expert opinion; and there is plenty of strong expert opinion on both sides of this issue.

Since the previous essay cast a relatively positive view, let's take a look at the other side. In an almost angry essay in *IEEE Spectrum* many years ago [Frosch69], Robert A. Frosch, then Assistant Secretary of the Navy and administrator for one of the largest U.S. research and development branches, tore into the pro position with a vengeance.

He kicked off the essay with his view in a nutshell: "I believe that the fundamental difficulty is that we have all become so entranced with . . . technique that we think entirely in terms of procedures, systems, milestones, charts, PERT diagrams, reliability systems, configuration management, maintainability groups, and the other minor paper tools of the 'systems engineer' and manager . . . As a result, we have developments that follow all of the rules, but merely fail."

Strong words. Frosch has lined up most of the process methodologies that one might use, independent of discipline, and mowed them down in one fell swoop! Does he support this opening salvo with some deeper thinking?

The answer is yes. Five pages worth. In words predictive of the failure of concepts like the waterfall (unidirectional) life cycle, he went on to say, "The PERT diagram and the milestone chart are excellent examples. These both essentially assume that the progress of development and design consists of doing step A, then step B, then step C, etc. Anyone who has ever carried out a development or a design (as opposed to setting up a management system for doing it) is well aware of the fact that the real world proceeds by a kind of feedback iterative process that looks more like a helix than a line." (Shades of the spiral life cycle, circa 1969!)

Frosch goes on: "The . . . procedures simply ignore the . . . nature of the real world because the process has been degraded to clerical reporting. To a large extent, this tends to constrain project managers from doing work in the real way toward doing it in a way that fits with their management tools. This is clearly nonsense."

So Frosch demolishes the old-fashioned way of managing, a way that we finally discovered, some 20 years after his pronouncements, was doomed to failure. But does his criticism apply to today's management techniques as well?

I think so. Here's Frosch's next sally: "We have come to a time when meeting certain targets seems to have become more important than producing a satisfactory system . . . Looking at what is actually happening in the development has been replaced by measuring it against a simplistic set of predicted milestones . . .

"The only thing I know that works is to obtain a competent man and his assistants, and make sure they understand the problem—not the specification of the problem, not the particular scenario written down, but what is really in the minds of those who have a requirement to be solved . . . "

Although Frosch is still specifically teeing off on milestone management approaches, the implication here is that too much focus on process detracts from our ability to build good product.

Is that a fair assessment of Frosch's viewpoint? I think it is. Here's the conclusion to his essay: "We have lost sight of the fact that engineering is an art . . . We must bring the sense of art and excitement back into engineering. Talent, competence, and enthusiasm are qualities of people who can use tools; the lack of these characteristics usually results in people who cannot even be helped by techniques and tools."

There it is—a second opinion on the relative worth of good process in building good product. According to this essayist, at least, all too often good process gets in the way of good product. The force of the author's words overcomes at least my intuitive reaction. Process, I believe Frosch is saying, must be wielded with extreme care. And the focus on product—including the role of people in building product—must never be lost.

This article contains some strong opinions on other, related, issues:

- Frosch supports the belief that "requirements specifications are considered harmful" (because they tend to make rigid something that must remain inherently flexible—he says "the idea of a complete specification is an absurdity").
- He supports the belief that "hard-part-first," not "top-down," is the appropriate way to attack problems.
- He argues for "satisficing" (finding a solution that works and is supportable), not "optimizing" (finding the best possible solution)—"optimization may merely be the definition of which catastrophe you want to undergo."

REFERENCE

[Frosch69] Robert A. Frosch, "A New Look at Systems Engineering," *IEEE Spectrum*, September 1969.

A CLOSE ESCAPE FROM GREATNESS

I recently reviewed a research paper that came within one turn of the author's mind of being of major significance. However, the author, bent on one research direction, failed to see that a turn in a different direction would have been profound. And something important was lost to our field.

Let met tell you about this paper, what the author wanted it to be, and what it might have been.

What the author wanted out of his paper was a study of the benefits of structured analysis and design during the maintenance phase. That is, if software was built using the structured approach, is it more maintainable, and if so, by how much? That's an important question, of course, one of vital significance to our field. It should have been asked nearly 20 years ago, back when structured approaches were first being introduced into academic curricula and into practice at an astonishing rate. Still, better late than never to correct flaws in our understandings of our field. The author's original intent for this paper was laudable and important.

The research approach was interesting. The authors, upon learning of a federally mandated change to the business rules that most enterprises build into their software (I've forgotten the exact issue, but it might have involved a basic change in the payroll tax laws, for example), contacted a bunch of enterprises with these questions:

1. What was the time/cost for making this change?
2. Was the software that needed to be changed built using the structured approaches?

If all had gone well, the author would have been able to define a nice, crisp relationship between whether the structured approaches made it easier to make this particular modification, across a lot of different software in a lot of different enterprises, and if so by how much. A finding like "software built with the structured approaches was 5% (or 35% or 150% or whatever) easier to modify than software that was not" would have been a unique and significant contribution to our field.

However, it didn't work out that way. First of all (and remember this point—we're going to return to it), the time to do the modification was all over the map. Some systems required only a few hours to change, and others required person-months. But more to the point of this research, there was no correlation between the time to do the modification and the use during development of the structured approaches.

Thus, the author's finding, the one that was highlighted in the paper, was this:

> The structured approaches make no discernable difference in our ability to make (this particular) modification to software systems.

Now that's an important finding, of course, albeit one that most of us would have some trouble with. I think most of us believe, deep down inside, that the structured approaches *do* make a difference in our ability to build and modify software. What most of us *don't* know, if we are honest about it, is *how much of a difference.* And this author has given us a finding that is memorable, in the sense that it's counterintuitive, yet forgettable, in the sense that we don't really believe it.

But remember back to the beginning of this essay; it is my belief that the author failed to see a major and even more important redirection for this research. I dropped a clue for you up above, when I said we'd come back to something that I discussed there. Do you see what I see here?

Here's where I believe the author failed. Remember that it took some enterprises only a few hours to make the government-required system change, but others took many person-months? Think about that a minute. Here are some software systems presumably doing rather similar things, yet the time to modify them for an identical change request was dramatically different. And the question the author failed to ask at that point was "Why?"

It is enough to say "the structured methods don't explain it." Something *does* explain it. But what?

At this point I'd like to say a few words about research approaches and goals, because I think it's very important in what's going on here.

The author in this particular study was using what some researchers call a "theory-based approach." It's an approach I think of as being like the scientific method, in which the researcher formulates one or more hypotheses based on some underlying theory, then conducts research to test the validity of the hypotheses (and thus of the underlying theory). It's a particularly admirable form of research, because it gets to the heart of our field (the validity of underlying theories) and addresses that heart in an orderly process (by evaluative research). Interestingly, it's an approach much more common in the information systems field than in the computer science field.

The goal in this research I would characterize as "process evaluation." That is, the author assumed that the structured approaches, which are about the process of building software, would have an impact on maintenance time/cost, and set about evaluating the hypothesis that that impact would be positive. So far, so good.

Product, Not Process

I would assert that what the author learned (but probably failed to grasp) midway through the study was that the systems in question differed profoundly in what they looked like and how they did what they did. What other possible explanation is there for the wide disparity in modification times? What is significant about this thought is that *it was not the process of building the system, but the product itself, which exhibited the major difference that became visible in the study.*

Let me repeat that in another way, to make the point I'm trying to make here. The author set out to measure the effects of process. There were no discernable process effects, according to the study; but there were profound product differences. And I believe what the author should have done, after winding down the process research, was to embark on a whole new question: What was it about these software *products* that accounted for the big differences observed?

Exploratory, Not Just Theory-Based

Perhaps I'll never know whether the author saw what was going on here and immediately began some new research directed toward this new issue. I suspect not. And the reason I suspect that goes back to the research approach issue I discussed earlier. Remember, this research study was "theory-based." But what the author learned midway through the study, I would assert, was that something was happening for which theory simply offered no answers. To investigate the product differences I mentioned above would have required an entirely different research approach, an empirical study of existing software products where the author probably had no idea of what they would learn during the course of the research. There *are* exploratory research approaches, of course, and that was what was needed here. But some tend to deride such approaches, calling them "fishing expeditions" because the author has not hypothesized a finding based on an underlying theory prior to conducting the research.

This has been a somewhat meandering essay, starting with a research study that learned some unexpected things but failed to transition that learning experience into something truly profound. So let me tidy up the ending by making a couple of points that summarize where *I* think I've been here:

1. It is popular now to focus on process and its effect on software product. However, there is reason to believe—and this particular research study nicely shows it—that the relationship between process and product is at best unclear, and at worst nonexistent. Although product-focused research is much more difficult to do, I suspect that we will never conduct successful process research until we first come to understand the role of product much better than we do now.

2. It is popular now to focus on theory-based research, and in general that is an important way for research to proceed. However, there are times, in a discipline as new as that of systems and software, when the gap between theory and practice is so large that there is not yet any theory to account for the realities of practice. Under those circumstances, theory-based research simply will not work, and exploratory research—the goal of which is to build theory that later can be tested by theory-based research—is the only way to make progress.

3. There was a profound learning experience for all of us in what this research failed to explore. I, for one, have no idea what that turn in research direction might have shown, but my message to researchers is this: If your research approach takes you through an area where you simply can't account for what you are learning, stop and take stock. You may be onto something much more important than what you set out to learn in the first place.

A MISCELLANY OF THOUGHTS ON SOFTWARE PROCESS

You never know where you're going to run across some interesting software insight.

You expect to find such insight, of course, in the learned papers in the technical journals of our field. But it is somehow a special pleasure, at least to me, when I run across some software insight in a more obscure source.

Take this quote, for example: "Focus on results rather than process." Does that sound like something out of a practical software engineering journal, perhaps one that has chosen to tee off on the SEI Capability Maturity Model work?

Well, it's not. That quote is from an article in, of all places, *The Wall Street Journal.* The title of the article is "Why Smart People Do Dumb Things" (December 21, 1992), and it's from a column called "Manager's Journal," by Mortimer R. Feinberg.

The gist of the article is this: Super-bright people need to be managed in a way different from run-of-the-mill people. But what way is that? The article presents some answers to that question.

The gist of the thought we quoted above is this: Super-bright people don't always do things the way the rest of the world does them. Don't try to force-fit their creative genius into the straightjacket of a formalized process. But make very sure, when they finally produce a product, that *it* has value; and review *their* progress along the way, using whatever process-checking makes sense under the circumstances.

Interesting, especially given the source.

Now, here's another instance of an interesting (and, as it turns out, similar) idea coming from an unusual source. The following quotes are from a letter to the editor—that's what makes the source unusual—from one of our own technical journals, *Communications of the ACM*. The letter is written by Edward S. Ruete, appears in the August 1990 *CACM*, and is in response to an also very interesting article written by Jonathan Grudin with the fascinating title "The Case Against User Interface Consistency." (In the Grudin article, the author had argued that application needs, rather than consistency alone, should drive interface design, and Grudin further suggested that following application needs will likely result in interfaces that are *not* necessarily consistent.)

In his letter, Ruete fundamentally agrees with Grudin. Midway through his letter, he adds some thoughts that link nicely to *The Wall Street Journal* quote above. Ruete makes the analogy that developing software is similar to creative writing, and says, "It does not matter how you do it, just so it is good. Once that principle is accepted, it puts all the tools and techniques of program development in perspective . . . The tools are good only insofar as their application results in good programs."

And, in a summing-up kind of paragraph, Ruete says, "In spite of the best efforts of software engineering theorists, including myself, to convince us otherwise, programming is essentially a creative activity. Standards can no more guarantee a good program than they can guarantee a good play, novel, or communications article."

Tools and standards are limited in their benefit to software people. An interesting additional thought.

Now here's a third piece of material from a strange source. This is from a paper submitted to the *Journal of Systems and Software* that, in a transmogrification, went on to be published. The draft was called "Controllable Factors for Programmer Productivity . . . ," and was written by Ali Mili and several others. "By contrast with all other industries, the productivity of the worker in the software industry . . . improves very little as a function of programming tools usage. According to measures taken by Boehm [in his *Software Engineering Economics*, 1981], the difference of productivity between a programmer who uses no tools at all and one who uses the most up-to-date, powerful tools . . . is no larger than 50%. To put this figure in perspective, one ought to compare it with the difference in productivity that exists between a car builder that has only screwdrivers and a car builder that has today's most sophisticated robots."

Once again, we see the opinion that tools (and thus process) are limited in their software benefit. However, the argument is placed in a particularly interesting context.

Finally, here's a fourth piece of material. This time, it's in a response in *IEEE Computer* to a Point/Counterpoint debate on the value of software process standards.

The response (*IEEE Computer*, May 1993) is by Norman F. Schneidewind, but most of the response consisted of quotations from interested readers. Here's a particularly relevant one:

Bill Dietrich of Atlanta says, "It is a widely accepted engineering principle that a good process produces a good product. Is it similarly accepted that a good design process produces a good design? Is the design process so well understood that it is ready to be standardized?

" . . . I am concerned that the fundamental nature of developing software is being misrepresented by those who would standardize the process. I understand their desire to make software development a measurable, repeatable, dependable process. But software development is mostly design . . . Where is the evidence that design activity is measurable or repeatable? What are the criteria for judging the goodness of a design?"

There you have it, four interesting viewpoints from four disparate sources. But what is especially interesting is that, I would assert, they all are saying a similar thing. If I may paraphrase, I see it as this. Process is not a universal software problem-solver. More important, it is not a panacea. Those who see it as one are simply not recognizing the facts available.

PROCESS VERSUS PEOPLE: GETTING TO GOOD PRODUCT

Good people are a way to good product. Many feel, in fact, that people are far more important than process in building software.

Is that just a philosophical disagreement of little consequence, or are there some real-world implications?

Twice now, when IBM set out to build an operating system (OS/360 and, more recently, OS/2), it employed hundreds of people to do the job. How well that approach worked out the first time was nicely documented in Fred Brooks' classic *The Mythical Man-Month*. It didn't work very well. The jury is, at this writing, still out on the more recent OS/2 story.

(It is interesting to note that the SEI Capability Maturity Model—the ultimate in process definition and focus—has its roots at IBM, where some of its key architects have a history dating back to OS/360.)

When that many people get into the act on a software project, good process is essential. Harnessing and steering hundreds of programmers toward a common goal becomes a major chore of its own. That's what process is all about. No wonder IBM and the Watts Humphreys of the world place heavy emphasis on process!

But is there another way? According to Microsoft and other, smaller software companies, there is. Those companies can't afford the Mongolian Horde approach to building software. They *have* to find another way. And, according to both press releases and annual reports, these companies see that other way as good people. Where IBM uses hundreds of invisible, process-driven people to build an operating system, the Microsofts of the world are using a few dozen at most. How can they do that? By choosing those few dozen very carefully. Microsoft uses such techniques as screening their hiring candidates (they even have to submit the code for a program they're proud of as part of their job application!) and getting rid of underperformers (peer votes result in those who aren't doing the work being dismissed). From hiring to firing, choosing good people is the most important part of the Microsoft way of doing business.

Is the Microsoft *et al.* approach working? In spite of the controversy surrounding the ethics of Bill Gates and his company (that's another chapter for another book), from a technical point of view one has to say a resounding "yes." The evidence to date is that the good people way is at least as sound, from production of product point of view, as the good process approach.

There is still an element of suspense to the issue, of course. The OS/2 vs. Windows NT battle has only recently been joined on the battlefield of real customer companies, as this is being written. Time will tell the winner of this particular software struggle.

But at this point, one thing seems clear. Good people got to good product a whole lot more cheaply than good process did. What remains to be determined is whether quality suffered along the way.

And do you know what? I'm betting on the quality of the product produced by those good people. It has always seemed to me that good product quality, for products of any kind, is most determined by the quality of the people building the product. Why shouldn't that be true for software as well?

But, of course, as you read this that battle is probably over. And you, dear reader, can give the final answer to the good people vs. good process question. What do *you* believe is the correct answer?

PRODUCT VERSUS PROCESS FOCUS: WHICH DO WE DO WHEN?

Some people are process people, and some people are product people. It just seems to be an innate human difference.

I once knew a man who loved kites. He loved to make them. Flying them didn't matter very much to him. It was the process, not the product, that he enjoyed. His kites were the most beautiful, best crafted kites I have ever seen. They were the kind that would win a "best looking kite" contest. Whether they'd win "best flying kite," however, was problematic—and more to the point, from this man's point of view it was largely irrelevant.

Most of us, in our vocations and professions, don't have the luxury this man had. Try telling your boss that your next program is going to win "best looking kite" but won't even place in "best flying kite," and he may tell you to go fly one! Process, in the world of work, is largely only a device for creating product.

So it is important to figure out when to focus on product and when on process. I would assert there are times for each; and I'd like to get somewhat specific about it. My overall going-in position is that we focus on product whenever we can, and we focus on process only when we can't see the product as clearly as we need to.

What do I mean by that? Well, take contracting for a piece of software, for example. I'm writing a contract with you that will be a vehicle for your building a software product for me. I want that product to have all the right quality attributes, and to meet my functional needs, and to give my users satisfaction, and to be built on time and within budget.

My job in writing the contract is to maximize the chance this is what will happen. Seems straightforward, but it's not. A lot of those things I want in my product are hard to specify in any legally binding way. For example, one of the quality attributes I'd like your product to have is that it be highly modularized, so that it will be easy for you—or the follow-on maintenance contractor—to understand and modify. But how do I specify that the code be modular? I must do it in such a way that, if we ever have to go to court, it is totally clear what I asked for, so that if you don't provide it the court will agree with me that I deserved it and didn't get it.

Think about that a little. It is a difficult issue. Modularity, a concept at the heart of what we know about good software engineering, is very hard to specify in a binding way. First of all, the contract is going to have to define module. Try doing that. Now try doing it with your hands bound so that you can't wave them! No matter whether you talk about functional cohesion, or low coupling, or single entrance single exit, or any of the usual things we use to describe good modularity, we keep running into the problem that one difficult-to-define term begets another.

Those who have tried to make a contractual definition of good modularity have, in desperation, sometimes ended up with a very bad one. They want a definition where it is obvious if it has been met or not, and as a result they often specify modularity by the number of lines of code clustered together. Something like "The program shall be divided into modules, such that each module satisfies one or a very few functional needs and is no more than 50 lines of code in length." A lot of software specifications have been written with that sort of contractual definition for module, especially in the U.S. Department of Defense world.

However, where is it written that 50 lines of code—or 100 or 200—makes a good module? In an effort to make a quantitative, checkable definition, we have resorted to absurdity. In fact, in [Card90], the author shows that quantitative definitions of module size tend to result in bad modules.

What is a contractual specifier to do? If you can't define the product, define the process. Invent and codify a series of checkpoints during product construction at which, among other things, conformance to a more vague yet more meaningful definition of module can be verified. It's the answer to the old conundrum, "I may not be able to describe good art, but I know it when I see it." Process is the way we get early visibility into seeing it.

And *that's* the role of process in a product-focused environment, I would assert. If you can't define the product as clearly as you would like, then make a clear definition of the process that will be used to achieve the product. Specify milestones. Specify intermediate products to be delivered or demonstrated at those milestones. Make sure that the intermediate products do indeed show progress being made toward the product. Evaluate the intermediate products with that goal as a yardstick.

Now, if over time we find a process that seems to make a lot of sense in building hard-to-specify products, think about formalizing it. When we build these sorts of products, we will use this kind of process. That formalization of process we can call a methodology. Notice that we have arrived at a definition of methodology in a sort of bottom-up fashion; that is, we have seen a problem (a product that is hard to specify), defined an approach to the problem (defining process to help us achieve product), evaluated the approach (by using it several times), and only then defined a methodology (by formalizing the process used).

(This left turn into a discussion of methodology may strike you as strange. But how many methodologies are developed top-down by gurus—or even graduate students—who haven't cut a line of code in 15 years [or a lifetime!]. Those who haven't built product to a process in order to evaluate the process should NEVER invent methodologies.)

After we have used the process-cum-methodology for awhile, we may even begin to think about some formalization on top of this formalization, (e.g. statistical process control). When we use this process, the following kinds of things normally happen. If those things are not happening, then we have a warning signal. For this product development, the process isn't working the way it usually does. That may be a problem, or it may not. However, it is a signal that investigation is warranted. Statistical process control is a useful tool, then, for detecting deviations from a norm.

There's one more important point to be made before we end this excursion. Good process does not *guarantee* good product. That is not the same as saying "good process doesn't lead to good product"; our intuition suggests it does. However, it has been popular, ever since the first guru invented the first methodology (formalized process, right?!) to say that the use of "my" methodology will guarantee that a good job gets done. Not only is that not the case, but we have some evidence that it is not. Tom DeMarco, he of many wonderful computing books and articles, reported at an International Conference on Software Engineering several years ago that he had studied software products built by people trained in and using a common methodology, and he found little if any similarity in the products they produced. And, in a case straight out of computing ancient history, the claims that structured programming produced error-free code were refuted some years back by the *New York Times* customers of the first major structured programming project, who are reported to have said, "If structured programming resulted in only one error per thousand lines of code, then the contractor owes about a million more lines." In other words, the reliability claims made for the benefits of structured programming at that point in time were grossly exaggerated.

Now, let's return to ground zero. The point of this essay is that there is a time for product focus, and there is a time for process focus. Product focus, at least in the workaday world, should always come first. Process focus, when the shape of the product is unclear, is a means to product focus. When we need it, we need it a lot. And when we have defined a process that really seems to work, there are some interesting formalisms we can layer on top of it.

REFERENCE

[Card90] DAVID N. CARD with ROBERT L. GLASS, *Measuring Software Design Quality,* Prentice-Hall, 1990.

"A productive symbiosis of human beings and computers will assign the nonprogrammable tasks to human beings and the programmable to computers. The nonprogrammable include the holistic, global activities involving heuristics, values, attitudes, emotions and humor, while the programmable include sequential step-by-step detailed algorithms."

—Moshe F. Rubinstein in *Tools for Thinking and Problem-Solving*, Prentice-Hall, 1986

2.6 INTELLECTUAL VERSUS CLERICAL TASKS

Let me tell you a story. The story is about the evolution of a research paper. (Don't stop reading now, there's more to this than you think!) It's a story about research the goal of which was to answer the question, "To what extent is software work intellectually challenging?"

Why ask that question? Isn't it obvious that software is complex, challenging work?

Unfortunately, the answer of a lot of people in our society is "No, it's not." All around us, we see evidence that people think this way. Managers wonder why their software maintainers take so long to make a "simple" change. Academic deans denigrate and sometimes eliminate computing courses and even programs from their curriculum on the grounds that they have "no intellectual content." (Don't laugh—it has happened at several A-grade institutions in the last decade!) Gurus announce that the latest computing fad or fancy will eliminate the need for programmers. Researchers seek funding for projects that will "automate" the process of constructing software. Governmental agencies seek contractors to produce "order of magnitude" improvements in our ability to build and/or maintain software. The list goes on. In one way or another, these people are expressing their belief that software is somehow easy to build and work with.

The mischief raised by those beliefs has done untold damage to the computing field. Outsourcing is a result. Closure of academic computing programs is a result. Failure to fund appropriate (as opposed to infeasible) software research is a result. Cost and schedule pressure to achieve the impossible is a result. Credibility loss is a result.

Now back to the story I want to tell. For some time, I puzzled over this strange disparity of beliefs. Not only did I wonder why people felt this way, I also—in the back of my mind—wondered what it would take to convince them otherwise. Perhaps an appropriately chosen research study on the subject could do the trick. But what kind of research?

Then I saw the tapes. What tapes? A couple of research colleagues were doing a protocol analysis study of software methodologies. To do that, they had videotaped some novice systems analysts in the act of studying a problem. For some reason that I can't recall, I put one of the tapes in the TV one day and, out of idle curiosity, watched it to see what happened.

What struck me as I watched the tape was the amount of time the analyst did absolutely nothing! It was an incredibly boring experience. And yet I knew, because the subject on the videotape knew that their work was being filmed and timed, that they were intently involved in problem-solving.

And then it hit me. The time the subject spent boring me out of my wits, doing absolutely nothing visible, was thinking time. And the time the subject spent acting on that thought, jotting down a representation of what they had been thinking, was by contrast clerical time. Here, on this tape, was a real-live representation of the issue of whether software work was intellectually challenging or not. Why not measure the amount of time each subject spent thinking, and the amount of time they spent writing or drawing?

We (my research partners and I) did just that. We studied the intellectual vs. clerical time for a number of subjects, we devised another scheme to measure the same kind of things in a different way just to run a consistency check on our findings, we wrote the paper, and we sent it off to a good journal.

Then a disappointing thing happened. What we had, we knew all along, was an excellent research issue pursued by a somewhat mediocre research approach. That is, there were flaws in the basic idea of the research:

1. Was inactivity, for example, really the same as intellectual time?
2. Was activity really clerical time?
3. Were novices appropriate subjects?
4. Were simple tasks appropriate vehicles to measure what we wanted to measure?

All of those legitimate issues were raised, as we knew they would be, by the reviewers for the journal to which we sent the paper. We hoped that the importance of the issue being explored would override the concern over research methodology. Unfortunately, it did not. The paper was rejected.

We sent the paper off to another journal, and—to make a long story at least shorter—this time the news was better. The paper was accepted and, after an appropriate period, it was published.

Then a particularly interesting thing happened. *InformationWeek*, a popular-press computing news magazine, published a brief mention of the paper's findings. Immediately, the phone began ringing. Over the next month or two, more than 100 phone calls came in, each from someone who was interested in the research findings, wanting to know more about them.

Only as I write this material has the number of phone calls dropped to zero. Whatever the quality of the research, the issue treated by the paper touched a nerve in the computing world.

That paper, as you might imagine by now, is in this book following this chapter introduction. In spite of the questionable research approach, its findings are startlingly consistent. Intellectual aspects predominate over clerical by a large margin. (To find out how much, read on.) Although more research studies are needed, there is no question—at this point—that those who believe that software is an easy task are clearly wrong.

And there you have it. A story about the evolution of a research project. And, as it turned out, one with a happy ending!

(P.S. There's more. Once the "intellectual vs. clerical" findings became public, another researcher interested in creativity—professor Dan Couger of the University of Colorado—contacted us and suggested extending the work to explore the extent to which software work is not just intellectual, but creative. (What could be more relevant to a book on creativity?!) With his help—he provided us with a good definition of creativity—we conducted a follow-on study. Those findings, though less dramatic than those of the original paper, are also here in this section.)

In all the other introductory material in this chapter, I've defined the key terms involved. Let's not move on to the remainder of the material until we have defined intellectual, derived from intellect: "the mind's power of reasoning and acquiring knowledge (contrasted with feeling and instinct)"; and clerical: "of clerks, the activity of copying or writing something out."

Now, on with an investigation of the intellectual vs. clerical (vs. creative) aspects of software.

Software: Challenging or Trivial to Build?

Robert L. Glass
Computing Trends

Iris Vessey
Pennsylvania State University

Introduction

The world view of the complexity of creating software is schizophrenic. On the one hand, we have numerous professional journals and much college/university coursework devoted to various aspects of software engineering and we hear such noted computer scientists as David

Parnas and Donald Knuth expressing their strongly-felt belief that "software is hard" to produce [Parnas86, Knuth89].

On the other hand, we have a popular view that developing software is easy. For example [MBA90] states:

"It is easier to teach a business person about technology than it is to teach a techie how to manage.

"MIS should be managed by a business generalist rather than a technology specialist. I can teach my mother to code."

Further, the current glamor of CASE workbenches is due largely to the notion that major portions of software development can be automated. For example, [McClure88] states:

"A workbench has integrated tools that automate the entire development and maintenance of software systems and software project management. The output of one life-cycle phase is directly and automatically passed on to the next life-cycle phase; the final product is an executable software system and its documentation."

This quotation conveys the message that humans can by replaced by tools in the software development process.

Clearly these opinions are poles apart. In one we see software as challenging even for finely-honed intellectual minds. In the other we see software as so easy that almost anyone can produce it. What is wrong with these pictures? Can they both be right? If not, which is wrong?

Of course, the complexity of software is intimately related to the complexity of the problem the software is to solve. So it is entirely possible that some software is trivially easy while some is exceedingly complex. But, in saying that, we have avoided coming to grips with the still-important question "How difficult is this software job, anyway?"

There are many possible ways to answer this question. Parnas' experience with the A-7 project shows that software construction is indeed a complicated task [see, for example, Parnas85]. With regard to automated methods for producing software, Rich and Waters [Rich88] refer to the "cocktail party" myth of automatic programming.

Empirical evidence is provided by [Fjelstad79] who shows that software maintainers spend 45 percent of their time seeking understanding of a change to be made and of the software to be changed, 35 percent of their time verifying the change once it is made, and only 20 percent of their time actually making the change. Effectively, they spend 80 percent of their time thinking about the problem and its solution. Further empirical evidence [Woodfield79] shows that for every 25 percent increase in the complexity of a problem to be solved, there is a 100 percent increase in the complexity of the software required to solve it. This data suggests that the complexity of software is a problem of scale: easy tasks are easy to solve, hard ones are very hard.

Yet there is little evidence beyond that. We find the question begged in statements like " . . . testing comprises a planning part and an operative part. While the latter can take great advantage from the support of automated tools, the planning part is mostly based on human ingenuity and competence" [Bertolino91]. There is little in the way of specific or quantitative answers.

It is important to find these answers. The current state of the art and practice of software shows that beliefs such as those stated above, that anyone can develop software and that anyone can manage software development, are prevalent, if not predominant.

If software is largely a clerical activity, then these beliefs are valid. If it is not, then these beliefs are a disservice to the field. Getting an answer to the intellectual vs. clerical question, then, is a high-leverage task.

In this paper we take an initial, exploratory step toward answering that question. We present the results of a two-pronged approach to examining the intellectual versus the clerical components of the software development process. In section 2, we examine the tasks involved in software development, and determine which of them require intellect and which are largely clerical. Then, in section 3, we present the findings of an empirical study in which, for a systems analysis task, a record was made of the amount of time subjects spent thinking as opposed to drawing diagrams. Finally, section 4 presents the conclusions and implications of the study.

Software Task Classification

In Tables 1 and 2 we present several taxonomies of the tasks of software. Table 1 shows tasks performed by CASE tools as documented in the CASE literature. Because those tasks have been automated, it is probably fair to say that they are somewhat more clerical than those that have not. Table 2 shows a more abstract view of tasks, independent of whether there is a CASE tool to support them.

In understanding how much of software work is intellectual and how much is clerical, it would be helpful to ascertain from these lists which tasks are intellectual and which are clerical. Then a simplistic analysis could be used to say something like "X percent of software's tasks are intellectual, and Y percent are clerical." This would still not tell us what percentage of overall software work falls into each category, but it would be a major step in understanding, if not quantifying.

There are several problems in doing this, however. First, as can be seen from the tables, there is little consistency, at least at the wording level,

TABLE 1 Tasks Performed by CASE Tools.[a]

Software task[b]	Code
Functionalities of representation	
Represent a design	i
Construct models	i
Customize the language or conventions used for representation	i
Represent relationships	i
Combine entities or processes	id
* Show an object's attributes	
Maintain descriptions	c
Provide naming conventions	i
Maintain single definition	c
* Move between models	
Redraw a diagram	c
Map onto functional description	id
Combine equivalent processes	id
* Simultaneously display several views	
Choose a model	i
Functionalities of analysis	
Test for model consistency	i
Check for structural equivalence	i
Check for unnecessary or redundant connections	id
Detect inconsistencies	id
Identify impact of design changes	i
Search the design for similar objects	i
Suggest resolutions	i
Estimate characteristics	i
Search design for specified characteristics	i
Simulate the production environment	i
Identify rules violations	c
Trace relationships	id
Identify differences	i
Recommend a general model	i
* Perform an operation on part of a design	
Functionalities of transformation	
Generate executable code	i
Convert specification	i
Transform a representation	i
Provide documentation	id
Perform reverse engineering	i
Generate screen mockups	i
* Import/export data	
Create templates for tasks and deliverables	i
Propagate a change	c
Functionalities of control	
Specify who can review work	id
Provide management information	id
Maintain a record of responsibility	c

TABLE 1 (Continued)

Software task[b]	Code
Maintain a record of changes	c
Provide management information on more than one project	id
Specify who can modify	i
* Freeze a portion of a design	
Manage quality assurance	i
Alter rules	i
Provide prioritizing assistance	i
Estimate tasks/projects	i
Remind team about deadlines	c
Merge versions	c
Produce metrics	i
Maintain list of requirements and how satisfied	c
* Temporarily ignore a problem so work can continue	
Functionalities of cooperative functionality	
* Maintain a dialogue with other tools users	
* Allow a group to work simultaneously on a task	
* Send message to others who use the tools	
* Allow concurrent use of dictionary/diagram/etc.	
* Provide group interaction support (brainstorming)	
* Attach electronic notes	
* Allow anonymous feedback	
Notify designer of changes	c
Build a catalog of macros	c
Facilitate design alternatives	i
Functionalities of support	
Provide quick reference aids	i
Provide instructional materials	i
Identify external sources of information	i
Build templates/examples for tutorials/demos	i
Browse in other segments of the tool	i
Explain why part of a design is inconsistent	
Anticipate user errors from past patterns	i
Allow undoing a series of commands	i
Generate outputs in a variety of media	id
Incorporate command macros	i
Generate reports and documents	id
* Provide change pages	
* Magnify a model to see greater levels of detail	
Build a library of customized models	i
* Prepare, edit, store, send, and retrieve documents	
Store versions of a design	c
* Link a design to a library for testing	
* Develop, run and store customized reports	

[a] Henderson, J.C., and Cooprider, J.G., "Dimensions of IS Planning and Design Technology," Information Systems Research, Vol. 1, No. 3, 1990, 227–254.

[b] technology-based tasks

* technology-based tasks not considered in this task analysis

TABLE 2(a)   Software Tasks Performed.[a]

Software tasks	Code
Software requirements tasks	
Requirements identification	
Context analysis	i
Elicitation from people	i
Deriving software requirements from system requirements	i
Task analysis to develop user interface requirements	i
Identification of constraints	i
Requirements analysis	
Assessment of potential problems	i
Classification of requirements	i
Evaluation of feasibility and risks	i
Requirements representation	
Use of models	i
Roles for prototyping	i
Requirements communication	i
Preparation for validation (criteria, techniques)	i
Managing the requirements definition process	i

[a] Brackett, J. W., "Software Requirements," Software Engineering Institute, SEI-CMU-19-1.1, 1989.

TABLE 2(b)   Software Tasks Performed.[a]

Software tasks[b]	Code
Overall software tasks	
Requirements analysis	i
Data flow analysis	i
Functional decomposition	i
Production of design and specification documents	i
Control of document updates	c
* Reusable design access	
New code development	i
* Reusable code access	
Analysis and modification of existing code	i
Restructuring of existing code	c
Removal of dead code	i
Design reviews	i
Code inspections	i
Personal debugging	i
Test case development	i
Test library control	c
Defect analysis	i
User documentation production	i
On-line help and tutorial production	i
User training	i

[a] Jones, T. C., "Why Choose CASE?" *American Programmer*, vol, 3, No. 1 (Jan 1990), 14–21.
[b] technology-based tasks

to the task lists. Second, to someone unfamiliar with software development it is not apparent which tasks are intellectual and which are clerical. Third, outside of a specific context, even knowledgeable software specialists may have some disagreement in categorizing the tasks.

To overcome these difficulties, we used a simple approach to create the desired categorization. We used two experienced software professionals to independently categorize the tasks based on their intellectual(i) or clerical(c) implications for software development. Tasks that shared characteristics of both intellectual and clerical tasks were classified as indeterminate(id). The two classifiers achieved 77 percent agreement. Differences were resolved by using a third independent classifier to establish a majority decision. The findings of that process are presented in the right hand columns of Tables 1 and 2.

The summary of these categorizations is presented in Table 3: the percentage of intellectual, clerical, and indeterminate tasks in the set of CASE and non-CASE tasks. From Table 3, we see that even for CASE tools, intellectual tasks predominate over clerical ones, 62 percent to 21 percent. For non-CASE tasks the breakdown is especially dramatic, 83 percent vs. 17 percent. Overall, intellectual tasks predominate 71 percent to 18 percent.

We see clearly, using this rudimentary taxonomy, that the predominant number of tasks in software work is intellectual. Given the limitations of the approach, however, it is important to see this finding as only one piece of evidence in the development of an accurate picture.

Experimental Findings

One drawback of the above results is that the findings are about numbers of tasks rather than time spent on tasks. In this section, we report an-

TABLE 3   Categorization of CASE and Non-CASE Tasks.

Task categories	Clerical	Indeterminate	Intellectual
CASE tool tasks Henderson and	14[a]	11	40
Cooprider (1990)	(21)	(17)	(62)
Non-Case tasks			
Brackett (1989)	0	0	13
			(100)
Jones (1990)	3	0	15
	(17)		(83)
Overall	17	11	68
	(18)	(11)	(71)

[a]The table entries are numbers of tasks in each category; the figures in brackets are percentages.

other approach to answering the intellectual vs. clerical question. We sought to observe how much time developers actually spend thinking and how much time they spend acting on that thought, while engaged in a software task.

A group of subjects involved in a study of systems analysis conducted for another purpose [Vessey92] was videotaped while problem solving. The purpose of the original study was to observe systems analysts using various methodological approaches to specify the information requirements for either one or two case studies. Subjects studied a problem statement, thought about how to represent the problem in the specification graphic of choice, and then drew the graphic (in this case, manually). It was possible, from the video tapes, to record thinking time vs. drawing time for the study subjects.

Table 4 shows the result of that study. There is a fascinating consistency to the results. Most subjects spent roughly 21 percent of their time writing (drawing graphics), and the remaining 79 percent of their time thinking. The range in thinking time is from 72 to 85 percent, certainly a narrow range for a group of subjects thought to have nothing much in common except for the pool from which they were drawn.

It is important to note, in spite of the interesting consistency of findings here, several limitations of this study. First, the subject pool consists of graduate students with little or no practitioner experience in systems analysis. Second, the findings are from a study conducted for another purpose; the experiment was not designed specifically to control any relevant variables. Third, the task of specifying information requirements is by na-

TABLE 4   Thinking Time Versus Writing Time During Systems Analysis.

				% of total time	
Subject	Problem	Total time (mins.)	Writing time (mins.)	Writing	Thinking
S3	1	153	23.1	15	85
	2	106	20.5	19	81
S4	1	117	24.2	21	79
	2	26	6.8	26	74
S6	1	108	18.7	17	83
	2	60	12.4	21	79
S10	1	51	11.0	22	78
	2	41	10.0	24	76
S11	1	61	12.8	21	79
	2	87	15.3	18	82
S12	1	61	16.9	28	72
	2	67	14.3	21	79

ture an unstructured and therefore intellectual task since it deals with formulating the initial model of the real world problem to be solved.

Because of the consistency of the findings, however, it is possible to say that, at least for a student population, intellectual time spent doing systems analysis is roughly four times the amount of time spent on relatively clerical activities.

There are several questions that still need to be answered: (1) Do the numbers differ for practitioner subjects? (2) Are the numbers similar for activities other than systems analysis? (3) Do the numbers depend on the case studies used in this particular study? (Note, however, that across the two cases examined here, the numbers vary little.) Answers to these questions would help in formulating a better understanding of the relationship between intellectual and clerical activities in software.

Conclusions and Implications

The issue of intellectual vs. clerical effort spent in software activities is an important one, and one that is somewhat controversial. Information bearing on the issue would help us to answer such questions as:

1. How much benefit can we REALLY expect from software automation?
2. Can we use relatively unskilled people (for example, untrained end users?) to build and maintain software?
3. How important are technical skills to the task of managing software?

In this study, we provide some initial, though diverse, evidence to resolve these important issues. The findings are interestingly consistent. From an examination of tasks performed, we see by analysis that intellectual tasks predominate over clerical ones in software work by roughly 71 percent to 18 percent, or almost 4 to 1. From an experimental study of time spent performing systems analysis, we see by observation that intellectual activities predominate over clerical ones by 79 to 21 percent, or almost 4 to 1.

The figures for the number of intellectual versus clerical software tasks and the amount of time spent on intellectual versus clerical activities in systems analysis are surprisingly similar. This initial exploration shows the tasks of software are considerably more intellectual than clerical. Thus, an early conclusion is that even simple software tasks are more intellectual than the "anyone can build software" viewpoint expressed in the introduction to this paper. The findings of these preliminary steps are certainly not definitive, however. Further work is needed to better differentiate and explore these findings.

Acknowledgment—The authors are indebted to Umesh Bhatia and Sue Conger for research assistance on this project. A modified version of this material was published in the journal Information and Management, November 1992.

REFERENCES

BERTOLINO91—"An Overview of Automated Software Testing," *Journal of Systems and Software*, May 1991; A. Bertolino

FJELSTAD79—"Application Maintenance Study: Report to Our Respondents," Proceedings of GUIDE 48, The Guide Corporation, Philadelphia, 1979; R. K. Fjelstad and W. T. Hamlen

KNUTH89—Keynote address, World Computer Congress, 1989, as reported in System Development, Dec. 1989; Donald E. Knuth

MBA90—"More on MBAs in MIS," letters to the editor in response to an article on whether the employment of MBAs in Information Systems positions helps or hurts organizations, Information Week, March 19, 1990.

McCLURE88—"The CASE for Structured Development," PC Tech Journal, August 1988, 51–67; Carma McClure

PARNAS85—"The Modular Structure of Complex Systems," IEEE Transactions on Software Engineering, March 1985; David L. Parnas, et al.

PARNAS86—Presentation at Seattle University graduate program seminar, 1986; David Lorge Parnas

RICH88—"Automatic Programming: Myths and Prospects," Computer, August 1988, 40–51; Charles Rich and Richard Waters

VESSEY92—"Specifying Information Requirements: Factors Influencing Problem Analysis," unpublished manuscript; Iris Vessey and Sue A. Conger

WOODFIELD79"An Experiment on Unit Increase in Program Complexity," IEEE Transactions on Software Engineering, March, 1979; Scott Woodfield

Software Tasks: Intellectual, Clerical ... or Creative?

Robert L. Glass
Computing Trends

Iris Vessey
Pennsylvania State University

Introduction

There have been few studies of the nature of software work. That is, there is little research evidence to support one or all of the following points of view:

- Software's tasks are easy and automatable.
- Software's tasks are intellectually complex and challenging.
- Software's tasks require large amounts of creativity.

What makes the lack of studies of these issues surprising is that each of the above viewpoints has intellectual and political support among some members of the computing community, and yet it is largely impossible for all three of these points of view to be correct.

For example, consider these statements:

- Managers of companies with significant computing activities have made public statements to the effect that "I can teach my mother how to code" [MBA 1990], conveying their belief that software's tasks are trivial.
- Gurus active in predicting the future of computing have taken the position that the future will see "application development without programmers" [Martin 1982], implying that software skills can easily be acquired by end users, or even "automated."
- Leading software engineering academics see software as the most complicated activity ever undertaken by humanity [USNRC 1990], implying that the search for order-of-magnitude improvements for the tasks of software is probably doomed.
- Authors of popular books in the field decry the advocacy of formal and disciplined processes for software development on the grounds that such approaches leave little room for the creativity essential to software design and construction (see, for example, [DeGrace 1993]).

The breadth of these conflicting beliefs and the depth of the underlying conviction of their supports begs a study of software tasks. Is it possible that all of these divergent points of view can, somehow, coexist? If not, which point of view is closest to the truth?

The objective of this paper is to present findings from a previous exploration of these issues and to report additional findings from a new and, to some extent, troubling study.

The paper proceeds as follows: The following section describes our previous study, which assessed the *intellectual* vs. *clerical* nature of software tasks. This is followed by a description of the current study, which assessed the *creative* nature of the tasks. We then analyze the findings of the two studies, while the last section presents conclusions.

The Prior Study

One way of approaching the issues presented above is to study the nature of software tasks by addressing the extent to which they are clerical, intellectual, and creative in nature.

This approach reduces the complicated issues identified in the preceding section to three surrogates. If we could somehow classify software tasks into one or more of these three categories, we would have a crisp—if perhaps simplistic—basis for tasks differentiation, leading to broader answers to the issues of concern.

In the prior study [Glass 1992], the authors used two approaches to answering this question:

- Measuring the amount of time taken by novice systems analysts in thinking about (intellectual activity), and carrying out (largely clerical activity), the tasks of specifying the requirements for some relatively simple software projects
- Evaluating, through expert judgment, the intellectual or clerical nature of several lists of software tasks appearing in the software literature and representative of all phases of the software development life cycle

Note that these approaches addressed part of the issue of concern (intellectual vs. clerical activities) via both a timing analysis and a task analysis, but did not address the creative nature of software tasks. That omission is rectified in the current study.

What was fascinating about the prior study was that the intellectual vs. clerical nature of the tasks consistently measured roughly 80–20 in favor of intellectual activity. That is, with several subjects being timed, a surprisingly consistent 80% of the subject's time was spent thinking (i.e., the subject was engaged in intellectual activity). With expert judgement applied to the nature of the tasks, once again—and coincidentally—80% of the tasks were considered intellectual.

In the current study, we undertook to pursue this research area further, and eliminate one of the shortcomings of the first study, the failure to consider the third issue of the intellectual/clerical/creative triad, the issue of the creativity needed for software tasks.

The Current Study

To address the issue of creativity, two things were necessary: a good definition of creativity as applied to software development; and a mechanism for evaluating the need for creativity in software tasks analogous to that employed in the first study, so that comparisons could be made.

The definition of creativity used in this study is based on the work on problem-solving presented in [Newell 1962] and used in most studies of creativity in software (e.g., [Couger 1990]). This work takes the position that to be creative, a solution must satisfy one or more of the following conditions:

1. The product of the thinking has *novelty* or *value*.
2. The thinking is *unconventional*, in the sense that it requires modification or rejection of previously accepted ideas.
3. The thinking requires *high motivation* and *persistence*, taking place over a considerable span of time (continuously or intermittently) or at high intensity.
4. The problem as initially posed was *vague* and *ill-defined*, so that part of the task was to formulate the problem itself.

The key words here—novelty, value, unconventional, high motivation, persistence, vague, and ill-defined—appeared sufficient to support a determination as to which software tasks were creative.

To solve the second part of the research problem—that is, to make this study comparable to the prior one—we used the same lists of software tasks as the first study, evaluating the tasks for their creative nature. Unfortunately, although we would also have liked to perform a timing analysis analogous to the first study, there was no way to identify in that research approach (protocol analysis recorded on video tapes) the amount of time spent being creative. Thus, in this current study of creative vs. intellectual and clerical tasks, we have classified the tasks of software into one or more of each of those categories, but we have not timed subjects to see how much of their time was creative as opposed to intellectual or clerical.

As in the first study, then, we used the judgements of experts to decide which tasks were creative. In the prior study, we used two experts, and for those tasks where the experts differed, a third expert resolved the differences. In this study, because we anticipated that the judgements might prove to be more difficult, we employed four experts. One expert had both academic and practitioner information systems experience; one was largely an academic information systems specialist; one was a software engineering academic specialist; and one had both software engineering and practitioner experience. Thus, the backgrounds of those participating in the study were reasonably diverse.

Tables 1, 2(a) and 2(b), and 3 present the findings of the study. (Note that the findings of the prior study are included in these tables as well.)

TABLE 1 Tasks Performed by CASE Tools[a]

Software task	Intellectual/ clerical code[b]	Creativity score
Functionalities of representation		
Represent a design	i	.25
Construct models	i	.75
Customize the language or conventions used for representation	i	.50
Represent relationships	i	.25
Combine entities or processes	id	.25
* Show an object's attributes		
Maintain descriptions	c	
Provide naming conventions	i	
Maintain single definition	c	
* Move between models		
Redraw a diagram	c	
Map onto functional description	id	.25
Combine equivalent processes	id	.25
* Simultaneously display several views		
Choose a model	i	.25
Functionalities of analysis		
Test for model consistency	i	.25
Check for structural equivalence	i	
Check for unnecessary or redundant connections	id	
Detect inconsistencies	id	
Identify impact of design changes	i	.25
Search the design for similar objects	i	
Suggest resolutions	i	.50
Estimate characteristics	i	.25
Search design for specified characteristics	i	
Simulate the production environment	i	.25
Identify rules violations	c	
Trace relationships	id	
Identify differences	i	
Recommend a general model	i	.75
* Perform an operation on part of a design		
Functionalities of transformation		
Generate executable code	i	
Convert specification	i	
Transform a representation	i	
Provide documentation	id	
Perform reverse engineering	i	.50
Generate screen mockups	i	.25
* Import/export data		
Create templates for tasks and deliverables	i	
Propagate a change	c	
Functionalities of control		
Specify who can review work	id	
Provide management information	id	
Maintain a record of responsibility	c	
Maintain a record of changes	c	
Provide management information on more than one project		

TABLE 1 (Continued)

Software task	Intellectual/clerical code[b]	Creativity score
Specify who can modify		
* Freeze a portion of a design	i	
Manage quality assurance		
Alter rules	i	
Provide prioritizing assistance	i	.25
Estimate tasks/projects	i	.25
Remind team about deadlines	i	
Merge versions	c	
Produce metrics	c	
Maintain list of requirements and how satisfied	i	
* Temporarily ignore a problem so work can continue	c	
Functionalities of cooperative functionality		
* Maintain a dialogue with other tools users		
* Allow a group to work simultaneously on a task		
* Send message to others who use the tools		
* Allow concurrent use of dictionary/diagram/etc.		
* Provide group interaction support (brainstorming)		
* Attach electronic notes		
* Allow anonymous feedback	c	
Notify designer of changes	c	
Build a catalog of macros	i	
Facilitate design alternatives	c	
Functionalities of support	c	
Provide quick reference aids	i	50
Provide instructional materials		
Identify external sources of information	i	
Build templates/examples for tutorials/demos	i	
Browse in other segments of the tool	i	
Explain why part of a design is inconsistent	i	
Anticipate user errors from past patterns	i	
Allow undoing a series of commands	i	
Generate outputs in a variety of media	i	
Incorporate command macros	i	.25
Generate reports and documents	id	
* Provide change pages		
* Magnify a model to see greater levels of detail		
Build a library of customized models		
* Prepare, edit, store, send, and retrieve documents		
Store versions of a design		.25
* Link a design to a library for testing		
* Develop, run and store customized reports	c	

[a]Henderson, J. C., and Cooprider, J. G., "Dimensions of IS Planning and Design Technology," Information Systems Research, 1 (3), 1990, 227-254

[b]i = intellectual task
c = clerical task
id = indeterminate task

*Technology-based tasks not considered in this task analysis

TABLE 2(a)   Software Tasks Performed[a]

Software task	Intellectual/ clerical code[b]	Creativity score
Software requirements tasks		
Requirements identification		
Context analysis	i	.75
Elicitation from people	i	.50
Deriving software requirements from system requirements	i	.25
Task analysis to develop user interface requirements	i	.25
Identification of constraints	i	.50
Requirements analysis		
Assessment of potential problems	i	.75
Classification of requirements	i	.25
Evaluation of feasibility and risks	i	.75
Requirements representation		
Use of models	i	.50
Roles for prototyping	i	.25
Requirements communication	i	
Preparation for validation (criteria, techniques)	i	
Managing the requirements definition process	i	

[a]Brackett, J. W., "Software Requirements," Software Engineering Institute, SEI-CMU-19-1.1, 1989.

[b]i = intellectual task
c = clerical task
id = indeterminate task

Tables 1 and 2 present the raw data, the codes assigned to each of the tasks by the expert judges, while Table 3 represents a summary of the findings shown in Tables 1 and 2. In Tables 1 and 2, the judgments of the experts on the creativity inherent in the tasks is added as a new column to the original intellectual vs. clerical coding of the prior study. For each expert who judged a task to be creative, a creativity score of .25 was assigned. If all four experts judged a task creative, the total score was 1.00.

In Table 3, the section labeled "creative tasks" represents the cumulation of the results shown in Tables 1 and 2. The first column represents the range of tasks judged to be creative by the four experts, from the lowest number of tasks identified by an expert as creative to the highest. The next two columns represent the numbers of tasks identified as creative by at least one expert ("some support"), and by two or more experts ("considerable support"). The final column represents a "weighted" average obtained by summing the creativity scores in Tables 1 and 2.

Table 3 tells us, for example, that for the CASE tool tasks of Table 1:

TABLE 2(b)   Software Tasks Performed[a]

Software task	Intellectual/ clerical code[b]	Creativity score
Overall software tasks		
Requirements analysis	i	1.00
Data flow analysis	i	1.00
Functional decomposition	i	.50
Production of design and specification documents	i	
Control of document updates	c	
* Reusable design access		
New code development	i	
* Reusable code access		
Analysis and modification of existing code	i	.25
Restructuring of existing code	c	
Removal of dead code	i	
Design reviews	i	.25
Code inspections	i	
Personal debugging	i	.25
Test case development	i	.50
Test library control	c	
Defect analysis	i	
User documentation production	i	
On-line help and tutorial production	i	
User training	i	

[a]Jones, T. C., "Why Choose CASE?" *American Programmer*, 3, 1 January 1990, 14–21.
[b]i = intellectual task
  c = clerical task
  id = indeterminate task

*Technology-based tasks not considered further in this analysis

- The range among the experts of the number of tasks considered creative was between 0 (one expert did not assess these tasks since they could be performed by CASE tools) to 18 (of the 40 intellectual tasks).
- There was some support (at least one expert) for 21 of the tasks being creative.
- There was considerable support for six of the tasks being creative.
- The weighted average number of creative tasks in Table 1 was 7.25.

What do we see in these tables? Perhaps the most dominant finding is that the experts viewed the tasks and their creative aspects in diverse ways. As opposed to the consistency of the intellectual vs. clerical classification, there was only marginal agreement among these four experts. Given individual tasks, for example, although there were some cases of strong agree-

TABLE 3 Categorization of CASE and Non-CASE Tasks

Task Categories	Intellectual/clerical tasks			Range	Creative tasks		
	Clerical	Indeterminate	Intellectual		Some support[a]	Considerable support[b]	"Weighted" average[c]
CASE tool tasks							
Table 1	14[d] (21)	11 (17)	40 (62)	0–18	21	6	7.25
Non-CASE tasks							
Table 2(a)	0	0	13 (100)	3–7	10	6	4.75
Table 2(b)	3 (17)	0	15 (83)	2–5	7	4	3.75
Overall	17 (18)	11 (11)	68 (71)	6–28	38	16	15.75

[a]Number of tasks identified as creative by at least one expert
[b]Number of tasks identified as creative by two or more experts
[c]Sum of creativity scores
[d]The table entries are numbers of tasks in each category; the figures in brackets are percentages.

ment—all four experts agreed that "requirements analysis" and "data flow analysis" in Table 2(b) were creative—there were often significant differences in the expert judgements.

Whereas one expert saw some modeling tasks as creative, for example, others did not. Note the predominance of .25 scores in the table; these indicate instances where only one expert ("some support") perceived a task to be creative.

The overall view of software tasks, presented in Table 3, also reveals considerable diversity. Percentages for the creative tasks are not given, since the clerical-indeterminate-intellectual figures in the table are from the prior study and already sum to 100%. (Note that tasks scored as creative almost always were those originally classified as intellectual.) The percentage of creative tasks out of the whole, however, is roughly 16%, with a range of 6%–29%. The wide ranges indicate that the experts did not agree on the extent to which software tasks are creative.

Analysis of Findings

Why did the experts differ so widely in their perceptions? There are several possible contributors to the problem.

First of all, the *task definitions* require considerable interpretation from the viewpoint of creativity. In spite of the fact that they are quite specific and represent a hierarchic decomposition to a fairly low level, there is still a great deal of room for doubt as to what they involve. One expert, for example, marked many tasks with a "?" regarding whether they were creative or not, and another scored many tasks as yes/no, implying that they might or might not be creative, depending on how one interpreted them. (It is interesting to note that, in spite of the fact that these "yes/no" votes were scored as no's in the tables, the expert who saw this ambiguity was the one who also saw the highest percentage of software tasks as being creative. In other words, if the yes/no votes had been counted as yes's, this person's overall scoring would have been far higher than 29%.)

Not only did the task definitions require interpretation; so did the *definition of creativity*. In spite of the fact that the definition is commonly accepted, the experts found it difficult to apply in the context of specific tasks. What constitutes "novelty," for example, or when is thinking "unconventional"? One person's "vague and ill-defined" problem might be another's oft-solved favorite. Personal experience probably played an important role in making judgements of this kind.

Finally, *personal bias* may also have entered into the expert judgements. Most experts already have a preconceived view of whether the work is creative or not. (Imagine trying to impanel a jury of professional peers who are impartial on the subject!) Thus, when interpreting a particular task in the context of an ambiguous definition of creativity, an expert might tend to favor their inherent view of the subject, rather than one formed at the time of the study.

Conclusions

This paper presents findings from a research study of an important issue; it sheds light on the issue, but does not resolve it. Clearly, some amount of the tasks of software require creativity. Just as clearly, there is little agreement—at least in this study—of what that amount is.

In spite of the lack of definitive results, some conclusions can, we believe, be drawn.

First, from the point of view of practice, the fact that creativity is an essential part of some software development tasks ought to refute the "I can teach my mother to code" and the "application development without programmers" viewpoints that perceive software work to be not very challenging. Clearly, these studies show that there are substantive intellectual tasks in the development of software, some (perhaps many) of which require creativity in their accomplishment. Given that we do not presently know how to automate creativity, and quite possibly never will, the fact that *some* creativity is involved in the work means that software tasks will probably never be completely automated or delegated to those with an absence of significant software skills.

Second, from the point of view of research, the fact that creativity is an essential part of the work of software development ought to motivate further studies into the subject. The issue of how creative software tasks are remains important but unresolved; and techniques for increasing and managing creativity might form an important focus for both software pedagogy and research.

Third, from the point of view of research funding, the fact that creativity is important for certain software tasks could motivate granting institutions to support proposals aimed at automating automatable tasks, rather than the less feasible current approach of automating all of the work of software development. Certainly, attempts to automate tasks requiring creativity are less likely to be successful than attempts to automate less demanding tasks.

These findings do lend support to the views expressed earlier in the paper, that software tasks are complex (note the sheer number of tasks defined in the tables—96 in all!), and that creativity is and probably always will be a key component of providing software solutions. The evidence is not as solid as we would have liked, but nonetheless, the evidence is there.

Acknowledgments

The authors wish to acknowledge the support of Bruce I. Blum, Dennis F. Galletta, and N. S. Umanath in the accomplishment of this work.

REFERENCES

[Couger 1990] J. DANIEL COUGER, "Ensuring Creative Approaches in Information System Design," *Managerial and Decision Economics*, Vol. 11, pp. 281–295, 1990.

[DeGrace 1993] P. DEGRACE and L. STAHL, *The Olduvai Imperative: CASE and the State of Software Engineering Practice*, Yourdon Press, 1993.

[Glass 1992] ROBERT L. GLASS, IRIS VESSEY, and SUE A. CONGER, "Software Tasks: Intellectual or Clerical?" *Information and Management*, Nov., 1992.

[Martin 1982] J. MARTIN, *Application Development Without Programmers*, Prentice-Hall, 1982.

[MBA 1990] "More on MBAs in MIS," *Information Week*, Fax Forum, p. 56. March 19, 1990.

[Newell 1962] A. NEWELL, J. SHAW, and H. SIMON, "The Processes of Creative Thinking," in *Contemporary Approaches to Creative Thinking*, H. Gruber, G. Terrell, and M. Wertheimer (eds.), Atherton Press, 1962.

[USNRC 1990] "Scaling Up: A Research Agenda for Software Engineering," Computer Science and Technology Board, U.S. National Research Council, 1990.

BUYING BREAKTHROUGH CONCEPTS FOR ALL THE WRONG REASONS

Each new software engineering idea that flows down the pipe from the world of research and the world of the vendor is heralded as the solution to all the productivity and quality woes of software.

And each new idea, once it hits the software shop floor, dissolves into a puddle of mediocrity.

What is wrong with this picture? Are software practitioners incredibly stubborn? Or stupid? Are researchers and vendors incredibly naive? Or wrong?

Whatever the answers to these questions, they are certainly well worth asking. Large sums of money are spent by management on each of these new ideas. Where *are* those promised benefits?

Oddly, there are few carefully thought-through answers to these questions. There are, of course, some very subjective ones. Researchers and vendors privately and quietly (and, on occasion, publicly and loudly) agree that, in fact, practitioners *are* incredibly stubborn and stupid. The whole premise of the "software crisis," in fact, rests on this belief.

However, this view does not really make sense. For one thing, today's practitioners—and yesterday's—have solved unimaginable problems in this new discipline, sending people into space, controlling the world's economic processes, and waging war in whole new ways. Furthermore, the software practitioners of today are the product of yesterday's academics. (That is, most practitioners by now have graduated from the same programs in which our researchers are the teachers.) How could the wiles of practice have subverted these students-cum-practitioners so quickly?

At the same time as researchers and vendors are wringing their hands about practitioners, practitioners are privately and quietly (less often publicly and loudly) agreeing that, in fact, their nemeses are incredibly naive and wrong. "Just leave us alone," they frequently tell the researchers and vendors; "we have enough troubles without *your* getting involved."

But this view also does not make sense. For one thing, today's researchers—and yesterday's—are incredibly bright people who have created concepts and defined approaches that are as mind-boggling in their own way as the applications built by the practitioners. To imply that they are naive and wrong about practice suggests that they have not even tried to understand it; certainly, it is inconceivable that they could have tried and failed.

So why is this phenomenon happening, again and again? Why are claims made for new technologies that dissolve into nothingness?

I think there's a fairly simple starting place to look for an answer. That starting place lies in an understanding of the intrinsic nature of software construction, and it attaches itself to the title of this section. It is important, in order to understand why software breakthroughs so frequently break down, to understand the distinction between intellectual and clerical activities, and the degree to which each is important.

First of all, consider this issue. Do we, at this point in time, know how to build software that dramatically improves the capability of human beings to think?

Then consider this issue: For those human tasks that are thought-intensive, do computers offer breakthrough support?

I would assert that, if we divorce those questions from the issue of software construction, the fairly clear answers are "no" and "no." Computers and software, for all the wonderful power they offer, are not tools that can broadly augment the human mind in pursuit of challenging intellectual tasks. Not yet, for sure (this point of view will be substantiated by the essay "Computer Support for Creativity" later in this book). Not ever, perhaps. Time alone will tell.

But what of all the CASE tools and 4GLs and other major technology changes for software, I hear you asking? We *must* consider these issues in the context of software. And there, you may be saying, the answers are somehow different.

Well, let's take CASE tools as a particularly interesting example of this phenomenon. There was an article partway through the hoopla of the CASE revolution [Bird91] that shed some light on this issue. It was a popular computing press article, I grant you, and the author didn't quite understand the significance of what he was saying, but nevertheless there's some fascinating insight in what he said.

"Many companies using the most popular CASE tools do all of the early work on whiteboards," the article said. "Only when everything is correct (or nearly correct) on the whiteboard do users employ the CASE tools. Is this what management bought into when spending $10,000 to $15,000 for the CASE software?" the author asks. "Surely management has a right to expect better tools for the creative phases."

"For the creative phases." There's the nub of it all. The software was purchased, the author of this article is clearly implying, as a tool to help human thought processes. And he's right, of course. The manager who spent those large sums of money expected, probably based on vendor promises, perhaps in turn based on researcher claims, that these tools would support the essential, intellectual, perhaps even creative work of software development.

And they don't. That's where the problem, and the truth, lies. Most CASE tools—especially the upper CASE ones that help the systems analysis and design process (arguably the most intellectual and creative of the life cycle phases)—do not, and were never intended to, replace the intellectual processes involved. They help the systems analysts and the software designers create and modify and keep *representations* of the result of the systems analysis and design process.

Let's say that again, because it's important. Most of these upper CASE tools are about supporting the representation process, not the intellectual process of creating those representations. They are two very different activities. The first, the one in which a problem comes to be understood and a design comes to be created, are deeply intellectual processes. The second, the one in which the drawings are made and the specifications and design are saved, is by contrast relatively clerical.

Seen in that light, a couple of things become clear. First, the expectations of the managers who bought the CASE tools were simply wrong. They may have thought they were buying intellect-augmenting capability, but they were not.

Second, the workers using the whiteboard before they used the CASE tool may very well have gotten it right. That is, they augmented their intellectual processes with a medium that (a) facilitated group work, and (b) permitted quick revision and rework. Most of today's CASE tools are not very good at either of those things. Yet group and heuristic processes, most would agree, are at the heart of the intellectually challenging parts of the software process.

What is the point of all this? We have done poorly, in our field of software, distinguishing between those parts of the job that are intellectually challenging/and those that are largely clerical. In the confusion resulting from that, we mistake capabilities that support one aspect of software work with capabilities that might help us with another.

Worse yet, we make that same mistake over and over again. We expect 4GLs to do away with the need for programmers, and we wonder why the need for programmers is even greater than it was in pre-4GL days. We expect CASE tools to automate the task of programming, especially systems analysis and design, and then we wonder why many of them end up as shelfware. We expect object orientation to be the next software panacea, once again reducing the work of software to something simple, and then we hear to our growing astonishment that object-oriented software developers probably need *more* skill and ability than their predecessors.

We spend a lot of money for breakthrough concepts, in short, that bring us small improvements—many say they average around 5–30%—but never the major change in productivity that we thought we were paying for. We end up angry and disappointed and suspicious. Upper management, wondering when the promised abolishment of programmers can finally happen, becomes impatient, then angry, and then loses all trust in computing organizations.

This cycle of breakthrough to bust is a vicious one, and it happens over and over again. This is because, I would assert, we understand our field so poorly that we have failed to distinguish between the software tasks that are intellectually complex and those that are not. Until software practitioners understand what they are buying; until vendors are honest enough to describe what they are selling; and until researchers are thorough enough to evaluate what they are advocating, we will continue iterating through this cycle of promised breakthrough followed by bust. And we will avoid making the incremental progress that *is* possible in our field.

REFERENCE

[Bird91] CHRIS BIRD, "CASE CROP A FLOP," *Software Magazine*, NOV. 8, 1991.

"Nobody knows how the Arab architect designed [the dome of the Masjid-I-Jami in Isfahan] but centuries before the necessary mathematics were developed he managed to create a dome of almost perfect proportion."

—Horace Freeland Judson, in *The Search for Solutions*,
Holt, Rinehart and Winston, 1980
(Reprinted by permission of Henry Holt and Company, Inc.)

"The Greek notion of science held it above vulgar pragmatics, leading to a pedantic tendency that tolerated intellectual laxity, sometimes with tragic consequences."

—Noah Kennedy, in *The Industrialization of Intelligence*, Unwin Hyman, 1989

2.7 THEORY VERSUS PRACTICE

When it comes to choosing up sides on the issue of software approaches, we find some strange bedfellows.

If the two predominant approaches are

- Disciplined/Formal/Optimizing/Quantitative/Process/Clerical

and

- Flexible/Heuristic/Satisficing/Qualitative/Product/Intellectual

(and how's that for a nifty reprise of all the section titles in this chapter so far?!) what we find is that theory people, for the most part, have chosen the first collection, and practice people, again for the most part, have chosen the second.

But isn't that a bit strange? Think of the nature of the work that theory people do. Theorists, in their work, do all of the things that they do *not* choose for practitioners, and they avoid all of the things that they *do* choose for them.

Imagine, for example, a disciplined, formal theorist who expected to produce, in his or her research, optimal, quantitative findings using highly clerical approaches. It just doesn't wash.

So why, then, is it the theorists of computing who advocate all those things for software practitioners that are just the opposite of their own behavior? I've thought about that a lot over the years, but I've never come up with a very satisfactory answer.

Could it be that they genuinely believe that the task of building software is so easy that these disciplined, formal, even clerical approaches will work?

Could it be that, in spite of not wanting to use the approaches themselves, they don't really see the weaknesses inherent in disciplined, formal, clerical approaches?

Could it be that they don't want to believe, as Parnas and Brooks would have us believe, that software work is the most complex that humanity has ever undertaken, because it would belittle their own work?

Or could it be that the quest for formal, disciplined approaches is such an interesting assignment that they pursue it in the absence of any knowledge or philosophy on whether it is the right thing to do on behalf of software practice?

I tend to side with the latter answer. After all, the chief motivator for a theorist is the pursuit of interesting (as opposed to useful) work (a later essay in another section will reprise that theme). What could be more interesting than inventing languages and formalisms, and defining discipline and methodologies, to be used by others? And if there is a slight suspicion that these approaches, although interesting, are the wrong thing to do on behalf of practice, that can quickly be overcome by reading the writings of other theorists—there are plenty of them—who belittle practice and make it sound easy and automatable. Plus, as the capper on the problem, most theorists have never experienced the world of practice, and have little or no basis on which to pass judgements upon it.

However, to give the devil its due, as we move more and more in the direction of domain-specific software approaches and increase our knowledge of how to solve very specific problems in very specific domains, there is a chance that we will identify some problems in some domains which can be solved by disciplined, formal, even clerical approaches. What are 4GLs, after all, if not problem-oriented languages for the report generation cum database access application domain? And don't 4GLs come about as close as we know how, at this point, to reducing software work to an automatable task? Thus, there is some justification for the collection of concepts that these theorists support, and that justification could very well increase over time.

But that will be then, and this is now. In the world of today, I would suggest that this is the appropriate status of the choosing up sides issues . . . a theory, you might say, about practice:

- Discipline vs. flexibility: Discipline is essential for programming in the large projects and useful for medium-sized ones, but can be a terrible burden on smaller ones. Flexibility? It is essential in *all* of those project categories. The "odd couple" must continue to live on!
- Formal methods vs. heuristics: Formal methods simply have not been shown to work in large projects or even medium-sized ones, and al-

though they can be used on smaller ones, there is little or no evidence that the approach is very beneficial. (Bear in mind that this is after nearly 25 years of research in the area!) Heuristic approaches, on the contrary, are used on all sizes of projects.

- Optimizing vs. satisficing: Optimizing solutions, though eagerly sought, are usually impossible for complex and significant problems. Settling for satisficing is the state of the practice. (Of course, these statements are problem-dependent. Some problems, such as those in the information systems area, are solved optimally if they are solved at all. The same is not true for, say, weather forecasting.)

- Quantitative vs. qualitative: The search for quantitative answers always takes precedence in practice over the search for qualitative ones ... even when it shouldn't! But, of course, the search for valid quantitative answers frequently fails, because many things in life cannot be meaningfully quantified. Oddly and dangerously, qualitative answers masquerading as quantitative ones are often misused.

- Process vs. product: Process has always been a focus of software practice, from the earliest days when it was called "techniques" or "methods." (Early issues of *Communications of the ACM*, for example, had a "Pracniques" column). The Software Engineering Institute's process modeling work has brought the issue into sharper focus in recent years and directed it more toward management process. However, the focus of practice, then and now and always, is on product.

- Intellectual vs. clerical tasks: Intellectual activities predominate in practice, at around the 80% level, as we saw in the previous section. Clerical tasks do exist—configuration management, change tracking, test case execution, and others—and they are very important to the field, but there are far fewer of them.

There, for what it's worth, is my own theory about software practice. I'd be interested to know how it compares with yours.

In the essays to follow in this section, I will explore further this theory vs. practice issue; but here, we will have a different focus. I want to look at the state of the theory and the state of the practice, and how they relate to each other. I think you may find some surprises here.

The Temporal Relationship Between Theory and Practice

"Theory: a statement of the principles on which a subject is based."
"Practice: action as opposed to theory; to be actively engaged in professional work." (Oxford American Dictionary, 1980).

The meanings of the words "theory" and "practice" are clear enough and accepted enough that we have little doubt about what someone means when they use them. But what about the temporal relationship between the two notions; that is, which comes first, theory or practice?

For most of us who have spent a decade or more in a school system, the answer is probably automatic; theory precedes and frames practice. But that automatic answer may be severely flawed, and in that automatic answer may be some profound misunderstandings.

Take, for example, this quotation from Christopher Alexander's *Notes on the Synthesis of Form* (Harvard University Press, 1964):

> The airfoil wing section which allows airplanes to fly was invented at a time when it had just been 'proved' that no machine heavier than air could fly. Its aerodynamic properties were not understood until some time after it had been in use. Indeed the invention and use of the airfoil made a substantial contribution to the development of aerodynamic theory, rather than vice versa.

According to Alexander, then, practice here preceded theory. Are there more examples of that perhaps surprising idea?

Another such quotation, astounding in its similarity to Alexander's, comes from D. D. Price's *Sealing Wax and String: A Philosophy of the Experimenter's Craft and Its Role in the Genesis of High Technology* (Proceedings of the American Association for the Advancement of Science Annual Meeting, 1983):

> Thermodynamics owes much more to the steam engine than the steam engine owes to thermodynamics. . . . If we look at the usual course of events in the historical record . . . there are very few examples where technology is applied science. Rather it is much more often the case that science is applied technology.

Two instances of practice preceding theory do not prove a case or even establish a trend, of course; but Price suggests that in fact there may be a trend here. Are there more examples?

Herbert A. Simon, in *The Sciences of the Artificial* (The MIT Press, 2nd Edition, 1981), says:

> . . . the main route to the development and improvement of time-sharing systems was to build them and see how they behaved. And this is what was done. They were built, modified, and improved in successive stages. Perhaps theory could have anticipated these experiments and made them unnecessary. In fact it didn't, and I don't know anyone intimately acquainted with

these exceedingly complex systems who has very specific ideas as to how it might have done so. To understand them, the systems had to be constructed, and their behavior observed.

In accordance with Simon, the notion that practice precedes theory is beginning to hit closer to home, in our own computing and software worlds. Let us look more at theory and practice in software.

I grew up in the practice of computing and software, and I recall many of the formative events in the field. This notion of practice preceding theory rings true to me. The origins of the computer, of course, go back to the early research labs in institutions scattered across North America and Europe. Yet by the mid-1950s, computing and software were beginning to thrive as professional fields. Practice, if not ahead of theory at the outset, in fact outstripped it as the field evolved. It was not until the 1960s that the academic field of Computer Science began to emerge. And the theory that came with these early academic pursuits probably did not begin to surface until the late 1960s or early 1970s.

Based on the personal recollections of an old timer in the field, then, the notion that practice precedes theory certainly seems credible. But experience, of course, can be a deceptive teacher. What one person experiences can be far different from what another experiences. Is there some other way to examine this issue?

Thus far I have discussed computing and software as if it were a single discipline, examinable as a whole. But what if, instead, we were to look at some of the constituent elements of that whole? Can we see a pattern of practice and theory emerge from that kind of examination?

How about programming style? Which came first here, practice or theory? Certainly, there were a lot of programs written before there were books on programming style. I recall vividly that some of those programs had excellent style, and some did not. I would suggest that style in practice was fairly well-developed before a theory of style evolved. (It is interesting to note that an early series of books on style, Ledgard's "Proverbs . . . ," were essentially a codification of good practice.)

How about compiler writing? The practice of compiler writing produced compilers for such languages as Fortran, Commercial Translator, FACT, and later Cobol well before there was a well-documented theory of compiler writing. Once again, I would suggest that compiler writing, now a topic at the heart of computer science academically, was fairly well-developed in practice before a theory began to emerge.

There are examples of practice leading theory even today. Simulation is a frequently used tool at the system level to help define requirements and extract a design for complex problems. The topic of simulation, on the other hand, rarely comes up in the computing research world. Recent interest in prototyping is not quite the same thing. (Note that simulation, as used in practice, is the creation of a tentative practical solution in order to establish a theory of the problem. Even here, practice leads theory!)

User-interface design, although firmly rooted in theory in its Xerox PARC origins, by now has moved forward more rapidly in (especially micro) computer practice than the theory that supports it.

Design itself is still poorly understood as the theory level. Courses in design frequently focus on methodology and representation, and yet most designers are aware that design is much more complex than simply having a framework for doing it and a way of writing it down. Once again, the practice of design is far ahead of its theory.

And in fact, the general notion of problem solving, which is what software engineering is really all about, is still in the early stages of theory building (see, for example, Simon's *The Sciences of the Artificial*, referenced earlier) even though the practice of problem solving (like that of design) is centuries old.

In other words, there is example after example of practice preceding theory. Does this surprise you? In spite of my historical perspective, it still surprises me. All of my academic background cries out for the notion that theory builds a framework upon which practice may construct things. If that notion is not true, then perhaps we should examine the implications.

Let us construct a diagram to show the relationship between theory and practice implied by this notion. What follows is my attempt at such a diagram. I believe, in essence, that given a particular discipline, practice comes first and evolves fairly rapidly at the outset; theory starts after there is a practice to formalize, and also evolves rapidly; and then there is a crossover point at which theory moves past practice. (See Figure 2.2.)

Let us assume for the moment that this relationship holds true. What are its implications? For one thing, the diagram suggests that in the early stages of a discipline, theory can best progress by examining practice. True, theorists must also be free to formulate new ideas unfettered by past ways of doing things; but, nevertheless, there is much to be learned by examining what practice is doing, particularly the best of practice. This is an important thought. For the most part, the development of computing and software theory has not followed the implications of this thought. Few computing theorists are former practitioners. There is little experimental, practice-simulating research in our field. And, except for some of the empirical studies of programmers' research, very little study is made of practitioners at work in evolving theory.

This thought suggests that at least the early approach to theory must

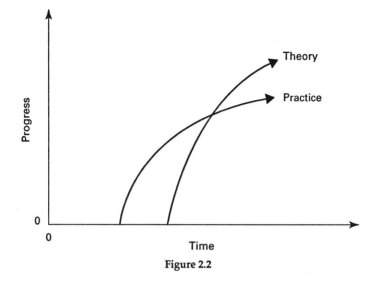

Figure 2.2

change. The lore of practical knowledge may be far too rich for theory to ignore it.

Another conclusion that can be drawn from the diagram is that there comes a point at which practice, having been surpassed by theory, must listen to it. The framework that theory can provide in such areas as data bases and data structures, for example, far surpasses the knowledge of most practitioners in those discipline areas. Once again, the state of the practice has not reached this point. Just as theory fails to study practice when it is appropriate, practice fails to listen to theory when that becomes appropriate.

In other words, there are some fundamental problems in the interactions between theory and practice that the above diagram can clarify; and the failure to understand the implications of the diagram is fundamental to the state of the art and practice of computing and software.

Probably the diagram is an oversimplification. In the most accurate of pictures, the progress of practice and theory is more likely an intertwining series of steps, where practice and theory alternately take the lead. But even with that more complex picture, there will be places on this new diagram (zoom-lens snapshots, perhaps) within which the simpler diagram is still valid.

Does practice precede theory? At some levels, and at some points in time, yes it does. Now it is time for both practice and theory to absorb the implications of that fact.

ACKNOWLEDGEMENT

I wish to thank Iris Vessey and Dale Dowsing for their help in the evolution of these ideas.

Theory versus Practice—Revisited

I imagine that anyone who comes out of our school system and begins to practice a profession forms some interesting opinions about what they learned, as opposed to what they wished they had learned.

My own personal trip from education to practice was through the field of pure mathematics. When I began working in industry, I was appalled to find that nothing I had learned in graduate school bore the slightest relationship to what I was asked to do on the job.

That began my career-long interest in the relationship between theory and practice. I see a massive "communication chasm" between the two and profound misunderstandings resulting from that chasm. And I see severe problems in both the products of theory and the products of practice resulting from that chasm and those misunderstandings. On occasion, in fact, my own job performance has been severely impacted by the chasm.

Out of this concern, I wrote an article entitled "The Temporal Relationship Between Theory and Practice." In it, I identified a relationship between theory and practice as shown in Figure 2.3—that is, initially practice leads theory, but later theory catches up with and passes it.

Subsequently, I had an opportunity to rethink what was in that essay. I think the essential truth it presented—that practice often precedes and helps form theory—is still true. But, like many things in life, I think it is more complicated than Figure 2.3 makes it appear.

Let me share with you the opportunity that caused me to rethink Figure 2.3. It was at World Computer Congress in San Francisco, and I was in the presence of greatness. Two speakers addressed this issue, and both were as brilliant in their thinking and presentation as any two speakers I have ever heard. The message, couched in different terms by each speaker, was essentially the same.

Donald Knuth of Stanford University, one of the keynote speakers, said, "Both theory and practice can and should be present simultaneously." He went on to say that blending the two has been "the main credo of my personal life."

Heinz Zemanek, retired head of the IBM Vienna Laboratory, speaking on "Formal Structures in an Informal World," said "We can only formalize

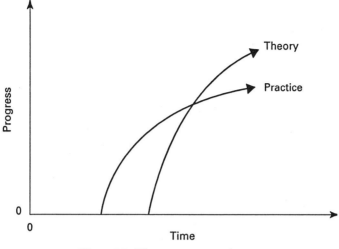

Figure 2.3   Theory versus practice.

what we understand at a basic level. We must start informally, then move to formalism."

In other words, informal practical thinking must precede—and proceed in tandem with—formal formulation of theory.

As Knuth gave examples of his credo from his experience, I thought back over an important one of my own. In the mid-1960s, after starting out as a scientific programmer, I was given my first data processing application—the job of writing three different report generators. There was a great deal of similarity between them, and as I struggled with the design problems of rolling totals and producing reports—problems that every data processing person has struggled with and by now mastered—I saw that the framework of those three products contained the nucleus of a generalized one. The result, when I finished delivering the reports, was that I produced one of the earliest report generator packages. But what is important in the context of this story is that my work in the specific construction of those report generators was an essential prelude to my ability to see the general problem that lay behind them. Without having done the informal or practical solution to those first three problems, in other words, it would not have been possible for me to form the formal, or theoretical generalized, solution.

That suggests to me two important corrections in my previous title and figure. It seems to me, with the benefit of the thinking of Knuth and Zemanek, that the title should be more like "Theory Plus Practice" rather than "Theory versus Practice," and that Figure 2.3 should be more like Figure 2.4.

Now we can see that, although often the first glimmer of a new idea comes from the world of practice (don't we say "necessity is the mother of invention"?), the act of maturing both the practice and the theory can and should go on in tandem. Attempts to do otherwise, as we have been trying to do in the world of computer science and software engineering, lead inevitably to weak theory and stuck practice.

Knuth left his audience with a fascinating "challenge problem" to cause them to explore their own blending of theory and practice. Study what your computer does in one randomly chosen second, he challenged, and then think about what you have seen there. He posed these questions to help frame and direct those thoughts:

1. Are the programs that were executing correct? (Most of those he looks at, Knuth said, have one or more errors in them.)
2. Do the programs use existing theory?
3. Would existing theory help these programs?
4. Would new theory help these programs?

Zemanek, too, left his audience with a fascinating thought. "Fifty years ago," he said, "we had masters of the language," people who were

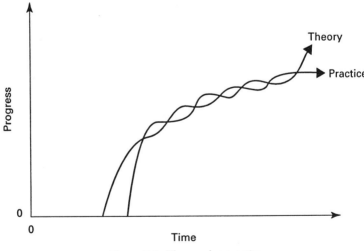

Figure 2.4   Theory plus practice.

articulate and even inspiring in their ability to speak. "Now," he went on to say, "we don't—and this is a very dangerous direction." The reason we don't, he said, is because our educational system has swung too far in the direction of formal methods and has neglected such informalisms as common sense and natural language communication.

Perhaps Knuth and Zemanek—and the others who care—can help us evolve theory and practice into a fundamentally sound working partnership.

THEORY AND PRACTICE: A DISTURBING EXAMPLE

The relationship between theory and practice has been dealt with philosophically in the preceding essays in this book. Here, I would like to illustrate that relationship by a real live example.

At a fairly recent prestigious computing conference, there was a paper presented on a very practical topic: how to decide when to terminate maintenance of older software and rewrite it. It is a topic at the heart of the maintenance effort, one confronted by every software organization in the world, dealt with in practice for over 30 years. Some companies, such as Ford Motor Company and Pacific Telephone, have created elaborate decision mechanisms just for this purpose.

However, this paper was written by academics. The research behind the paper was, in fact, done by an information technology department at a major university, and took no account whatsoever of the 30 years of practical history devoted to this "rewrite or maintain" decision. Instead, the researchers wrote the paper based on their analysis of projects described in the computing literature.

What was the result? Some academics who heard the paper congratulated the authors on a job well done. They had, after all, tackled an important topic with wisdom and insight.

But others in the audience, myself (and, I am happy to say, the academic discussant assigned to critique the paper) included, were dismayed. The paper not only was not based on the accumulated experience of our field, but it was patently erroneous in its conclusions.

The conclusions, in fact, are worth stating here. The researchers based their analysis of the decision to rewrite or maintain purely on a mathematical analysis of cumulative maintenance costs for the software product. Their assumption was that as software reached the point of rewrite, maintenance costs would be exploding upward. But that conclusion is naive. Often software reaches the point of rewrite because its original design envelope has been stretched to the point at which additional enhancements are simply impossible. At such a point, maintenance costs, far from going up rapidly, actually drop!

Additional conclusions, peculiar in themselves, were also presented by the researchers:

1. Software should be rewritten "less than halfway through its projected lifespan."
2. Software operational life:
   a. decreases with initial size (the bigger the software, the shorter its lifespan)
   b. decreases with structuredness (the more structured the software, the shorter its lifespan)
   c. increases progressively as the software is repeatedly rewritten (the more it is rewritten, the longer its lifespan)

Some of these conclusions are amazingly counterintuitive and counterexperiential. Could the researchers really have believed that, with findings like these, their analysis was correct?

What's the point here? There are topic areas where practice is far ahead of theory. In the 1990s, software maintenance is one of those topics. Researchers ought to be aware of what those topic areas are, and rely on practice to help build theory. Not only do most researchers not do that, they do not even seem to be aware that they could or should.

The result is weak theory that gets laughed out of the halls of practice. The flip side is stuck practice that does not upgrade to match the legitimate findings of theory. Neither theory nor practice is well served by what is happening.

What was my personal reaction? I quietly told the researcher, after his presentation, that he should go no further with his research until he considered the implications of practice. And I gave him a couple of names of software practitioners who could help him.

I wondered at the time if he would follow through. To get the contact points for the names I gave him, he would have needed to call me up, using the business card I left with him.

He never did.

THE FLIGHT OF THE BUMBLEBEE

I first heard about it in the fourth grade, and I've heard it said many times since.

"There's no scientific reason," the saying goes, "why a bumblebee can fly."

What people who say that mean is that the theories of science do not hold an explanation for why this bulky, heavy bee with the stubby wings can do what it does.

Whatever you may think about this strange statement, one thing is clear. When we consider the puzzle of the flight of the bumblebee, it does not occur to us that the practice—the flight—is wrong. We all know intuitively that there is something wrong with the theory.

Perhaps there's a broader lesson here.

THEORY VERSUS PRACTICE: A VARIETY OF LAMENTS

The issue of the relationship between theory and practice is a complicated one. But what is at least as interesting as its complexity is the number of viewpoints—and the emotional laments that arise from them—that we find if we explore the topic.

In a fascinating interview with Harlan Mills in *IEEE Software*, July 1988, Mills is quoted as saying "It's too bad that hardware grew so fast. You know, if we'd had these new processors . . . for 50 years at least, mankind could really have learned how to do sequential programming. But the fact is, by the time that [Edsger] Dijkstra comes out with structured programming, we've got all kinds of people using multiprocessors with interrupt handling, and there's no theory behind that, but the IBMs, the DECs, the CDCs, and so on, they're all driving forward and doing this even though nobody knows how to do it."

What a wonderful acknowledgment that early on in a discipline, practice leads theory, and a lament that it does, all at the same time! However, just as there are those stuck in the world of practice who would prefer that theory go away, Mills illustrates that there are theory people saying "slow the world down, it's moving too fast for theory to keep up." Of course, both viewpoints are wrong. The world will move at its own pace, urged onward by practice and theory in turn, and none of us have the power to stop it. Would we really want that power?

Not all academics adhere to the Mills viewpoint, of course. Quite the opposite of Mills' lament is one expressed by Manfred Kochen [Kochen85] in a paper called "Are MIS Frameworks Premature?" Here, Kochen suggests that research has been guided erroneously by the belief that the construction of definitional frameworks should precede theory and experiment, with the application of theory coming last. He points to the mathematical notion of derivative, noting that it was first used, then discovered, then explored and developed, and finally defined, as the correct model for theory development in any new field. Kochen laments, in fact, something the opposite of Mills—that the search for definitional frameworks, given the state of the practice, is premature, and that "such a search diverts effort from problem-solving activities which, despite its imperfect definition and in absence of a framework, are likely to be more fruitful."

There are other lamentations in our field. David Parnas, in a surprising essay on computer science education [Parnas90], found major flaws in our pedagogy, many of them related to this same issue of theory vs. practice. "Academic departments and large conferences," he says, "are often battlegrounds for the 'theoretical' and 'applied' groups. Such battles," he concludes in a meaningful warning, "are a sure sign that something is wrong."

What does Parnas see as wrong? Plenty. "Computing science," he says, "focuses too heavily on the narrow research interests of its founding fathers . . . The separation between academic computing science and the way computers are actually used has become too great. CS programs do not provide graduates with the fundamental knowledge needed for long-term professional growth."

Returning later to the value of practice in both pedagogy and theory, Parnas says, "Students do not get the feedback that comes from having a product used, abused, rejected, and modified. This lack of feedback is very bad education."

In another part of the computing forest, information systems specialist Peter G. W. Keen says something similar [Keen80]. "No one should be involved in MIS research," he says bluntly, "who is not a craftsman in some aspect of computer technology and techniques . . . To want to be 'scientists' may be a praiseworthy goal, but if this involves an explicit disdain for 'application,' 'business,' or 'practice,' one wonders about the sense of ethics of the researcher being at a business school."

And, as the conclusion to this article, Keen says, in no uncertain terms, " . . . the world of practice is central, not peripheral" to that of MIS theory and research.

In a more emotional and controversial article, Rustom Roy, quoted in an article in *Newsweek* [Roy91], questions the very value of research. Roy, the interview says, finds that "Many programs still have it backward. They start with basic principles and only eventually . . . work up to application." Roy objects to that approach. "Only that which is connected to life will be remembered for life," he is quoted as saying.

Roy's objection seems more than a simple lament at times. He decries the quality of the theory development that *does* take place, noting that of the top-quality papers (by reviewing standards) published in various scientific fields, 45% were never referenced by other researchers in the five years following their publication. "The implication," says *Newsweek*, "is that nearly half the scientific work in this country is basically worthless." Roy calls researchers who believe they have a right to be supported by government funding "welfare queens in white coats."

Not all laments are that emotionally tipped. However, as we can see here clearly, when it comes to the issue of theory vs. practice, there is plenty of room for discussion—and strong opinion.

REFERENCES

[Keen80] PETER G. W. KEEN, "MIS Research: Reference Disciplines and a Cumulative Tradition," *Proceedings of the International Conference on Information Systems,* 1980.

[Kochen85] MANFRED KOCHEN, "Are MIS Frameworks Premature?" *Journal of Management Information Systems* Vol. II, No. 3, 1985.

[Parnas90] DAVID LORGE PARNAS, "Education for Computing Professionals," *IEEE Computer,* January 1990.

[Roy91] "Gridlock in the Labs," *Newsweek,* January 14, 1991; from an interview with Rustum Roy.

P.S. In a quotation that is peripherally related to this discussion, Steven Jones, one of the Brigham Young University physicists involved in the controversial nuclear fusion experiments, said this: "We have an experiment but not a theory. We have Cinderella, but we don't have her shoe." Dare we characterize practice as Cinderella without the shoe? Or is it perhaps the other way around?

A TABULATION OF TOPICS WHERE SOFTWARE PRACTICE LEADS SOFTWARE THEORY

I've been saying for several years now that, in a new discipline, sometimes practice leads theory. I've said it in print, and I've also said it in person before lots of audiences. Most of the audiences, be they practitioners or academics, listen with rapt attention and sometimes a furrowed brow, as if to say, "This is all very interesting, but do I really want to believe this nonsense?"

However, in front of one audience, a particularly rapt and furrowed listener finally challenged me on the subject. "OK," he said, "that's an interesting theory, but get specific. *Where* in computing and software does practice lead theory?"

That's a fair question, of course. Now it was my turn for a bit of rapt and furrowed. It's all well and good to express a theory about theory vs. practice, but could I make it become real in a practical sense?! (Do I detect a bit of something similar to recursion here?)

I'm not a terribly creative thinker standing on my feet in front of an audience. All that adrenalin that surges through my body parts to get me into a high-energy mode for speaking seems to sap the brain power needed to do new things with a few dozen or a hundred people watching. On the occasion when the listener challenged me, I mumbled some things about creative design and graphical user interfaces being areas in which practice led theory, but then I hastily looked at my watch, harrumphed about being behind schedule, and went on with my prepared speaking materials.

Back in the safety of my own office, after the adrenalin had calmed from a waterfall to a trickle, I began thinking about that question some more. Where, indeed, does practice still lead theory? Here are some of the thoughts I had.

Software Design

People have been doing software design now for four or more decades. Many of those designs have been successful, some phenomenally so. Those designs that have succeeded have been the product of creative minds focusing on fairly complex problems; remember the Fred Brooks quotes about software being "the most complex task mankind has ever undertaken?" So there's plenty of evidence that the practice of design is a thriving enterprise.

What about the theory of design? Look at any textbook on software design, and tell me that you see there. I'll bet it's a bunch of stuff on methodology and a bunch of stuff on representation. Follow these methodological steps, the textbook implies, and you'll have some thoughts worth drawing with this representation. Well, not good enough. There's many a creative step twixt the methodology and the representation, and what's in the textbook leaves all of that out.

Plus, think about this: When did methodologies and representations arise in the software world? How about the 1970s? And when did practice start designing real production software? How about the 1950s? No matter what sword you use to slice it—a historic one or a contemporary one—practice has led and continues to lead theory here.

However, I think it is important to admit that theory is playing a good game of catch-up on this topic. The research into cognitive design by Bill Curtis and his folk, and Elliot Soloway and his, brought theory well into a position to catch up with practice on creative design. But that happened in the 1980s, and is still not well acknowledged in the textbooks and theory work of our time. For a little while, at least, I would assert that the practice of software design still leads its theory.

Software Maintenance

The first job I got in industry, over 40 years ago now, was one doing software maintenance. I wasn't very good at it then, but after getting lucky—I was given software by some pretty superb software developers to maintain—I was making significant strides in my maintenance maturity within a few years.

What did computer science and software engineering have to say that would help me do that software maintenance at the time? Absolutely nothing! In fact, there was no computer science or software engineering then, in an academic/theoretic sense. Those disciplines were to first grace the halls of ivy over 10 years later.

But is all of that ancient history still relevant today? I would assert that it is, and for a particularly sad reason. The theory world of software, until very recently, actually disdained the subject of maintenance. It wasn't just behind practice, it was refusing to try to catch up! The literature of software displayed an amazing paucity when it came to theoretic contributions to maintenance. I recall one academic making a presentation at a software conference the content of which was clearly behind, and could have bene-fitted from an understanding of, the state of the practice! (That story was told earlier in this chapter.)

That is beginning to change now. Still it is sad to note that the places where the change is happening—the University of Durham in England, the University of West Florida, Arizona State, De Paul University, and a few others—can be counted on the fingers of one, or perhaps barely two, hands. There is still very little solid interest in software maintenance in the world of theory.

Now, there is a very well understood theoretic approach that theory can use—in any discipline—to catch up with leading practice. It is called "empirical studies," and it involves studying the best of practice in order to evolve theory. But software theorists have, to date, exhibited little interest in using that very effective bootstrapping approach, and as a result it is fair to say—as of the publication of this essay—there is little evidence that theory is making much progress at all in catching up with the world of software maintenance practice.

User Interfaces

Here is a nice example of an area in which theory and practice are proceeding neck and neck, and there is every reason to believe that theory is pulling out ahead. Still, it is an interesting example of what happens during the phase when theory catches up with practice.

The pioneering work in user interface development, as any computer-crazed schoolchild knows by now, was done at Xerox PARC a couple of decades or so ago. Now, how do we count that work? Was it theory work? (It was done in an industrial setting.) Or was it practical? (It was done by theorists who, except for their industry identification, had all the trappings of academe.) It seems to me fair to take the position that this pioneering work was a mixture of theory and practice.

What happened next? Much of the work transitioned out into industry, where Apple made it into an industry standard, and based most of its long-term economic success on continuing to use and further develop the Xerox PARC concepts. Theory development continues, of course, but it is probably fair to say that the great theoretical/practical leap forward that happened all those years ago has not been equalled to date in either theory or practice.

Programming in the Large

Pragmatic programming has always seemed like programming in the large. That is, every generation of practitioners has had the feeling that the software they were building was severely stretching their intellectual capabilities, and those of the hardware they were developing it on, to the absolute limit.

And, of course, every generation of practitioners has been trampled in the dust by the onrushing complexity of the problems tackled by the next generation. I still find it difficult to believe—but I can't refute the numbers—that software systems were 50 times larger, on average, in 1990 than they were in 1980 [Dekleva91]. That is a staggering commentary on the rate of change in the world of software practice.

What, in the meantime, has been happening in the world of theory? In most places, theory development is still based on small studies of small projects. Practitioners make fun of that approach by calling it "toy projects," but I would prefer to give it a little more dignity by calling it "research in the small." There are a few counterexamples of people and places doing research in the large—the work of Vic Basili at the University of Maryland and Chris Kemerer at M.I.T. and a few people at the Software Engineering Institute comes to mind—but for the most part, theorists are stuck trying to extrapolate findings from research in the small to programming in the large. And, as most people in software engineering have known since the term "software engineering" was invented over a quarter of a century ago, it just won't work.

Now here, of course, theory has a severe problem. It costs a lot of money to do research in the large, and most software researchers haven't developed access to the kind of money needed. So it is easy to understand why the world of theory has not grown to match the needs of practice.

However, at the same time, it is not unknown for some insensitive computing theorists to poke fun at practice for being stuck using old technologies and concepts. I sometimes wonder what would happen if computing practitioners poked the same kind of fun at theorists for doing the same thing?! I don't imagine that progress in the field would be helped by that kind of social interplay; but still, isn't there something about "sauce for the gander"?

It is time for the world of software theory to graduate to something that Vic Basili calls "full professor research." What does he mean by that? My interpretation is this: New professors tend to do research that involves making in-depth studies of disciplinary minutiae. That kind of work is consistent with what they did in their graduate studies, and is necessary to get them tenure. But the time comes when someone—preferably those who have leaped the tenure hurdle—ought to do more in-breadth examination of the key issues of the discipline. Full professors, and others senior in the field, are in an ideal position to do that.

Who is doing full professor research? In addition to those named above, it is interesting to examine the work of Mary Shaw of Carnegie Mellon, who has studied the origins and evolution of the various engineering disciplines for an understanding of the evolution of software engineering. There is a lot, she has observed, to be gained in understanding our own field through that approach.

With a stronger commitment toward research in the large, and/or full professor research, and with a large dose of funding thrown in to help make it happen, it is possible to get the world of research in the large moving faster. Perhaps, with enough help, it can even catch up with the practice of programming in the large.

Modeling and Simulation

If you have ever worked on a large real-time software project, you know how much a part of the development of that kind of software modeling and simulation are. Models are developed and simulations run in order to:

1. Analyze the concept of the system before starting to build it
2. Run design studies to check the viability of design approaches

3. Allow the execution of target computer software on a host computer with a different instruction set (because the target computer is not yet available, or not capable enough to support debugging)
4. Substitute for the real test environment during early environmental testing
5. Produce approximate test oracles for checking the test results produced by the as-built system during system test

That is a lot of modeling and simulation. The technology, you can see here, is an essential part of the real-time software practitioner's world.

How is the world of theory doing here? My own observation is, not much. When I judge by the number of courses that theorists introduce into their curricula, for example, I see virtually nothing on this subject. Yet in practice, instruction-level simulators and environment simulators and all the others we talked about have been absolutely essential in doing business for decades.

Modeling and simulation are, of course, heavily used in some fringe areas of computer science theory, especially those having to do with manufacturing applications; but that is far from the mainstream of computing theory. When they do appear in an academic discipline, in fact, modeling and simulation are usually taught in some other college, not the one housing computer science or even software engineering.

This is what I call a "gap" subject in contrasting theory and practice: a subject where practice has a presence and theory does not, thus identifying a gap in the underlying theory. And when there are gaps in the theory, it will take an awful lot of playing catch-up for theory to even begin to approach practice.

Metrics

This is a field where bifurcation has occurred. What theory is doing with respect to measurement of software work and what practice is doing are on two different planes, planes that are shifting in different directions.

Take a look, for example, at the encyclopedic theory work on metrics by Zuse, and compare it with the practical books by Grady. Or take a look at the complexity metrics work done by Halstead and McCabe, contrasted with the quality metrics work funded at the Rome Air Development Center (and documented in lots of studies filed with the National Technical Information Service). It is almost as if the two areas have given up communicating with each other.

I had the good fortune, as the editor of a software engineering journal, to read the comments that an anonymous theorist reviewer passed on to a theorist author of a paper on metrics. The message was basically this: Why are you bothering to propose unverified additional theoretic metrics when (a) the theory world is already full of other unverified metrics, and (b) the practice world has given up on all of this unevaluated theory and is rapidly moving on in its own directions? My personal bias is that this reviewer/theorist—who was unwilling to be identified because his theoretic colleagues might crucify him—is one of the few who has grasped what is happening in software metrics.

There is, of course, a bit of theory/practice overlap. Many enterprises doing software maintenance are using the commercially available CASE tools built to calculate the various theoretical metrics such as those of Halstead and McCabe, and say that the identification of complex code segments that they obtain in that way is very helpful, especially in planning reengineering activities.

However, there is another strange faction in the metrics world. There are many, both theorists and practitioners, who have explored the various complexity metrics and found them to be dubious when theoretic justification is attempted, and of little value in a practical setting.

Perhaps the best summation for the topic of metrics is that here is a field where there is much turbulence in the relationship between theory and practice. However, I think it is fair to say that practice is very slowly beginning to evolve some practical, useful metrics, and that theory is still trying to decide whether its own work has merit at all. This is an area, I would assert, poised for explosive growth once these early difficulties can be sorted out.

There, then, is my response to my rapt and furrowed questioner. At least in these areas—software design, software maintenance, user interfaces, programming in the large, modeling and simulation, and metrics—software practice leads software theory.

Like all us human beings, it's the response I wish I had been able to make on the spot during my lecture. But perhaps, if that listener has happened to run across this essay, he'll recognize his question, and be glad for this belated answer!

REFERENCE

[Dekleva91] An article in *Software Maintenance News*, February 1991, reporting on a survey conducted by Sasa Dekleva

---

"A peculiar division of labor has established itself between East and West, a silent arrangement in which the United States and Europe do the basic science, and Japan turns their discoveries into marketable products."

—Horace Freeland Judson, in *The Search for Solutions*, Holt, Rinehart and Winston, 1980 (Reprinted by permission of Henry Holt and Company, Inc.)

2.8   INDUSTRY VERSUS ACADEME

How does this section on industry vs. academe differ from the previous one on theory vs. practice?

In the previous section, we explored intellectual differences between the world of ivy walls and the world of profit motives. In this section, we will explore their behavioral differences.

It is true, of course, that much of theory is produced in academe, and nearly all practice is done in industry. However, even those somewhat absolute statements deserve the qualifications I gave them. I have done "research and development" work in industry (we called it "R&D," and tended to do a whole lot more R than we did D, so that it came out to be very close to the kind of theory work academic people did), and I have worked on practical projects in academe (mostly directing graduate-student projects, where a secondary goal was to produce something that might be useful in the marketplace).

There is, then, a logical reason for distinguishing theory/practice from industry/academe. It is possible to mix and match who does what where.

But a far more interesting theme here, I think, is how people in the academic world differ from those in industry. I've had an ideal career for exploring that question. After nearly 30 years in industry, doing most of the different kinds of things that industry people do (software development and maintenance and management and R&D), I've spent another decade or so in various facets of the world of academe. I've done teaching on a tenure track and contract basis. I've done research and had it published in some pretty good journals. I've done committee work and curriculum development and all the other lesser baggage that is part of academe. In short, my career has spanned these two very different worlds.

As an acid test of my bipolar background, I spent a year at the Software Engineering Institute. Whatever else you may think of the SEI, I think it is fair to say that it is a strange and somewhat unsuccessful mix of the worlds of industry and academe.

People from academe are directing and working on projects that have a major impact on industry. People from industry give input to projects with a largely academic focus. Different organizational entities in the SEI are populated largely by people from one particular camp or the other. Many of the industry people are those who spent much of their industry career doing the R of R&D, making them really only semi-industry people.

Why do I say the mix is somewhat unsuccessful? Because industry people struggle to be heard at the SEI. Because real industry practitioners tend to lose out to industry research people. Because academic people display so much disdain of industry people that it is difficult for an industry person to gain sufficient respect to help steer what the SEI does. If a cultural study of computing ever looks at the behavioral and intellectual worlds of industry vs. academe, and how successfully or unsuccessfully they work together, the SEI is the perfect cultural melting pot in which to conduct the study—except that the melting pot contains undigested chunks whose cultural identities have never really been melted into the whole (a comparison with Bosnia comes to mind!)

In the absence of such a study, the collection of essays that follow is my attempt to make a small initial contribution to the field of computing cultural anthropology.

Before we start reading on, let's do the definition thing:

Industry, my dictionary says, is "the production or manufacture of goods; the quality of being industrious." (Notice, once again, how the smokestack America philosophy is solidly imbedded in the dictionary!)

Academe, by contrast, is related to academic: "of a school, college, or university; scholarly as opposed to technical or practical; of theoretical interest only, with no practical application."

Surely, more than the other word pairs we have dealt with in this chapter, the dramatic contrast between the two is self-evident in the definitions.

On to the essays . . .

The Interesting/Useful Dichotomy

Everyone should have an ethic.

It gives the person a touchstone, a cause, and even an enthusiasm.

There is, however, a problem with ethics. By their very nature, they are rarely subject to personal compromise. Name your favorite ethic. Are you willing to discuss the possibility that it may be faulty?

Even that rock-steadiness of ethics is both good and bad. It's good because it makes people relationships dependable and predictable. But it's bad because it makes people relationships over the subject of ethics inflammatory and divisive.

Enough philosophy. What does ethics have to do with software?

Let's take a look at the academic world of software, and the industrial world of software, for a while, and the relevance will soon become clear.

In the academic world, the researcher pursues those subjects he considers to be *interesting*. He is rewarded for doing so by the esteem of his peers.

In the industrial world, the researcher pursues those subjects he considers to be *useful*. He is rewarded for doing so by the esteem of his management.

The dichotomy between studying things which are interesting or useful is not a small dichotomy. The academician looks with some disdain on things which are merely useful. The industrial worker looks with some disdain on things which are merely interesting. Thus each side is making judgements about the basic goals of the other.

In fact, the pursuit of interesting work is an ethic to the academician, and the pursuit of useful work is an ethic to the industrial worker. It is an ethic so strong that it brooks little compromise. Believers in each of the ethics question the wisdom and even the morality of the other.

Are there some less philosophic examples of this dichotomy? Yes, all around us in software.

Is proof of correctness interesting? Yes. Is it useful? No.

Is testing interesting? No. Is is useful? Yes.

Are requirements languages interesting? Yes. Are they useful? Not yet.

Are requirements reviews interesting? Largely, no. Are they useful? Yes.

Is symbolic execution interesting? Yes. Is it useful? Not very.

Is peer code review interesting? No. Is it useful? Yes.

The dichotomy is all around us, and it is very real.

It is also very bad. Because the researcher who pursues primarily interesting problems communicates badly, if at all, with the researcher who pursues primarily useful ones. Mutual disdain is a poor basis for sharing knowledge.

The dichotomy is made worse, not better, by the researcher who works interesting problems believing erroneously that they are useful, or who works useful problems believing erroneously that they are interesting. The bridging of the dichotomy must be genuine, and not contrived. It must be based on knowledge, and not ignorance.

It is time for academic and industrial people to review their ethics. It is legitimate to work interesting problems. It is legitimate to work useful problems. What is not legitimate is to represent one as the other. What is not legitimate is to disdain those who make the other choice.

There is a fascinating concept we all grew up with that I call "local loyalty." We all knew our grade school was the best in the city. And so was our high school the best in the county. And so was our college the best in the state. And so was our city, and county, and state the best in the country.

Our religion is the best in the world. And so is our ethic.

Local loyalties are useful. They are also absurd. The likelihood that my personal grade school, or high school, or college, or city, or county, or state is *really* best . . . is nil!

Understanding is the answer to overcoming absurd local loyalties. It is also the answer to overcoming conflicting ethics.

Everyone, as we said at the beginning, should have an ethic. Everyone, perhaps we would now agree, should mesh that ethic with a large dose of understanding.

The Individual/Team Dichotomy

The boundary layer between the academic world and the industrial world is subject to turbulence.

Some of the turbulence is well known—the student moves from learning to earning as the prime motivator, for example.

Some of that turbulence is not so well known.

This is a note about one of those less well known areas.

In the academic world, the student functions as a competing individual among competing individuals, and group activity is often thought of as cheating.

In the industrial world, the employee functions as a team member, and group activity is the primary way things happen.

In the academic world, the individual is given credit for what he or she does.

In the industrial world, the individual's role often dissolves into anonymity.

In the academic world, building on the work of others is questionable.

In the industrial world, building on the work of others is common sense. (The other alternative is called, with considerable disdain, "re-inventing the wheel".)

In the academic world, copying is wrong.

In the industrial world, cutting and pasting from previous documents to make new ones is expeditious and wise.

The transition from wrong to right comes suddenly. The transition from competition to cooperation is unexpected. The transition from individual importance to individual anonymity may be painful.

Whatever else the transition is . . . it will be turbulent. Boundary layers are like that!

TWO POP CULTURE SAYINGS. . . .

One of the things computing academics say about software practitioners is that they do too little thinking about what they are about to undertake. The pop culture saying for that is:

Ready, Fire, Aim

Practitioners, stung by that criticism, might be pardoned if they found a similar accusation for academics. Given their propensity to find fault with practice, the pop saying for that might be:

Ready, Blame, Fire

Of Understanding, Acceptance . . .
And Formal Methods

I made a fool of myself at a computing conference last winter. I argued with a speaker. I disrupted the session. I did all the things I hate when someone else does them.

What happened? Why did I get so involved?

The speaker was explaining a concept. It was a spirited presentation of the concept, and, in the spirit of the moment, he was expressing exasperation that not everyone agreed with his concept, and in fact began to put down those who did not. Since I didn't agree with the concept, I became increasingly uncomfortable. Finally, I couldn't take it anymore. I spoke out, trying to point out that it was possible to understand what the speaker was saying but still not accept it.

The more I spoke, the more the speaker sought to explain his concept; and the more he explained, the more disagreement I expressed. We were mired in a difficult loop that finally flamed up in anger. The remainder of the attendees and speakers in the session grew quiet. Discomfort settled heavily around the room. When the session ended, I slunk from the room, wishing I hadn't been there.

As I ruminated afterward over what had happened, I began to realize that the speaker and I were operating under two different communication models. In his model, it was sufficient to make me *understand* the concept he was presenting. If I did not accept the concept, it was because I didn't understand. If I didn't understand, then more explanation was in order.

And if I still didn't understand, it must have been either because I was pretty stupid, or because I wasn't listening carefully.

However, in my communication model, two notions were decoupled. The first notion was understanding, the one the speaker was working on. But the second notion, one entirely separate from understanding, was acceptance. I *understood* the concept he was presenting; I simply did not *accept* that understanding.

As I mulled over the problem, I related it to some deeper social implications, and I began to realize that there was a problem of more general interest here. (This is my rationale for including a conference squabble in these pages!) Through the early part of our lives, as our maturation process is led by authority figures, the notions of understanding and acceptance are, in fact, identical. The parent or teacher explains a concept, and the child or student accepts it. But as the student or child matures, a gap slowly begins to emerge between understanding and acceptance. It is not enough for the parent of a teenager, or the teacher of a graduate student, to present an understanding of an idea. They must also seek its acceptance, a far more taxing and complex task. This is because understanding is accomplished simply by absorption of conceptual material, whereas acceptance is about fitting the concept into the framework of other understandings. The richer the listener's framework of past understanding, the more difficult the task of reaching acceptance becomes.

(The typical authority-figure reaction to the growing decoupling of understanding and acceptance in the maturing person is perhaps best typified by the plaintive cry that all parents will relate to—" . . . because I'm your mother, that's why!")

I remember when this distinction first became important to me. I had finished reading, several years (decades?) ago, Shirer's *Rise and Fall of the Third Reich*. And I realized, as I ruminated over what I had read, that I understood what Shirer had to say about Hitler's reasons for killing the Jews, for the Holocaust.

And I was horrified. Because, in my personal history to that date, I had equated—as a child or student must—understanding and acceptance. Did I accept Hitler's rationale for the Holocaust? Of course not—I rejected it with all my being. And yet I understood it. At that moment, the decoupling of the terms became totally necessary.

Now let me return to my more recent ruminations, and try a little harder to make this discussion relevant to systems and software. Frequently, in the computing literature, I find a discussion of some new concept (e.g. formal methods) followed by the exasperated statement that those involved in the practice of software have not adopted this new concept *because they are ignorant of it.*

However, I think I understand the practice of software fairly well, and it is my belief that practitioners may or may not be ignorant of such concepts, but it matters a lot less than whether they accept them or not. And it is frequently the case—formal methods are a particularly good example here—that the *real* basis for lack of adoption by the world of practice is not lack of understanding, but lack of acceptance.

What happens when an academic begins to realize that their new concept is not being used? They work harder at explaining the concept. They seek understanding. And when they provide that understanding, and find that the concept is still not accepted, in exasperation they blame the practitioner for being stupid or not listening. (Sound familiar?) After all, in the world of authority figures, isn't understanding equal to acceptance?

The message imbedded in these thoughts is this: It is necessary for authority figures, as well as students and children, to decouple understanding and acceptance. The degree to which the authority figure permits the student or child to decouple the two notions is symptomatic of how well the authority figure respects the maturation of the student or child and has achieved some personal maturation of his or her own.

Once that decoupling occurs, the authority figure can then go about the *two* important tasks for which he or she is responsible:

1. Explaining a concept in such a way that it can be understood
2. Supporting that understanding with a rationale for why it should be accepted

I believe that there is an absence of an evaluative component to most contemporary software research. My view of the current state of the art in our research is that it involves a lot of definition, a lot of explanation, a lot of advocacy, and very little evidence to support that advocacy. Evaluative research, whose purpose would include providing such evidence and which is a rich part of the tradition of our more scientific brethren, is largely absent from our research.

(The one piece of evaluative research on formal methods with which I am familiar shows a 9% benefit in "total development cost" to the use of the formal specification language Z [Ralston91]. In the larger world of cost-benefit tradeoffs, where formal methods must compete with 4GLS and CASE tools and methodologies and downsizing for management attention and funding, a technology that promises a 9% benefit and large learning costs simply isn't going to rank high in the technology transfer queue.)

Perhaps the near absence of evaluative research is partly due to our authority figures not yet decoupling understanding and acceptance.

Perhaps there is a general feeling, not well understood and certainly not articulated, that the job of the researcher is simply to provide understanding. Perhaps this is partly because the authority-figure researcher has not really accepted yet the increasing maturity of the software practitioner. Therefore, they do not yet see the need to supplement explanation with rationale.

Over the years, I have mused about the differences between the world of academe and the world of practice. I believe, for example, that academics are often poorer listeners (the typical lecture hall setting is not conducive to building listening skills in the lecturer) and less goal-oriented (academics do in order to learn, rather than learning in order to do). And perhaps, now, I should add to those differences my belief that practitioners have done a better job of decoupling understanding and acceptance than academics. (Try selling a new concept to upper management on the basis of understanding alone, and you won't make that mistake more than once!)

Ah, well, enough of these ramblings. The truly important question is, what's the bottom line regarding that conference squabble? Well, I really do believe that I made a fool of myself, but I can't quite bring myself to be sorry that I did it!

REFERENCE

[Ralston91] T. J. RALSTON and S. L. GERHART, "Formal Methods: History, Practice, Trends and Prognosis," *American Programmer*, May 1991.

THE DRIFTING TALK/LISTEN RATIO

One of the nicest guys I had ever met had just walked into my office. I was pleased to see him, and told him so. However, the message from my gut, the one that told me how I really felt, was somewhat different. There was a queasiness there, and I wondered what it was all about.

This nicest of guys was a faculty member, the one who had the office next to mine. He taught in one of the engineering disciplines; over the ensuing years, I have forgotten which one. He was a caring, thoughtful kind of guy. What possible reason could there be for my stomach to launch a rebellion?

I was relatively new to academe at the time. After nearly 30 years in industry, it was fun to try a new field. I had loved my software-building and software-maintaining experiences over those industry years, but in the back of my mind there had always been this career alternative—teaching.

Now, I was trying out that alternative. I was a software engineering faculty member at a university that had chosen to make a splash in software engineering. I was in the right place at the right time, and I was loving it.

The conversation began between this nicest of guys and me. We chatted pleasantries, sampling a few of the relevant conversational topics *du jour*, and we moved toward the more interesting subjects slowly, as conversationalists usually do. Finally, we launched into a deeper topic, one we could truly wrap our minds around. Ah, these were the kind of conversations it was worth joining the academic world to have!

But then it began to happen, so slowly that I didn't see it coming at first. The tilt of the conversation, well-balanced at the outset, was beginning to slide in the direction of the nicest of guys. As time went by, his talk-listen ratio climbed higher and higher, and mine (commensurately) fell lower and lower. It was happening all over again, as it had happened before. My visitor loved to talk, but not to listen. My stomach growled an "I told you so."

My pleasant smile began to freeze on my face, as I tried to be nice to this nicest of guys; but I was rapidly losing interest in the conversation, in the guy, in all of it. What had begun as a two-way conversation had turned into a LECTURE. And I was no longer enjoying it.

As the conversation moved on without me, I began to muse over what was happening. Certainly, I had run into people who talked but didn't listen before, but what I was experiencing with this nicest of guys was an experience I'd had before, with other academics, not as nice as this guy, of course, but still reasonably nice people. There seemed to be, my new insight was trying to tell me, an epidemic of talk-not-listen in the academic world. What had been an occasional problem in industry was a thriving disease in academe.

How strange, I thought to myself, the smile still frozen on my face. There seems to be something in the environment of a university that causes people to lose their listening skills. What could it be?

The answer was fairly obvious, of course. What do academics tend to do for a living? They lecture. Who do they largely do it with? Undergraduate students. And there, as I teased those two facts around a bit, lay my obvious answer. Academics talked instead of listened because that's what they were paid to do, trained to do, best practiced at doing. Their motivation to listen was low because the people they normally talked to (I was beginning to think it was really talking at, not to) had much less to contribute to an equal conversation than the lecturer. Everything in the workaday world of the academic moved him or her in the direction of talking and away from listening.

There is, of course, a problem with this mindset. The mind that fails to listen rarely obtains new insight; and without insight, a mind can atrophy. And that, of course, is the worse possible thing that can happen to an academic. If the mind does not personify what the academic offers to the world, what does? An academic with an atrophied mind is a wasted academic.

My mind had drifted far enough down this path, as the conversation wore on, that I almost failed to notice that the conversation was coming to a halt.

"Gotta go now," the nicest guy was saying. And, with a genuine and warm smile, he left the office. I came back to reality with a start.

Two starts, in fact. One, that I had returned to the world of participation, and it was up to me to begin to do something, to take some action. My time of passive listening had ended for awhile.

And the other start? This one came as a shock. As I realized how much I had tuned this nicest guy out during our talk, as I realized that I missed the last two-thirds of what he was telling me, the horror of what that meant began to wash over me. I had been an academic just long enough, I could see now, that my own listening skills were atrophying. I hadn't learned to compete at the talk level, but I was certainly losing my ability to listen actively. My reverie about talk-not-listen was a symptom that I had begun the voyage to that undesirable land already.

I resolved, that day, to fight that tendency. But who knows how well I have succeeded at it? I can't seem to get anyone to talk with me long enough to find out. Could that mean . . . ?!

Postscript

There is a particular aspect of this problem that really troubles me. I believe, and I have believed for decades now, that there is a communication chasm—not just a gap—between the academic and industry worlds of computing and software. Academics don't listen to practitioners, and practitioners don't listen to academics. How does this chasm manifest itself?

1. Practitioner jargon and academic jargon don't mix very well. The academic, who can point to the origins of his or her jargon in the textbooks and papers of the literature of the field, doesn't understand why the practitioner can't use the proper terms, the proper language. Academics sometimes say, "They got it wrong." That can mean a lot of different things, but one of them is, "They don't speak the correct language." Although the academic who says that may in a sense be correct, the lack of understanding that underlies such statements can be a real deterrent to meaningful dialogue.

2. Academics seem to genuinely believe that practitioners don't know very much. They talk about "dumbing down" presentations to practitioners, they speak of a "software crisis" as if some large percentage of practitioners don't know what they are doing, and they pay little attention to the system-building and system-maintaining skills that the practitioners *do* excel in. How do these academics think we succeeded in reaching out into space, for example, if there weren't some capable, even brilliant, practitioners doing their thing successfully?

3. Academics don't seem to know what they don't know. Somehow they have come to believe that if they are aware of the state of the art, as it is defined in the literature of the field, then they are totally knowledgeable about the field. They do not seem to be aware that there is a state of the practice, which is sometimes—perhaps even frequently—ahead of the state of the art, and is certainly, in real and important ways, different from the state of the art.

4. In short, some academics—a small but disturbing number of them—are arrogant and ignorant.

That is, of course, a fairly one-sided picture of the communication chasm at work here. Practitioners who don't read the literature and who ignore powerful new ideas must carry their share of the blame, too.

But still, it is interesting for me to muse, sometimes, about how much of the chasm lies in this very simple difference between academics and practitioners: academics, I believe after sampling both worlds, have decidedly atrophied listening skills. And that, of course, doesn't bode well for overcoming the chasm.

THE NON-GOAL-ORIENTED COMMITTEE MEETING

The faculty committee meeting droned on. It was our third meeting on the same subject, and I was beginning to think we were never going to get anywhere. Little did I realize at the time how right that thought was going to be.

The meeting was about defining a core curriculum. It was an important meeting. Whatever we decided would be in our core, all of the university's undergraduates from then on would be required to take. No matter what their major. It was hard to imagine a more important committee assignment than this one.

Why, then, was our progress so slow? There was the usual internecine warfare, of course, as the different disciplines tried to force their way into—or out of—the core. (I hadn't yet realized what a drag so-called "service courses"—courses given to non-majors in the subject—were to the professor. Teaching those students who *had* to take a course was the worst teaching assignment possible, I was to learn. No wonder some disciplines wanted none of their material in the core.)

However, it wasn't politics that was the real problem. The real problem seemed to be—and here, I still have to fumble for words, looking back on the experience a decade later—that no one really cared whether we got anywhere in the meeting or not. There was a joy in collegiality among the meeting attendees, to be sure, but there was little if any sense of mission.

Collegiality, not mission. That's a cumbersome way of saying what I really want to say here. What I really decided, after experiencing it so many times in my academic life that there was no doubt in my mind that it was true, was that academic people simply weren't goal-oriented. Whereas a meeting in industry would have come to order, come to the point, and been dismissed, these academic meetings seem to exist of and for themselves.

At one level, I still see that as an accurate conclusion. At another level, I suppose, it is unfair. After all, what industry has for goals and what academe has for goals are very different. Academics do in order to learn, we have probably all heard by now, whereas industry people learn in order to do. Academics pursue things they find interesting, whereas industry people pursue things that are useful. Those are not just words, they are profound social differences; and they affect a lot of what people in each area do.

However, there is nothing like working toward a common product to motivate people to get on with what they are doing. And my colleagues at this core curriculum committee meeting simply didn't see the final product as being important enough to spend a lot of energy working toward.

(Later I came to see the problem as even deeper than that. When industry people disagree over methods or approaches, the eventual need to produce a final product forces them to overcome their differences and row in the same general direction. When academics disagree over methods or approaches, there may be nothing to pull them together. Without the need to strive for a communal product, there is little to force diverse interest groups to work together. Disputes can smoulder unresolved in the academic world for ludicrous amounts of time. The fact that teaching students and performing research are the real underlying institutional goals doesn't help overcome these differences, since teaching is generally regarded as something of a necessary evil, and research is often individual and thus not dependent on group agreement.)

The fourth and fifth meetings of the core curriculum committee brought us only slightly closer to our stated goal, defining an agreed-upon core. And then, wonder of wonders, the summer holidays intervened. We could not meet during the summer, of course; presumably, we would return to our task in the fall.

And then an interesting thing happened. During the summer, by a process that none of us could ever see or feel, the core curriculum in fact got defined. When we came back in the fall, there were no longer any committee meetings. It seemed a blessing too good to be true.

Or was it? What in fact seemed to have happened, I concluded with the advantage of hindsight, was that the administration went ahead, over the summer, to define *their* notion of a core; a notion that they probably had had all along. However, and this is important, it was a notion that no one on the committee now had the least inclination to oppose, because in fact we didn't want to hold any more committee meetings!

So what had really happened here? The core curriculum committee had been, in the jargon of technology transfer and change management, an instrument of grass-roots involvement. The faculty members of that committee had had the opportunity to affect the process, to steer toward a goal. The fact that they had not reached a goal, and had left a rudderless ship at the end of the spring semester, had in fact been very predictable. However, the net effect was a decision made by the goal-oriented administration that had the look and feel of involvement at the faculty level, a decision that the faculty could feel some sense of participation in. Not only had the faculty members not been terribly goal-oriented, but their administrators had known it would be that way—and had taken advantage of it!

However, I am afraid we digress here. The preceding analysis is about the effects of this fundamental industry-academe difference; but this essay is about the difference, not the effects. And that difference is goal orientation. Industry people are generally well-focused on their goals; academics either are not focused on goals, or have a kind of goal so different that it is not at first apparent that goals are even involved.

And any attempt to build bridges across the industry-academe communication chasm had better take this difference into account.

Postscript

There is another interesting way in which this difference in goal orientation manifests itself in industry and academe. We have already seen that industry people are product-focused, since the product, for most disciplines, is clearly the goal that matters.

It has become common in recent times for academe to take the position that process is the best way to achieve good product. With that thought, a great deal of effort is focused on defining better process. The whole of the Software Engineering Institute Capability Maturity Model work for example, is focused, on that premise.

However, it is important to be careful here. The natural tendency of the academic world is to focus on process over product. That's part of "doing in order to learn," it's part of "interesting rather than useful." The fact that academics tell us that good process is the best way to good product should be seen as what it is: the natural tendency of a non-goal-oriented group to focus on things of interest to *themselves*, not necessarily of usefulness to their more goal-focused colleagues.

In other words, it is OK for industry people to focus on process, but never to the exclusion of product. And goal-oriented industry practitioners should never lose track of that fact.

"There clearly follows the impossibility . . . of increasing machines to immense size . . . enormous ships, palaces, or temples."

—Galileo in *Dialogues Concerning Two New Sciences*, as
quoted in *The Search for Solutions*, Horace Freeland Judson,
Holt, Rinehart and Winston, 1980
(Reprinted by permission of Henry Holt and Company, Inc.)

2.9   FUN VERSUS GETTING SERIOUS

Now it's time to really get down to it. All the rest of that talk in this chapter, about discipline and satisficing and qualitative reasoning and process, is just mental gymnastics. This is where the truth really comes out!

Software development is and always has been fun. That's what makes the field of software go round. You do it, and if it goes well you feel good. It just don't, as the beer commercial says, get any better than this.

Take it from an old-timer. I got in on the ground floor of computing, way back in the 1950s. In those days, those of us in computing had to be in it for the fun of it, because there was a price to be paid in society for being a computist.

What price? We were, to put it simply, considered weird. We were doing something with our minds that most everyone else did with their hands—crafting a product and making it do phenomenal tricks (in our case with the aid of a box of mysterious electronics that few people understood).

It wasn't the same as today's hackers. Hackers do a fairly normal thing in fairly weird ways. We pioneers did what were considered to be weird things, and no one cared much how we did them. We pioneers were weird to the core of our professional selves; hackers engage in weird behavior, but their profession itself goes unquestioned.

I can still remember the first time, flying on a business trip, that I discovered a seat mate who spoke computerese (it was in the '70s, on a flight from Albuquerque to Austin). I had been in the field for a couple of decades by then, and had never before met anyone who had anything meaningful to say on the subject. Contrast that with today's social world, where the chance that you will meet someone who knows nothing about computers and has no opinions on them is virtually nil.

That weirdness was part of the fun of the field. We really were pioneers, doing something that most people couldn't even imagine. Our frontier was invisible and had no shape or weight. Even explaining it to non-computer-people was a task doomed largely to failure! What fun all of that was.

But that fun paled in contrast to the fun of doing software things: figuring out how to use some new instruction in the instruction set of the latest computer; figuring out how to rewrite last year's software and make it better using this year's computer (we did it all the time, because the pace of computing hardware change then was far faster—believe it or not—than the pace of change now); debugging a program, playing detective and trying to ferret out mysterious clues to determine what they were telling us; and seeing the results of our handiwork in the form of real answers, correct answers even, spilling out onto our printers or terminals.

Most of that fun persists today. We may be figuring out some feature of a new programming language instead of a new instruction on the computer. We may not have to rewrite our software on a regular basis (and we're probably thankful for that!). However, we still feel the joy of the chase in debugging, and the pleasure of creation in results. I sometimes marvel at how lucky I was to find myself getting paid to work in a field that was so much fun. Do we really need money to do this sort of thing?!

But something has gone wrong over the years, and I can't quite figure it out. Computing, as you will see in the final essay in this section/chapter, isn't as much fun anymore. Is it me who's changed, unable to mix frivolity and productivity? Or is it the field that's changed, driving software people to distraction with impossible cost and schedule targets? I don't know the answer, although I suspect it's some of both. If this is a theme that interests you, I'd love to hear from you.

Be that as it may, let me stand aside here and let you get on to the material at hand. Do we need to define fun? Why not: "light-hearted amusement." (Imagine yourself not knowing our language, and trying to make something out of *that* definition! Light-hearted indeed.)

What about serious? "Solemn and thoughtful, not smiling; sincere, in earnest, not casual or light-hearted."

That does it . . . we're going to have to look up light-hearted as well: "cheerful, without cares; too casual, not treating a thing seriously."

Talk about overloaded words. Which would you rather be, a fun person or a serious one? Somehow, that part about "not smiling" says a lot to me.

But enough wordplay. On to the subject at hand.

Torn Between Fun and Tedium*

Bruce I. Blum

Like many software engineers, I am (professionally) torn between fun and tedium. There are lots of things about my work that I like. The input pile labeled "FUN" never seems to build up. But there is also a lot of tedium in my job. I really enjoy building systems—or at least the first 90% of them. I just wish I could pass my brilliant foundation on to someone else to finish; after all, haven't I already done the hard part?

Some time ago, I produced a chart that puts the software process in perspective. I began with the old 40–20–40 rule in which 40% of the effort is allocated to developing the requirements and design, 20% to implementing the design (i.e., "code and debug"), and 40% to seeing that we get it right. Recognizing that we spend more money after installation than we do on development, I then added maintenance to this 40–20–40 base. To keep the arithmetic simple, I assumed that maintenance accounted for half the total life cycle cost of a product.

The resulting distribution is shown on the left of Figure 2.5. In it I decomposed the first 40% (now 20% because of maintenance) into three components, and then I added a "zero cost" item called selling the concept. (Actually, if one is unsuccessful in selling the concept, then this category represents 100% of the project cost.) Usually, of course, this zero cost is part of our overhead.

What is really interesting about the figure is the emotional quotient shown on the right. It provides a subjective measure of the distribution between fun and tedium for each step in the process. For example, selling the concept is almost all fun. It's problem solving in its freest, most stimulating form. With a wave of the hand almost any objection can be overcome. Only narrow-minded persons devoid of insight will miss the potential splendor of this . . . whatever. The only tedium here is trying to find nonstop flights, making the last-minute changes to the visuals, and working with narrow-minded people.

Assuming that we have been successful, we must prepare a statement

*From the *Software Practitioners*, May, 1991 used with permission

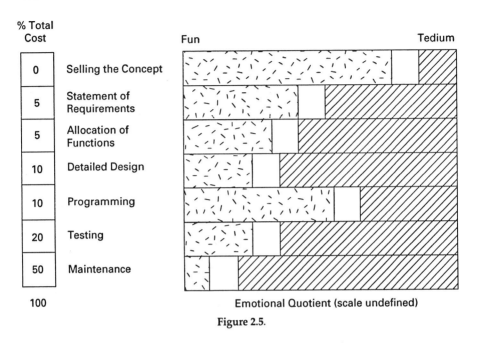

Figure 2.5.

of requirements. This is equally divided between fun and tedium. The fun part is the stimulating problem solving and the sense of creating a new system. The tedium is writing it all down and making sure that what has been written is accurate, will work, and conforms to the promises already made. Still, at this early stage a lot can be done with a wave of the hand.

Next comes the top-level design, or allocation of functions, and we can see the tedium creeping in. There are promises to keep, and now we have to find out how to keep them. As the amount of documentation increases, we lose the freedom to make up solutions on the spot. The source of the growing tedium is obvious. All those documents have to be read, more documents have to be written, and—most distressing of all—we have to be sure that what we are saying is consistent.

It certainly seems as if someone else has made a lot of dumb decisions that make my job more difficult. (You mean I wrote that? Then obviously I was given some mighty poor input!)

Look at detailed design. It only gets worse. But hope is around the corner. Programming is mostly fun. That's why it is a hobby; that's why *Byte* is so thick and filled with advertisements. You know, whenever things get to be too bad, I just go to the computer and write some programs. It's therapeutic; it makes me feel better. (Reminds me of the joke from a bubble-gum cartoon. Panel 1, one lady to another, "Whenever I'm down in the dumps, I get myself a new hat." Panel 2, the other lady, "I always wondered where you got your hats.")

Sooner or later we designers must move on to testing, which we find about as much fun as detailed design. The fact that the program didn't bomb ought to count for something. But no, some of those testers want to keep trying to find faults. Frankly, I get defensive in an adversarial situation in which someone tries to find fault with my work. Most of the time they just find unimportant nits that I am sure I would have found myself if I didn't have to spend so much time on this darn testing. I'm sure that if they looked at it from my perspective (that is, how I understood the problem when I created the code) they would recognize that I had a mighty clever solution. Certainly for a designer testing isn't much fun, although I must admit there is great satisfaction in uncovering a fault in the requirements and then producing an effective response.

Now that the software is installed, I can move on to a new project. Of course, there still is maintenance. This is almost pure tedium, which initiates a primitive emotional reaction: rejection. We can't tie up our best designers with maintenance, or they would just leave us. Therefore, let's assign maintenance to our new employees. Maintenance is good training. It shows them how we write code. After a few years, when they have paid their dues, we'll move them up to (junior) design tasks. If they can make it here, we'll let them advance to the senior design tasks. (I'll be in management by then.) If they don't do well, perhaps we can transfer them to the quality department or back to the maintenance section. We'll use sensitivity training and make them feel happy about their new assignment. (Remember *Brave New World*? "I'm glad I'm a beta. I'm glad I'm not an alpha. I'm glad I'm a beta, . . . ")

I think that this is a fairly accurate picture of the software process. It is optimized for design. Hence, the best people in the organization are assigned the most critical 10% of the work, and it is assumed that the post-coding 70% can be done by anyone. I'm not saying that this is what *ought* to be, but I think this is how management and tradition have structured the process. Furthermore, I believe that this view has influenced software engineering to a greater degree than we may have realized. After all, the management of the software process is really only the management of the tension between fun and tedium. Let me explain.

In the beginning, there were the ones and zeros, and then the mnemonic codes, and then the macros. And each was good. Then man created the high-level language, and it was very good. So good, in fact, that writing programs ceased to be the bottleneck; the problems now were in developing large systems. Thus, when the first of the NATO Conferences on Software Engineering met in 1968, the concern was for projects involving hundreds of people. One goal was to apply what had been learned in writing programs to the task of developing systems. Unfortunately, the differences between the models of computation represented in programs and the domain processes embodied in systems are so great, that—even today—we cannot transform what we know about programming into viable techniques for system design.

Unable to formalize the system development process, software engineering instead turned to eliminating some problems in its conduct. When, in its earliest days, programming was a small-scale, problem-solving activity, the emphasis was on optimizing the human role in problem solving. Because the experience base was thin, there were few firm requirements. Programmers worked with prototypes and used them to extend their understanding of the technology as they created new products. In doing this, they maximized fun, and went from selling the product, perhaps to some fun-charged form of requirements analysis, and then directly to programming. Given the degree of uncertainty in the requirements and design methods, any other approach would have been foolish.

Yet, as the programming technology matured and larger systems were being designed, the inherent problems of this ad hoc approach became obvious. Teams of 100 programmers could only work if there were fixed requirements and designs. Thus, software engineering turned to the optimization of process conformance rather than fun. One would not allow the allocation of functions step to begin until the statements of requirements was complete. Programming could not start until detailed design was finished. This, of course, was depicted in the waterfall diagram. Here, a hardware engineering process model was modified for software development. (Actually, the only change was that the hardware phase called "Fabrication" was now called "Code and Debug.")

Clearly, the discipline introduced by this first phase of software engineering did improve the process. It instituted a form of mathematical rigor. The requirements were taken as the axioms, and the designs were produced as theorems that built on each other until enough was known to produce the programs. Just as one cannot accept theorems without a verification based on the existing foundations, one would not allow programs to be developed without the prior definition of the properties they would exhibit. The logic was undeniable, and this shift to a disciplined process proved to be very effective for large and constrained projects. In particular, when much of the system's behavior can be defined by a set of fixed external interfaces, this remains the most appropriate process model.

Alas, success again changed things. Computer technology had improved to the extent that we felt confident in undertaking projects so complex that we couldn't be sure of how the systems would work until we used them. As the scope of automation expanded, moreover, new demands emerged. For example, consider the transition from the early days of VisiCalc to the modern spread sheet program. The changes include both the details relating to the man-machine interface and the perceptual shifts in expected functionality. Indeed, some people now use their spread sheet program as if it were a word processor. The evolution took place as incremental changes involving feedback from the user community (i.e., by software maintenance for those firms that were responsive and survived). For other classes of product, however, uncertainties must be resolved before the first release.

Here, then, is the underlying problem. A software process optimized for fun is only good when the tasks are small and the motivation for quality is based on an individual's insight. A software process optimized for phased compliance, on the other hand, is only valid for firm and stable requirements. It fails when there is uncertainty regarding the requirements. (How would you like a mathematical system in which half the axioms had the word "probably" in them?) It also fails when the requirements are not stable. (How often do we deliver products, years in the making, that are correct with respect to their requirements but no longer reflect what the organization needs?) Thus, both the natural intuitive approach and the managed response to it have proven to be poor models for controlling the software process.

Perhaps you would like to know how software should be developed. Actually, the answer is simple. What we need is a structured, object-oriented, knowledge-based prototyping paradigm based on formal specifications and proofs of correctness that combines the main features of composition and decomposition in a CASE environment using methodology-independent methods and visual programming in Ada. As soon as my grant is approved, I'll show you how it works; it really makes computing fun. (In fact, there is a product that automates the tedium of the software process, which is a plug for my *TEDIUM and the Software Process*, MIT Press, 1990.)

Until better paradigms are tested and available, keep in mind this stress between fun and tedium. It provides considerable insight into what is good (and bad) about the waterfall flow. It is more important to know why we do something than how it is done. The waterfall provides a discipline that structures a project according to what needs to be done rather than what is the most fun. Unfortunately, the waterfall model assumes that we can begin with a thorough and valid set of requirements. For many projects, this is no longer a reasonable assumption, and we must find ways of addressing this new challenge. Changing a process model is difficult and steeped in risk. It requires us to discard much of our historical experience and to develop new tools and techniques. Perhaps understanding why we choose our process models will help us make better choices. Moreover, if we recognize why we shortchange quality and maintenance, we may be able to discover how to improve both our processes and products. One last piece of advice: don't wait for my grant; tools alone cannot solve our software development problems.

Can You Help Me Find It?

Fun. That's what software is all about, right? Those of us who eat, sleep and breathe computing and software do it because it's fun.

Oh, sure. We also do it for the money, the status, the professional advancement, and all those other mundane things that people write books about. But basically, we're in it for fun. That's why no one has ever written a book called *The One-Minute Programmer* . . . not because programming takes longer than that, but because who could ever quit after one minute?

Now that I've said that, though, I have a confession to make. Software *used to be* fun for me. After 30 years, it's not nearly as much fun any more. And as I work my way into my third mid-life crisis, I'm trying to figure out why. I'm writing this story to see if any of you readers out there can help me.

Here's where I've gotten so far. I've established some candidate explanations to try on for size.

1. *Employers think 30-year people are too valuable to let them program.* The last time anyone *really* asked me to write a program for money was so long ago I can't remember when. Oh, sure, I get to study requirements, or write proposals, or do research, or write papers. But it's not the same. The fun in programming is programming. Nothing else really hacks it (cough). And employers believe that a fresh young programmer is just as good as an experienced older one.

2. *Programmers suffer burnout.* What's fun about programming is also what's awful about it. It's weaving a thousand tiny, intricate details into a functioning tapestry, an executable work of art. And after awhile, tangling with those details becomes less like fun and more like work. Why else would so many programmers aspire to become managers . . . what's the fun in that?

3. *The older you get, the more uptight you get.* Now *there's* a truly revolting thought! Have we learned so little about life, we experienced folk, that it becomes *more* of a burden as we live it, rather than *less*?

Growing older should, in part, be a refinement of the ability to have fun. Looking about me at my age-peers, I don't believe I see that happening.

The list could be longer. That's one thing I'm counting on from you, dear reader. But let me wrap up this story by telling you what brought this issue to a focus.

I don't know how better to put this: I now have a second-generation programmer. Thirty something years ago I had a son, and darned if he didn't decide to follow in his father's footsteps, cow pucky, program bugs, and all. So now there's a new generation programmer out there with my name on him. And as I watch his career progress, I see him having fun. Nostalgia and déjà vu . . . just like I used to.

It was his write-protect-ring story that got me. There he was, sitting around on a laid-back Friday afternoon at his particular employer's software factory, mellow after a week of hard work. And darned if one of the crew didn't throw a write-protect-ring at someone else (you know the write-protect-ring? The badly-named plastic gizmo that allows you to write on a tape when it's present, and protect it from writing when it's absent?). And, as will happen among spirited folk, the volley was returned. Write-protect-rings were flying through the air like bugs in an undebugged program. Even the corporate vice president got into the act (you know how small some of these contemporary software houses are, and how young their executives!). There was my son, a big smile on his face, happily telling me this story. And there was me-the-listener, analyzing my reaction and finally identifying it as *envy*. What was flashing through my mind was those halcyon days at the beginning of *my* career, when I swapped stories, shot rubber bands, and played ten-second chess on the job just like God intended us to do. So what happened?

What happened, indeed? I got more experienced. I got paid more, got to feeling more responsible, somehow. I wrote some books, authored a column or two. I did research, wrote a paper or two. I got *successful*, just like All-American boys and girls are supposed to dream about.

But somewhere along the line, I think, I lost something. Can you help me find it?

3

GETTING DOWN TO BUSINESS: A MORE FORMAL VIEW OF SOFTWARE CREATIVITY

> *"The most creative human problem solvers have an unusual capacity to integrate the two modes of conscious functions of the two [brain] hemispheres, and move back and forth between the holistic and sequential, between intuition and logic, between the fuzzy field of a problem domain and a clear specific small segment of a field. Such people can be outstanding artists and scientists because they combine the strong attributes of both . . . Leonardo da Vinci . . . and Einstein."*

> —Moshe F. Rubinstein, in *Tools for Thinking and Problem-Solving*, Prentice-Hall, 1986

Chapter 2 constituted a philosophical and motivational trip through creativity land. We stood back and looked at creativity from a lot of different points of view, and pontificated informally on some underlying conflicts between creativity, in a variety of guises, and more disciplined and formal approaches, also in various guises.

We discussed contemporary conflict surrounding the subject, acknowledging that conflict on this issue is probably a sign of disciplinary health, and moved gradually from a too-liberal, all-creative view of the work of software, to a more balanced, creativity plus discipline view. And we noted that the contemporary too-conservative view of software as discipline and formality to the exclusion of creativity probably also needs to make a similar movement.

However, all of that is pretty general stuff. It's time, in this chapter, to get down to brass tacks. Where, in the software process, does creativity *really* need to get into the act?

There are undoubtedly many answers to that question. For now, let's just take a quick look at some possible answers:

- Translating fundamental needs of the business enterprise into problems for computer solution
- Trying to resolve a problem definition posed by several different organizations in an enterprise, each of which wants a slightly different variant of the same problem solved
- Designing a solution to a complex and (perhaps) well-defined problem, but a problem significantly different from any encountered before
- Establishing a reasonably necessary and reasonably sufficient set of test conditions and cases that will do at least an adequate job of verifying an already-constructed software solution at both the white-box and black-box levels
- Making a major enhancement change to an existing software system that was not originally designed to accommodate this particular change

In other words, as we can see from the above list, the need for creativity emerges not just at a point or two in the software life cycle, but throughout it. There are instances, in that list, of a need for creativity in concept definition, in requirements determination, in design, in testing, and in maintenance. And that is not an exhaustive list!

What would be nice is if, in this chapter, we gave an example of a more specific need for creativity at all of those points in the life cycle, and more. But that approach might lead to redundancy and reader boredom. Instead, we have done this:

There are two sections in this chapter. One of them focuses on the need for creativity in the design process, and how that need manifests itself. (The paper talks more about "cognitive" rather than "creative" approaches, but I believe that, in the context of this particular paper, the two are largely interchangeable.) The other paper in this chapter focuses on the need for creativity earlier in the life cycle, at concept definition, as it discusses creativity in the definition of strategic (alias competitive advantage) systems.

The first paper gets quite specific about where creativity enters into the design process, basing its findings on some empirical studies of, and some interviews with, good or top designers. The empirical nature of these findings is particularly compelling: design is clearly one of the facets of software construction where practice still leads theory, and where formal and disciplined approaches simply fail to deal with the essence of the problem.

The second paper, by Professor Dennis Galletta of the University of Pittsburgh, presents a model of a process for coming to grips with strategic systems, a process that takes place even prior to the beginning of our software life cycle. The model examines some specific aspects of the innovator, the task to be performed, and the environment in which the work will be done. It finds flaws in contemporary approaches, and suggests at least an interim strategy for improvement.

And the point of these two papers, again? This is the "get real" portion of the book, the chapter where we translate from vague entreaties into specific information and recommendations. We hope you will find this material both interesting and useful.

3.1   CREATIVITY AND SOFTWARE DESIGN: THE MISSING LINK

Abstract
Formal processes are increasingly recommended to those who build software. But in an analysis of the methods used by top software designers, we see that cognitive, creative processes—in some ways the opposite of formal processes—are closer to the essence of the design task. Further analysis of the work of these top designers exposes some additional facts about design that are counter to traditional, textbook views. The implications of these findings to those who build software are explored.

There is tension and conflict growing between two polar software points of view. The first point of view is that the construction of software is best done using formal, disciplined processes. The second point of view is that software should be constructed using creative, freeform processes.

This conflict is seen in presentations at software conferences and papers in the software literature, as well as in the approaches used in software-producing organizations. At this writing, the dominant voice in the software literature is one that advocates formalism. Formal methods are seen as *necessary* for the construction of large-scale software, and *appropriate* to software of any scale. We see papers on formal approaches saying such things as " . . . Software engineering leaders are beginning to call for more systematic approaches: more mathematics, science, and engineering are needed" [CSTB90]. Creative approaches, from this formal point of view, are seen as counterproductive—sometimes effective, but more often unpredictable.

However, the counter view is also beginning to appear in this same literature. We find a growing questioning of formal approaches. For example, in [Denning91] we find, "There is nothing wrong with formality. It has demonstrated remarkable technological power. I am saying it limits what we can accomplish. We need to go beyond formality . . . "

Nowhere is this conflict more focused than in the topic of software design. The formal, disciplined approach to design is generally seen as:

1. Follow a life-cycle methodology, a series of steps calling for activities performed in a particular order, with specified deliverables produced at the end of each step. The steps involving design are called such things as preliminary, or logical, design, and detailed, or physical design.
2. During design itself, attack large problems by decomposing them in hierarchic fashion into smaller, more manageable problems. Within those smaller problems, employ high cohesion (focus each solution on a cohesive set of problems) and loose coupling (make each solution stand as much on its own as possible).
3. When the design is complete, represent the design in some formal, often graphical, language. Candidate languages include dataflow diagrams, structure charts, and program design language (pseudocode).

Those who favor more creative approaches say that there, in design, is where the problems of the formal approach are most easily seen. Although the steps of a methodology, and the use of a representation, are an important part of the design process, these people say, there is clearly something missing. Nothing in the methodological steps and the representational techniques is actually a design activity. Instead, they represent preparation for design and completion of design. Where, this point of view says, does design *really* take place?

With that question in mind, over the past ten years several software researchers have begun exploring ways of discovering the actual design process. This search has been characterized by some as the pursuit of a "missing link"—the link between methodology and representation—that represents the true act of design.

In Pursuit of the Missing Link

In pursuit of this missing link, these researchers have looked to the best of practice. After all, successful software designs have been produced for over 30 years. Even though the theory of design, these people say, has a missing link, the practice of design does not. Peter J. Denning [Denning91] says, "The time has come to pay more attention to the murky, imprecise, unformalizable domains of everyday practice, which is, after all, where design is judged."

That is precisely what these researchers have done.

Two approaches have been taken to examining design through its practice. In one, an interviewing approach was used, identifying and talking to top designers about their perceptions of design. In the other, actual design sessions were videotaped, and the process used by these designers was abstracted into a theoretical description of the process. The two approaches, though rather different, have produced some interesting resonance in their resulting findings.

In the interviewing approach, again, two rather different approaches were used. Veteran software specialist John Nestor, at the time working at the Software Engineering Institute, identified what he believed to be the top ten software designers (based on his experiences in working with them) and set out to interview them, presenting the results in an internal SEI briefing. Journalist Susan Lammers, on the other hand, interviewed a collection of successful microcomputer software entrepreneurs, and published the result in a book [Lammers86]. We will present a quick summary of Nestor's findings here; the Lammers' findings, on the other hand, will be presented scattered through the remainder of this paper.

What did Nestor learn from his top designers? He asked several questions, including "What is design?" and "What makes great designers?" He got answers like the following:

- Great designers have a large set of standard patterns.
- Great designers have lived through failing projects and have learned from those failures.
- Great designers have absolute mastery of their tools.
- Great designers have a strong predilection for simplicity.
- Great designers are able to anticipate more kinds of possible change.
- Great designers are able to put themselves in the user's shoes.
- Great designers have no fear of complexity.

There are flaws, of course, in research conducted as subjectively as this. The choice of designers and the choice of conclusions was entirely dependent on one person's view of design. Still, there are some fascinating themes to Nestor's findings. Top designers apparently must have had some experience, including experience at failure, and must have been able to abstract from those experiences a collection of models for use in future design efforts. (I like to think of these top designers as carrying a pack on their back full of analogies into which they can reach to find a starting point for a new design. The more full their analogy pack, the better they are at design.) Top designers are also able to tackle extremely complex problems and try to find simple solutions. There is no doubt that, in spite of the subjectivity of the approach, Nestor's findings are important.

The Videotaping Approach

The videotaping approach, the second approach to researching the nature of design through an examination of practice, escapes the dilemma of subjectivity. The process for this research was as follows:

1. Individuals or groups of designers are videotaped while designing a solution to an assigned problem.
2. During individual design sessions, designers are quietly urged to "think aloud" so that the thought processes employed can be captured.
3. Videotape sessions, although inevitably intrusive, are designed to interfere with the design process as little as possible.
4. Results of several video sessions with several design groups are reviewed to identify common themes and activities.
5. A theoretical description resulting from the above reviews is constructed.
6. The theoretical description is tested by applying it to further videotaped sessions to see if it matches what is happening.
7. The theoretical description is exposed to the design session participants to see if they agree that it describes the process they used.

This series of steps is called "protocol analysis," and is used in many kinds of observational research. The researchers who used it in pursuing the question of software design include Elliot Soloway, then at Yale University (and more recently of the University of Michigan), and Bill Curtis, then at the Microelectronics and Computing Consortium (MCC) (and more recently of the Software Engineering Institute). The findings of this research were published in the late 1980s [Curtis87, Guinon87, Adelson84, Adelson85, Soloway87].

What, in fact, did these investigations into the nature of design discover? There were two levels of findings:

In the first, the researchers found that design involves

1. Understanding a problem
2. Decomposing the problem into goals and objects

3. Selecting and composing plans to solve the problem
4. Implementing the plans
5. Reflecting on the design product and process

At this level, the findings were interesting but not terribly illuminating. Some, in fact, have criticized these findings on the grounds that they describe the general process of problem-solving, rather than the specific process of design. That criticism seems warranted—looked at objectively, these steps are really another wording for the concept of the software life cycle, a notion well defined and understood long before this research was begun. If this level of findings had been all that these researchers produced, their findings would have died a quiet death.

Striking Paydirt

But it was at the next level down that the researchers struck pay dirt. They explored more deeply the issue of "selecting and composing plans," to see what activities that task implied. And there they found what many now believe to be the essence of creative design.

People composing design plans, they found, performed these steps:

1. Build a mental model of a proposed solution to the problem.
2. Mentally execute the model to see if it does indeed solve the problem. Often this mental execution (also called a "simulation") takes the form of providing sample input to the model to see if it produces correct sample output.
3. If the sample output is incorrect (as will often be the case in the early stages of design), the model is expanded to correct its deficiencies, then executed again.
4. When the sample output finally becomes correct, another sample input is selected, and steps two and three are repeated.
5. When sufficient sample inputs have passed the test in step four, the model is assumed to be a suitable design model and representation of the design begins.

It is important to note two things about this process. The first is that the process is entirely cognitive—that is, all of the steps are conducted inside the mind, at mind speeds. This is important because the design activity must occur extremely quickly in order to succeed. Use of pencil and paper, or even computerized support, at this stage would significantly slow down and thus degrade the design process.

The second thing to note is that the process is iterative. That is, a designer repeats certain steps in the process in a trial-and-error fashion until a potentially successful design is achieved. Researchers call such a trial-and-error process a "heuristic" method.

What is especially significant about both of these things is that they are, to some extent, at odds with the more formal, methodological approaches. Since the steps of the design process occur inside the mind, it would be difficult—and counterproductive—to subject them to any formal, disciplined process. Since they are heuristic, they are almost exactly the opposite of formal approaches (formalists often mention heuristic approaches as the "erroneous" opposite of their preferred formal methods). Thus here, in this cognitive essence of design, we have found one point at which formal approaches simply are not useful.

This finding did not surprise those who have been concerned about formal approaches all along. For example, H. Dieter Rombach has said [Rombach90], "While formalization . . . is a solution for more mechanical processes . . . it is not feasible for design processes." Here, we can see why.

Let us return for a moment to the other research approach to studying design, that of conducting interviews. Recall that the results of one set of interviews was recorded in a book [Lammers86]. It is interesting to note some quotations from that book:

"The first step in programming is imagining. Just making it crystal clear in my mind what is going to happen. In this initial stage, I use pencil and paper. I just doodle . . . because the real picture is in my mind." (This from Charles Simonyi, designer of the Multiplan spreadsheet product.)

"At some point, the [design] gets explosive and I have everything inside my brain at one time . . . All sorts of things go on in my brain that I can't put on paper because I'm always changing them." (Gary Kildall, designer of the CP/M operating system.)

"You have to simulate in your mind how the program's going to work . . . When you're creating something . . . and you have that model in your mind, it's a lonely thing." (Bill Gates, founder and CEO of Microsoft.)

"You constantly try to hold the state of the entire system you're working on in your head. If you lose the mental image, it takes a long time to get it back into that state." (John Page, designer of PFS:File.)

The resonance between these interview findings and the findings of the videotaped protocol analysis process are almost amazing! The interview subjects put into lifelike words the more analytic findings of the researchers. It is particularly interesting to note that the interview subjects used words like "model" and "simulation," and talked about the "loneliness" of the creative designer who, during the act of design, must not "lose that mental image." Clearly, these words describe a creative, not formal or disciplined, process.

Empirical Research

Research of this kind based on an examination of practice is generally known as "empirical." Many of the findings of these empirical studies were originally presented at a series of conferences devoted to empirical research, known as the "Empirical Studies of Programmers" conferences. (The unfortunately chosen acronym, some in the formal methods community have noted, is "ESP"!) It is important to note that the findings of this empirical research have moved well beyond this discovery of heuristic approaches.

For example, ESP researchers have stepped back from the details of the cognitive design process to examine its broader elements. They have found that design involves several components:

- Those oriented toward the problem to be solved
- Those oriented toward the nature and notion of design itself
- Those oriented toward the involvement of the human designer
- Those oriented toward the use of computer tools to support the designer

In this list of the components of design, some ESP researchers are becoming more and more convinced that the difficult problems of design are not those involved in the design process itself, but those involved in designing a solution within the context of a particular application problem. For example, the designer must know not only some basic facts about the application domain (problem-oriented) but also some specialized facts about design approaches unique to that domain (design-oriented). (For example, designers of report programs must understand how to produce columns of figures totals lines, with multiple levels of totals of totals; and designers of scientific programs must understand how to perform iterative mathematical solutions on a finite-precision computer.)

The Designer as Human Being

However, perhaps the most fascinating components in the design process are the contributions and limitations of the designer as human being.

Recall that the inner nucleus of the design process is a cognitive, heuristic activity. What advantages and disadvantages does the human mind bring to this activity?

To begin with, psychologists have discovered that the human mind consists of two different portions, "short-term memory" and "long-term memory." (The analogy between these components and a computer's main memory and external memory is interesting.) Short-term memory is exceedingly fast but has limited capacity; long-term memory is comparatively slow but appears to have unlimited capacity. The capacity limitation of short-term memory is, in fact, extremely severe; researchers from the 1950s (and since) have found that this portion of the mind can hold only about five to nine distinctions at any one time. (Psychological researchers have referred to this as the "magic number 7 plus or minus 2.")

Because cognitive design must happen at lightning speed, it must happen in short-term memory; but this magic number 7 constraint is a severe limitation on the designer. Fortunately, according to psychologists, the mind has developed a workaround solution for that limitation. It performs an act called "chunking," in which several distinctions are "chunked" together into one, and the mind can then hold seven of *these* things. (For example, when humans identify another person, they do not remember the looks of that person through a set of lower-level facts like "lip shape" and "eye color" and "facial hair," but rather they form and remember a gestalt or chunk, perhaps one called "face.") Thus, designers are able to overcome part of the natural human limitations on short-term memory by chunking. However, in spite of that, the constraints of memory are a serious problem to the designer. For example, recall the "loneliness" of the designer who cannot be interrupted for fear of losing the state of a design. Here we see the volatility and low capacity of short-term memory at work: A short-term memory interrupted is a short-term memory unable to reconstruct its contents, and the problem is made all the worse because that short-term memory was necessarily full of complicated chunks of information rather than a large number of simple facts.

There are two other important findings of these empirical researchers regarding design. The first has to do with the beginning of design, and the second with its ending.

Beginning of Design

One of the key findings of the ESP researchers is that designers begin a design, whenever possible, with the reuse of an existing design. (Recall the "analogy pack" on the designer's back, where he or she reaches for a past design used in a similar problem.)

That first model used in the heuristic process of cognitive design may very well be a reused model rather than one created by the designer in response to this particular problem. Visser discovered that, for problems encountered before, designers employ an "example program" as their starting point, and then observed, "Designers rarely start from scratch" [Visser87]. This was echoed in one of the interview findings from [Lammers86], where veteran mainframe and microcomputer software designer Butler Lampson is quoted as saying, "Most of the time, a new program is a refinement, extension, generalization, or improvement of an existing program. It's really unusual to do something that's completely new ... "

There is another interesting empirical finding about design. Although textbooks and the literature frequently refer to design as a top-down process, design is in fact rarely top-down. Bill Curtis has said, "The unperturbed design process is opportunistic"—that is, rather than proceed in an orderly process, good designers follow an erratic pattern dictated by their minds, pursuing opportunities rather than an orderly progression. Some say that design is really "hard-part first" design—that is, the designer seeks out sub-problems that appear to be difficult to solve, and solves them before any easier problems, in order to be sure that the complexity of an unknown solution does not come along to destroy the predictability of earlier, known solutions. It is interesting to note that David Parnas, a noted computer scientist, has recommended "faking" a top-down process—that is, even though design does not take place top-down, the recording and representation of that design *should* be top-down, because only in that way can observers or reviewers understand the design product.

Again, this notion of "opportunistic" or "hard-part-first" design is echoed by the interviews in [Lammers86]. We find these quotations:

"You start at the point where you think it's too hard to solve, and then you break it down into smaller pieces," says Gary Kildall, designer of CP/M.

"Once I've dealt with the hard parts in isolation—maybe by writing a little program to prove out some theory—I can go about structuring the program," says John Page, designer of PFS:File.

Ending of Design

If the beginnings of design, involving reuse of existing designs and an opportunistic, hard-part first approach, were a surprise when compared to textbook views of design, what have ESP researchers learned about the ending of design? There are some surprises here as well.

The textbooks tell us that design proceeds down to the level at which a competent programmer can begin writing code. But what does that really mean? Top designers seem to have a well-defined criteria for ending design—they quit when what remains to be designed is analogous to something they've already done before, and done it so many times that they can code it with no further creative thought. They call these presolved problems "primitives." But the question naturally arises, "Do all designers have the same set of primitives?"

Clearly, the answer is "no." A designer's primitives emerge not just from their knowledge of design, but (as we saw earlier in this paper) from their knowledge of one or more application domains and domain-specific design approaches. Thus, designer "A," when designing a data processing report generator, might stop at a fairly high level of design if he has designed and coded many of them before, whereas designer "B," who might have just as much experience as designer A but be inexperienced in report generation, might produce a much more elaborate, detailed design. This produces no problem, of course, as long as the person who writes the code is the same as the person who produced the design. However, more and more often, particularly in very large systems, there is a handoff from the designer to the coder. If the primitive set of the designer matches that of the coder, this handoff can go smoothly.

But consider two situations where the primitive sets do not match:

The designer has a stronger primitive set than the coder: Here, the designer stops at a fairly high level, but the coder cannot write code from that level of design and must do further design work before writing code.

The coder has a stronger primitive set than the designer: Here, the coder may be offended by what he or she may perceive to be an unnecessary level of design (and, in fact, the design may be erroneous or more complicated than the coder knows to be necessary), and the coder discards portions of the design before writing the code.

The point here is that the end of the design process is far from the simple "competent programmer" textbook solution. It is often true in practice that when a design handoff occurs, further design or discarding of design takes place.

There is one other consideration at or near the end of the design process. It is a characteristic of software design that, on occasion, some difficult design problem lurks at the lowest level of design, such that the entire design solution to that point is found to be infeasible, and the designer must discard it and begin again. What happens in this case is that the designer has overlooked a "hard-part" portion of the design, waiting to do it last, only to find that the design-to-date does not allow a solution to the hard-part problem. Most designers confess to having encountered this problem on occasion, but no research has been done to try to characterize the types of problems that cause this effect, or to define warning signs to allow anticipating such problems.

Once again, these thoughts are echoed by quotes from [Lammers86]: "Carry the design down to a level . . . where two things are true. First, I already know about the primitives I write the programming in—they have been implemented many times before . . . Second, I understand the primitives well enough to estimate within a factor of two or three how much memory they are going to cost . . . I can be fairly confident that it's possible to implement a function, and I can roughly estimate its performance. Of course, it's possible to do that and overlook something very important. There's no way around that," says Butler Lampson.

Summary

What is it possible to say about the nature of software design as a formal process and as a creative process? Certainly, we can say that the formal processes of methodologies and representations form an important underpinning for design; but just as certainly, it is clear that they do not get at the *essence* of design.

The essence of design, it has been discovered by researchers looking at the best of design practice, involves:

1. A heuristic, cognitive process not susceptible to formal approaches
2. The need for experience in constructing suitable reusable design starting places
3. An opportunistic rather than top-down approach to the steps involved in design
4. A person-dependent, primitive-dependent process for determining when and how design shall end
5. The possibility of lurking, unspotted "hard-part" problems that can destroy an apparently complete design at the last minute

This set of findings may be upsetting to those who believe that formal approaches are the only way to build software, but the realization that formal processes must be supplemented with creative ones may be the beginning of a more complete understanding of what is necessary to build superior software products.

REFERENCES

[Adelson84] B. ADELSON and E. SOLOWAY, "A Model of Software Design," report from the Dept. of Computer Science, Yale University, October 1984.

[Adelson85] B. ADELSON and E. SOLOWAY, "The Role of Domain Experience in Software Design," *IEEE Transactions on Software Engineering,* October 1985.

[CSTB90] "Scaling Up: A Research Agenda for Software Engineering," a report of the Computer Science Technology Board of the National Research Council," *Communications of the ACM,* March 1990.

[Curtis87] MCC Technical Report Number STP-260–87, "Empirical Studies of the Design Process: Papers for the Second Workshop on Empirical Studies of Programmers," B. Curtis, R. Guindon, H. Krasner, D. Walz, J. Elam, and N. Iscoe, September 1987.

[Denning91] "Technology or Management? An Editorial," *Communications of the ACM,* March 1991; Peter J. Denning.

[Guinon87] MCC Technical Report Number STP-283–87, "A Model of Cognitive Processes in Software Design: An Analysis of Breakdowns in Early Design Activities by Individuals," R. Guindon, B. Curtis, H. Krasner, August 1987.

[Lammers86] *Programmers at Work,* Microsoft Press, 1986; Susan Lammers.

[Rombach90] "Design Measurement: Some Lessons Learned," *IEEE Software,* March 1990; H. Dieter Rombach.

[Soloway87] "E Unum Pluribus: Generating Alternative Designs," Dept. of Computer Science, Yale University, E. Soloway, J. Spohrer, D. Littman, 1987.

[Visser87] "Strategies in Programming Progammable Controllers: A Field Study on a Professional Programmer," *Proceedings of the Empirical Studies of Programmers, Second Workshop,* Ablex, 1987; Willemien Visser.

3.2 THE ROLE OF CREATIVITY IN IDENTIFYING STRATEGIC INFORMATION SYSTEMS

Dennis F. Galletta and Jeffrey Lynn Sampler

Introduction

Academics and practitioners have dedicated much time and effort in recent years to understanding a range of phenomena associated with the identification of strategic information systems (SIS). One of the main goals in SIS development is to provide a particular, significant competitive advantage. In highly publicized cases, this advantage has on occasion lasted for decades and accounted for millions of dollars of profits. The most vivid examples to date illustrate dramatic increases in market share and decreases in the potency of competitors. Wiseman takes this scenario to its logical conclusion, and warns that a firm failing to develop SIS "may find itself at risk", lost in a state of competitive disadvantage [Wiseman88, p. 15].

Competitive applications* now appear to be widespread; there is talk of new systems appearing each month. Wiseman describes over 100 early published cases of SIS, further emphasizing the importance of investigating potential strategic uses of information systems; it appears that SIS development has become a tactic for survival. As a result, there has been a great deal of interest in providing guidance for identifying strategic applications.

Other scholars note the difficulty of achieving *sustainable* competitive advantage (e.g., [Clemons91]) because enterprises have learned the importance of responding quickly to a competitor's SIS. This suggests that, in addition to being able to create *original* SIS, it is also vital to be able to create *responsive* SIS.

The creation of either original or responsive SIS is, of course, a significant intellectual and technical challenge.

Most writers have offered us frameworks or techniques for understanding and identifying opportunities for achieving effective and sustainable competitive advantage. All of these frameworks make it explicit that their major goal is to identify ideas for becoming more competitive in the marketplace. These ideas can involve dramatic increases in market share, decreases in cost, or increases in customer loyalty.

It is difficult to determine cases in which following those frameworks has allowed practitioners to develop creative approaches to strategic systems. At the same time, it is peculiar that none of these frameworks is explicit in addressing the role of creativity in generating ideas, and none cites any of the many creativity techniques available. One would expect frameworks intended to be used for generating ideas to employ idea-generation techniques! Perhaps the frameworks are not, in fact, effective in uncovering truly creative SIS applications, due to their lack of a foundation in creativity.

It is time to inform the SIS identification process with creativity techniques and principles. This paper reviews SIS frameworks and creativity,

---

*Throughout this paper, references to "SIS" or "strategic systems" are intended to apply to strategic applications that result in competitive advantage. Although they are less specific, the shorter terms are used to improve readability.

and presents some recommendations for applying what we know about creativity to the task of SIS development.

The SIS Frameworks

Several frameworks have been used by consultants and authors in the search for SIS ideas. These frameworks became very well known at about the same time, and many writers have considered the 1980s to be the decade of SIS. Although the 1980s have passed, and there has recently been less attention paid to SIS for competitive advantage, there is still a need for identifying creative SIS for competitive advantage. It is analogous to the fact that even though the 1960s have passed, there is still a need for developing effective reporting systems. Each of the frameworks will be described in turn.

Two frameworks proposed by Porter and colleagues have been widely used. An analysis of a firm's competitive forces [Porter80] allows a strategist to pinpoint targets for creating competitive advantage. Porter contributed structure to the search for competitive advantage by categorizing general competitive forces into five dimensions. These forces were applied to information systems by Cash, McFarlan, and McKenney (1983, 1988), who developed questions aimed at discovering SIS applications in each of the five areas. Potential SIS adopters should ask themselves if information technology (IT) can (1) build barriers to entry; (2) increase customer switching costs; (3) build power in relationships with suppliers; (4) achieve dramatic cost reductions; or (5) generate new products or services. By identifying these all-important targets and their interrelationships, opportunities for new business practices can be revealed.

Later work by Porter and Millar (1985) focused attention on the "value chain," where a product or service can be traced through a firm's activity cycle, from receipt of raw materials to operations to distribution to marketing and, finally, to service. This tracing is done from the points of view of the corporate infrastructure, human resource management technology development, and procurement. By going through the value chain from each point of view, SIS opportunities might be uncovered.

A concept related to the value chain is the "customer resource life cycle" [Ives84] where the focus is on how customers of a firm specify, acquire, maintain, and retire resources they purchase. The authors' intention is that by forcing examination of 13 stages of this life cycle, enough detail will be provided to trigger new SIS opportunities that will result in competitive advantage. Their focus on customers results from the critical role the customers play in virtually all SIS applications.

Building on some of the above work, Wiseman and MacMillan (1984) and Wiseman (1988) offered another model that is intended to provide focus in identifying potential SIS applications, the "strategic option generator." The earlier approach asks five questions, each having either two or three possible answers. The total number of permutations of these answers is 108 ($3 \times 3 \times 2 \times 2 \times 3$). The questions are: (1) What is our strategic target? (suppliers, customers, competitors); (2) what strategic thrust can be used against the target? (differentiation, cost, innovation); (3) what strategic mode can be used? (offense, defensive); (4) what direction of thrust can be used? (usage, provision); and (5) what information system skills can we use? (processing, storage, transmission).

Finally, Wiseman (1988) later revised the option generator to a 37-cell grid plotting strategic thrusts (differentiation, cost, innovation, growth, and alliance) against strategic targets (arenas including suppliers, channels, customers, and rivals; and users including the enterprise, suppliers, channels, customers, and rivals). Users of either option generator are expected to pinpoint a particular set of concerns to trigger ideas for SIS applications. According to Wiseman and MacMillan, such an approach should help managers "uncover new options for competitive advantage" like the "physicists who discovered a new class of atomic particles" [Wiseman84, p. 49].

All of these frameworks can certainly be of some assistance to the task of attempting to identify ideas for strategic systems. However, there is no explicit use of creativity techniques other than simple brainstorming [Rackoff85] in any of the frameworks.

To present a more unbiased picture, it should be noted that there is some confusion over the need for innovative ideas in identifying SIS. Although some researchers acknowledge the need for innovative thinking [Johnston88] for generating "blockbuster ideas" [Rackoff85, p. 292], Emery asserted that "strategic systems come through a long-term adaptive process, rather than through a major breakthrough that brings quick rewards . . . we cannot set out to develop an SIS" [Emery90, p. vii]. As evidence of his assertion, Emery notes that most of the strategic systems are simple extensions to well-designed transaction processing systems, and that no one is intelligent enough to have planned such systems from the start. Ciborra goes so far as to claim that most of the publicized systems considered to be strategic were the result of low-level "tinkering" that accidentally led to significant competitive advantage [Ciborra91]. Starbuck warns *against* attempting to strategize, largely because of our faulty approaches to forecasting [Starbuck91].

Our perspective is that yes, it is true that we do not yet have convincing *evidence* of systems that were developed on the basis of deliberate attempts to create sustainable competitive advantage. However, the lack of evidence just might support the assertion that we need to develop an effective creativity-based strategy for identifying opportunities. Had such a strategy existed in the past, perhaps we would be discussing an entire array of systems that were *not* simple extensions to transaction-processing systems. Therefore, the lack of evidence might be a symptom of a problem, not a reason to abandon efforts to refine our frameworks.

The creativity literature and cognitive science literature can be useful in generating several guidelines for identifying creative SIS opportunities. The next section will provide a survey of findings from those areas.

Advice from the Creativity Literature

Work in creativity can be helpful at both the individual and group levels, in light of the goal of identifying SIS applications. Although there is a vast amount of literature, we attempt here to be frugal in our references.*

Creative people.   There are many important questions that one might raise about creativity and the individual. How do you find creative people? How can creativity levels of individuals be increased? What role does motivation play in creativity? These and other questions will now be explored.

Several researchers have attempted to identify individuals who are creative. In general, the studies focus on innate creativity, factual expertise, and motivation.

Innate creativity is a sought-after but elusive trait. It would be useful for many organizations that embark on creative missions to be able to indicate who is likely to be creative and who is not. Although it is common to hear people confidently proclaim the creativity of themselves or others, it is a nontrivial issue to verify or determine the level of a person's creativity.

Personality factors were investigated in the early literature, perhaps as an easy, visible indicator of innate creativity. Unfortunately, mere possession of such traits as independence, self-discipline, curiosity, energy, nonconformity, and so on will not guarantee the production of creative products [Amabile83]. More formalized instruments have also been developed to better focus on creative abilities, but there is some controversy about their efficacy [Epstein85, Mischel82]. Tests such as the Adaption-Innovation scale [Kirton87] and the Torrance Test of Creative Thinking (Torrance, 1974) were developed to quantify the extent to which a person

---

*Those seeking a more detailed, formal review of the literature at the individual level, along with formal research propositions, should refer to [Galletta92].

has innate creative ability. At best, these instruments should represent one of a variety of assessments of the creativity of individuals.

Factual expertise is another element of a creative person. If a person is expected to develop an innovative approach to an existing problem, he or she should possess a certain amount of knowledge of the problem domain. An interesting paradox is that people with high levels of expertise might be "set in their ways" when approaching what might seem to be a routine problem (Adelson, 1984; Elam & Mead, 1987), and that an intermediate level of expertise might allow a fresh look at a situation.

Relating a set of seemingly unrelated facts is also a valuable attribute of a creative person. Not only is it helpful to have the facts themselves at one's disposal; it is perhaps even more important to be able to relate those facts. For example, basic awareness of the ability of computers to communicate over voice telephone lines can be coupled with everyday knowledge about touch-tone phones to form the basis for the ideas of a touch-tone customer ordering system. Most people possess both kinds of knowledge, but few would relate them immediately.

A person's ability to solve a problem is also dependent on several external factors. The problem's size, structure, decomposability, and stability are important factors that interact with the person's abilities and experience. A problem with a large number of elements (e.g., organizations with many divisions, offering many different products and/or services, or facing many competitors) and possible solutions can be very difficult to understand, and it might be difficult to generate a comprehensive list of alternatives. Problems that are low in inherent structure make it difficult to understand cause-effect relationships, and therefore difficult to predict effects of proposed actions. Decomposable problems ease the problem-solving process, because they are broken down into smaller, more readily understood problems. Finally, problem instability might be seen as a negative factor for effective solution, but instability often causes the need to redefine the problem; problem redefinition is a creativity tool that can introduce a fresh look and new opportunities.

Interestingly, there is a facilitating effect of environmental uncertainty on creative problem-solving to some threshhold, and then uncertainty reduces problem-solving creativity after that point (Schroeder et al., 1968). This "inverted-U" relationship is perhaps the result of the lack of need or opportunity for creativity in situations of low uncertainty, and futility in situations of high uncertainty. Unfortunately, we cannot adjust environmental uncertainty to the problem-solver's ability levels.

There is not much that can be done about problems being too large or unstructured, either. Any difficulties with a person's problem-solving ability can be alleviated somewhat by creativity tools. Limitations in a person's ability to manipulate or remember a large number of facts can be overcome by using notes, pictures, diagrams, and analogies (Larkin & Simon, 1987; Kotovsky et al., 1985). Such tools can be powerful in easing the acquisition or manipulation of difficult material. Notes are widely used, and their benefits need hardly be described. Many creativity techniques employ written lists at many stages of idea generation.

Pictures and diagrams can help a decision-maker reconceptualize a problem in a new way or visualize the interrelationships between a set of dimensions. For example, seeing a plot of sales history versus advertising dollars, sales promotions, and new product introductions can make vivid the relative effectiveness of and interrelationships between each marketing approach. A diagram reduces the search for information by localizing related information, removes considerable need for text, and provides perceptual enhancement (Larkin & Simon, 1987). Also, in developing diagrams the problem-solver typically abstracts a subset of the properties of the problem to form the representation (Novak, 1977). This subset might contain the critical features of the problem, which may enable a crisp focus on cause-and-effect relationships. Thus, diagrams can enable the problem-solver to constrain his or her search and focus on some of the critical problem attributes.

Analogies are also very useful for giving instant understanding of some aspects of the problem, and have been recommended in both the creativity (VanGundy, 1981) and cognitive psychology literatures (Carbonell, 1986; Gentner, 1983). Analogies reduce the amount of time spent in the rule familiarization stage of problem-solving (learning cause-and-effect relationships and other detailed information) and significantly reduce the cognitive burden (Kotovsky et al., 1985). For example, when considering how consumers might interact with a touch-tone purchasing system, it might be useful to consider the analogy of how a store is separated into departments and aisles. This makes it easier for a shopper to navigate through the store, as it might make it easier for a telephone shopper to navigate through the electronic store. Other useful analogies that might bring out interesting and useful dimensions might be: braille systems, for valuable guidance on how to maximize economy of inputs and outputs; an audio tape recorder, for its set of playing, rewinding, and erasing functions; and a television remote control, for its button-pushing orientation. If the problem-solver is able to relate the current problem to information already in long-term memory (LTM), this will reduce the amount of learning necessary for the problem, and thus should quicken the arrival at a solution.

Motivation has been found to be an important but neglected key to creativity. According to Amabile, a manager should be aware of two different types of motivation and their effects [Amabile83, 88]. People can be motivated by external (extrinsic) rewards or by internal (intrinsic) value systems. Extrinsic factors like monetary rewards or peer recognition have not been found to be effective in leading to creative behavior. On the other hand, tasks that are inherently rewarding to a person appear to engage them more intensely and push them to expend the greater effort that is required to generate a large set of alternatives. This line of research has lent some scholarly evidence to the well-known expression that weighs the relative merits of "perspiration" and "inspiration" when creating something new, tipping the scales toward the former.

Creative groups.   Groups are used in most organizations to "brainstorm" ideas for solving problems. It is important to ensure that the makeup of a group is appropriate for creativity, and that the group processes support creative problem-solving.

Because it is sometimes advantageous for persons to have different levels of expertise and points of view to promote individual creativity (Adelson, 1984; Elam & Mead, 1987; Newell et al., 1962), it follows logically that groups have special potential at times in taking creative approaches to solving problems or identifying opportunities. Many interesting relationships between seemingly unrelated items can be uncovered in group discussion. For example, AT&T's attempt to purchase TCI represents a gamble of millions of dollars to provide new markets that have not yet been created. It will take creative sessions including specialists in both telephone and entertainment technologies to invent new products and services that will eventually be desired in the marketplace, because we have little or no experience with interactive cable systems. Previous market tests were performed in limited areas, with limited services or limited technology. There might be a substantial market in coupling banking, grocery shopping, or video rentals with television cable services.

Many consultants and researchers have found that the creativity of groups can be increased by using a wide variety of techniques; the majority of the 67 creative problem-solving techniques reviewed by VanGundy are intended for use by groups rather than by individuals [VanGundy81]. Although most readers will immediately think of brainstorming (Osborne, 1963) as a creative group process, there are many other techniques. Several examples are in order. In "boundary examination" exercises, groups can question assumptions of a situation. "Wishful thinking" allows a group to assume anything is possible and then search for substitutes for impossible aspects of its solution. "Goal orientation" is a process by which the problem is identified, and then needs, obstacles, and constraints are specified and scrutinized. "Reverse brainstorming" involves the generation of potential solutions and group discussion to point out difficulties with them (ruling most of them out). The use of the "nonlogical stimuli" procedure encourages or forces participants to introduce unrelated or random elements into a discussion, so that unusual and valuable approaches are uncovered. The "nominal group technique" (NGT) involves individual generation of ideas, group discussion and clarification of these ideas, preliminary voting, discussion of the results, and final voting.

VanGundy's review can be indispensable for those who wish to explore a wide variety of such techniques in great detail. The reader should also consult Galletta et al. (1992) for a modest survey of more detailed examples of how to apply the techniques to the information systems domain, and Couger (1990) for a description, in great depth, of how a small number of techniques might be employed at various life cycle stages.

Creative organizations.   There are many considerations that concern organizational practices in fostering the creative uncovering of strategic systems. Substantial organizational commitment must accompany any decision to employ creativity techniques, even on an experimental basis. It is necessary to provide resources not only in the time required to perform the steps, but also in providing an environment that is consistent with those techniques.

Because motivation is a key component of creativity (Amabile, 1988, 1983), the motivational environment should be healthy. As described above, a healthy motivational environment is one that focuses on intrinsic rather than extrinsic motivation. While it is difficult to make tasks inherently worthwhile for people, there is an abundance of temptation to provide undue focus on extrinsic factors like bonuses and awards, and desire to meet overly ambitious deadlines. Well-established research has shown that these extrinsic factors tend to decrease one's intrinsic motivation (Amabile et al., 1986; Deci, 1971; Lepper et al., 1973). Interestingly, time constraints can decrease creativity when they become extreme, but the lack of time constraints can also decrease creativity (Hogg, et al., 1983). Perhaps the challenge of having a modest time constraint is motivating, but removing it altogether might remove too much of the challenge.

Groups need adequate resources for developing creative plans of action. These resources include not only the obvious time required for practicing one of the many creativity-enhancing techniques, but also a plan for ensuring the diversity of group members described earlier. Other barriers to creativity are conspicuous evaluation, surveillance, restrictions on choices, emphasis on the status quo, organizational disinterest, and competition.

It might be very difficult to gain the time required for group idea generation, and it can be even more difficult to convince managers to build in diversity, withhold premature evaluation, allow independent work, provide freedom in group deliberations, demonstrate commitment, and downplay any intragroup competition that might exist. These actions are nevertheless crucial in nurturing creativity.

There is also hesitancy as a result of the overall culture of the organization, preventing people from crossing departmental lines and preventing them from taking risks.

Cross-functional perspectives are important for developing ideas that are integrative across functions or departments, and there should not be incentive systems that pit departments against each other. For example, a new sales approach that would increase the level of custom orders would be likely to reduce measured efficiency in the production department while it enhances prospects in the sales department. Incentive systems that reward the production department based on unchanged efficiency measures would present formidable barriers to what would otherwise benefit the organization.

In many organizations, risky decisions are often avoided because of severe punishments for failure. An interesting idea proposed by Peters is to support risky decision-making [Peters88]. Rather than punish a manager for a failed program, Peters suggests that a reasonable percentage of a manager's decisions should represent failure; otherwise, he or she is being far too conservative. Many SIS decisions represent large risks to the organization, but there is also risk in being too conservative. The organizational culture should support risk-taking to some extent to avoid falling behind other firms.

Creativity and SIS Identification

Figure 3.1 integrates the preceding discussion and defines a framework for interpreting how the upcoming guidelines fit together. It is assumed that competitive pressures on organizations led to the development of the SIS frameworks. Simultaneously, the organization holds certain values for creative problem-solving and supports the use of creativity tools in problem-solving. Both the SIS development frameworks and creativity tools intend to diminish the effects of cognitive limitations and increase the efficacy of SIS ideas. Effective utilization of the frameworks and tools are unfortunately also affected by cognitive limitations.

To summarize much of the preceding discussion, there are eleven specific pieces of advice that can guide an organization to apply creativity principles to the task of SIS identification:

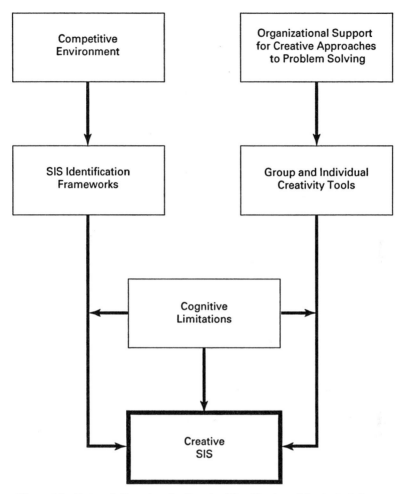

Figure 3.1   Factors influencing the Creative Identification of Strategic Information Systems

1. **Use SIS frameworks.** Make use of one or more of the SIS identification frameworks. There are many concepts within each that can trigger ideas for SIS.
2. **Use creative people.** In SIS identification tasks, use individuals who score well on creativity tests and/or who are otherwise known to perform in creative ways.
3. **Use people with some depth.** Use individuals who are knowledge-

able about the business, but not those who are so expert that they
have predetermined responses to problems.

4. Use people with some breadth. Use individuals who perform well at
   relating seemingly unrelated facts.

5. Use cognitive aids. Use tools such as notes, pictures, diagrams, and
   analogies in creative sessions.

6. Promote intrinsic motivation. Limit emphasis on extrinsic factors
   such as bonuses, awards, and overly ambitious deadlines to maximize intrinsic motivation and creativity.

7. Provide group diversity. Form groups that provide a variety of expertise and experience levels.

8. Use creativity techniques. Make use of one or more creative problem-solving techniques.

9. Support the group. Provide adequate resources for the group, such
   as realistic deadlines, freedom in group deliberations, and commitment to the goal; and limit early evaluation, supervision, and intragroup competition.

10. Remove organizational barriers. Explicitly support cross-functional
    perspectives.

11. Encourage risk-taking. Promote reasonable levels of risk-taking and
    failure.

It is an important and illuminating exercise to determine which of
these pieces of advice are included in the oft-cited frameworks for SIS identification. Table 3.1 summarizes the advisories and compares the SIS frameworks for their explicit handling of each.

Each advisory will be addressed in turn, with the exception of the
first. None of the frameworks addresses the makeup of the people who
must develop SIS ideas. The competitive forces and value chain frameworks each use one basic diagram, and thus provide very limited support
via cognitive aids. The recommended procedures for using the option generator (Rackoff et al., 1985) include extensive lists of ideas and procedures
for voting, as well as one basic diagram, so there appears to be some use of
cognitive aids. None of the frameworks addresses intrinsic motivation or
group diversity. Only the option generator procedures make use of creativity techniques (limited to brainstorming) and recommend substantial support for group activities. All of the frameworks appear to promote breaking
down organizational barriers, but none of them addresses the importance
of encouraging risk-taking.

TABLE 3.1   Examination of How Four SIS Frameworks Address Creativity Advisories

Advisory	Competitive Forces	Value Chain	Option Generator	Customer Resource Life-Cycle
1. Use SIS frameworks	Yes	Yes	Yes	Yes
2. Use creative people	No	No	No	No
3. Use people with some depth	No	No	No	No
4. Use people with some breadth	No	No	No	No
5. Use cognitive aids	Limited	Limited	Yes	No
6. Promote intrinsic motivation	No	No	No	No
7. Provide group diversity	No	No	No	No
8. Use creativity techniques	No	No	Limited to brainstorming	No
9. Support the group	No	No	Yes	No
10. Remove organizational barriers	Yes	Yes	Yes	Yes
11. Encourage risk-taking	No	No	No	No

Conclusion

The lack of evidence of systems that were deliberately deployed to create competitive advantage might be a testimonial to the need for application of creativity techniques and principles. The existing SIS frameworks can be seen as an important part of the process of SIS identification, but not as complete strategies for idea generation.

Existing SIS identification frameworks seem to concentrate heavily on the business and/or information systems content of the problem, but do not present many recommendations for increasing the creativity of the ideas generated. This paper has reviewed the literatures of SIS and creativity, and presented 11 advisories that can foster creativity in SIS identification.

In short, these advisories recommend using SIS frameworks, using creative people with some depth and breadth knowledge, using cognitive aids such as diagrams and analogies, promoting intrinsic motivation, providing group diversity, using creativity techniques, providing adequate resources for the group, removing organizational "walls," and encouraging risk-taking.

The advisories might be useful for ensuring that there are substantial resources for and commitment to idea generation. There is probably little doubt that success is based not only on effort, but also on good ideas. It is quite curious that there has been very little research devoted to the relationship between idea generation and competitive advantage. Perhaps this review can provide an important but modest step toward establishing and refining our knowledge of that relationship. Perhaps when creative ideas begin to increase, the stakes will rise in developing and responding to strategic systems for competitive advantage.

REFERENCES

ADELSON, B. "When Novices Surpass Experts: the Difficulty of a Task May Increase with Expertise," *Journal of Experimental Psychology: Learning, Memory, and Cognition,* 1984, Vol. 10, No. 3, pp. 483–495.

AMABILE, T. M. "Social Psychology of Creativity: A Componential Conceptualization," *Journal of Personality and Social Psychology,* 1983, Vol. 45, pp. 357–376.

AMABILE, T. M. "A Model of Creativity and Innovation in Organizations," in *Research in Organizational Behavior,* Vol. 10, ed. by Cummings and Staw, Greenwich, Connecticut: JAI Press, 1988.

AMABILE, T. M., HENNESSEY, B. A., & GROSSMAN, B. S. "Social Influences on Creativity: The Effects of Contracted-for Reward," *Journal of Personality and Social Psychology,* 1986, Vol. 50, No. 1, pp. 14–23.

CARBONELL, J. G. "Derivational Analogy: A Theory of Reconstructive Problem Solving and Expertise Acquisition," in R. S. Michalski, J. G. Carbonell, & T. M. Mitchell (eds.), *Machine Learning: An Artificial Intelligence Approach.* (Vol. 2), Los Altos, California: Morgan Kaufmann, 1986.

CASH, J. I., MCFARLAN, F. W., and MCKENNEY, J. L., *Corporate Information Systems Management: Text and Cases,* Homewood, IL: Irwin, 1983.

CASH, J. I., MCFARLAN, F. W., and MCKENNEY, J. L., *Corporate Information Systems Management: Text and Cases,* (2nd ed.) Homewood, IL: Irwin, 1988.

CIBORRA, C. U., "From Thinking to Tinkering: The Grassroots of Strategic Information Systems," *Proceedings of the Twelfth International Conference on Information Systems,* New York, December 16–18, 1991, pp. 283–292.

CLEMONS, E. K., "Strategic Systems Debate," panel session comments, *Proceedings of the Twelfth International Conference on Information Systems,* New York, December 16–18, 1991, pp. 409–410.

COUGER, J. D. "Ensuring Creative Approaches in Information System Design." *Managerial and Decision Economics,* (11), 1990, pp. 281–295.

DECI, E. L. "Effects of Externally Mediated Rewards on Intrinsic Motivation," *Journal of Personality and Social Psychology*, 1971, Vol. 18, pp. 105–118.

ELAM, J. J., and MEAD, M. "Designing for Creativity: Considerations for DSS Development," *Information and Management*, 1987, Vol. 13, pp. 215–222.

EMERY, J. C. "Misconceptions about Strategic Information Systems," *Management Information Systems Quarterly*, V. 14, N. 2, June, 1990, pp. vii-viii.

EPSTEIN, S. & O'BRIEN, E. J. "The Person-Situation Debate in Historical and Current Perspective," *Psychological Bulletin*, (98:3), 1985, pp. 513–537.

GALLETTA, D. F. and SAMPLER, J. L., "Creativity: The Missing Ingredient in Identifying Strategic Information Systems," working paper WP-703RR, University of Pittsburgh, Katz Graduate School of Business, September, 1993.

GALLETTA, D. F., SAMPLER, J. L. and TENG, J. T. C., "Strategies for Integrating Creativity Principles into the System Development Process," *Proceedings of the 25th Annual Hawaii International Conference on Systems Sciences*, January 1992, pp. 268–276.

GENTNER, D. "A Theoretical Framework for Analogy," *Cognitive Science*, 1983, 7, pp. 155–170.

HOGG, J., COREY, S., FOREMAN, K., & PRANGE, H. "The Effects of Time Limitation upon Creativity," unpublished paper from University of Washington, 1983.

IVES, B. AND LEARMONTH, G. P. "The Information System as a Competitive Weapon," *Communications of the ACM*, Vol. 27, No. 12, December 1984, pp. 1193–1201.

JOHNSTON, H. RUSSELL, and CARRICO, SHELLEY R. "Developing Capabilities to Use Information Strategically," *MIS Quarterly*, Vol. 12, No. 1, pp. 37–48.

KIRTON, M. J. *Kirton Adaption-Innovation Inventory Manual* (2nd Ed.) Hatfield, UK: Occupational Research Centre, 1987.

KOTOVSKY, K., HAYES, J. R., & SIMON, H. A. "Why Are Some Problems Hard? Evidence from Tower of Hanoi," *Cognitive Psychology*, 1985, 17, pp. 248–294.

LARKIN, J. H. & SIMON, H. A. "Why a Diagram Is (Sometimes) Worth Ten Thousand Words," 1987. Reprinted in H. A. Simon, *Models of Thought*, Vol. 2. New Haven, Connecticut: Yale University Press, 1989.

LEPPER, M. R., GREENE, D., & NISBETT, R. "Undermining Children's Intrinsic Interest with Extrinsic Rewards: A Test of the 'Overjustification' Hypothesis," *Journal of Personality and Social Psychology*, 1973, Vol. 28, pp. 129–137.

MISCHEL, W. & PEAKE, P. K. "Beyond Déjà Vu in the Search for Cross-Situational Consistency," *Psychological Review*, (89:6), 1982, pp. 730–755.

NEWELL, A., SHAW, J. & SIMON, H. "The Processes of Creative Thinking," in H. Gruber, G. Terrell, & M. Wertheimer (Eds.), *Contemporary Approaches to Creative Thinking*, New York: Atherton Press, 1962.

NOVAK, G. "Representations of Knowledge in a Program for Solving Physics Problems," *IJCAI*, 1977, 5, 286–291.

OSBORN, A. F. *Applied Imagination*. New York: Scribner, 1963.

PETERS, T. M. *Thriving on Chaos: Handbook for a Management Revolution*, Harper and Row, 1988.

PORTER, MICHAEL E. *Competitive Strategy: Techniques for Analyzing Industries and Competitors*, New York: The Free Press, 1980.

PORTER, MICHAEL E., and MILLAR, VICTOR E. "How Information Gives You Competitive Advantage," *Harvard Business Review*, July-August 1985, pp. 149–160.

RACKOFF, NICK, WISEMAN, CHARLES, and ULLRICH, WALTER A. "Information Systems for Competitive Advantage: Implementation of a Planning Process," *MIS Quarterly*, Vol. 9, No. 4, December 1985, pp. 285–294.

SCHROEDER, H., DRIVER, M., & STREUFERT, S. *Human Information Processing.* New York: John Wiley, 1968.

STARBUCK, W. H., "Strategizing in the Real World," panel session comments, *Proceedings of the Twelfth International Conference on Information Systems*, New York, December 16–18, 1991, pp. 409–410.

TORRANCE, E. P. *Torrance Tests of Creative Thinking: Norms and Technical Manual.* Bensenville, IL: Scholastic Testing Service, 1974.

VANGUNDY, A. B. *Techniques of Structured Problem Solving.* New York: Van Nostrand Reinhold Company, 1981.

WISEMAN, CHARLES. *Strategic Information Systems*, Homewood, Illinois: Richard D. Irwin Co., 1988.

WISEMAN, CHARLES and MACMILLAN, IAN C. "Creating Competitive Weapons from Information Systems," *Journal of Business Strategy*, Fall 1984, Vol. 5, No. 2.

4

MAKING CREATIVITY HAPPEN

"There are two main phases in the . . . creative process . . . and in the . . . development of new ideas; an imaginative phase and a practical one. In the imaginative phase, you generate and play with ideas. In the practical phase, you evaluate and execute them.

"In the imaginative phase, you ask such questions as 'What if?' 'Why not?' 'What rules can we break?' 'What assumptions can we drop?' 'How about if we looked at this backward?' 'Can we borrow a metaphor from another discipline?' The motto of the imaginative phase is 'Thinking something different.'

"In the practical phase, you ask such questions as 'Is this idea any good?' 'Do we have the resources to implement it?' 'Is the timing right?' 'Who can help us?' 'What's the deadline?' 'What are the consequences of not reaching the objective?' The motto of the practical phase is 'Getting something done'."

Roger von Oech, in *A Whack on the Side of the Head*, Warner Books, 1990

It is one thing to believe that creativity is an essential part of the work of software. It is another to make creativity happen. If the earlier chapters of this book have been about philosophy and motivation, both formal and informal, then this is the "how-to" chapter!

Much has been written in both the popular press and the more serious journals about how to make creativity happen; but very little has been written, as we are about to see, in the computing literature. It is as if the focus on disciplined, formal, quantitative approaches to software development that we discussed in Chapter 2 of this book has blinded us to the need for more creative approaches as well.

Fortunately, one academic has seen this problem and set out to overcome it. In this chapter, we present some material excerpted from the work of Professor J. Daniel Couger of the University of Colorado at Colorado Springs. Couger's interest in creativity in the field of computing has resulted in both significant research in the topic area, and in the founding of a Center for Research in Creativity (CRC) at his institution. As a matter of fact, this work has led Couger to prepare a book on creativity which is being written at about the same time as *Software Creativity* and which should be in print as you read this. Given that you have read this far in this book—and especially if the material in this chapter interests you—I strongly recommend that you buy and read Professor Couger's book as well.

But enough mutual admiration and plugging! Let's return to how-to. Let's suppose, for the moment, that you've become convinced by all the prior material in this book that creativity is, at least to some extent, an essential part of the process of building software. Let's further suppose that you're in charge of a group of software people, and you're eager to increase the creative capabilities they possess. What do you do next?

That's where Professor Couger's material comes in. In the first paper to follow, he presents a solid academic framework for thinking about creativity in information system design, and then he moves quickly to a discussion of where and when and how in the software process creativity can and should be important.

In the second paper, he gets more specific. He presents a set of techniques for enhancing creativity, discusses a program that taught those techniques, and elaborates on what happened at the enterprise in question when they were taught and applied. Although we tend to think of innovation entering an organization top-down, in this paper Professor Couger talks about making it happen bottom-up, and even suggests that it may work better that way!

However, if creativity can and should enter the organization bottom-up, what is the manager's role in all of this? In the third essay of this chapter, we find a familiar name and an unfamiliar subject. Watts Humphrey, he of software process fame, wrote on the management of innovation in software development before his better-known work on software process appeared in the general literature. Humphrey's insights here make an interesting complement to the work of Couger. From Humphrey we learn that managing for innovation requires some new thinking from software managers, and he talks about what form that new thinking should take. If this short summary of Humphrey's earlier book whets your appetite, I strongly recommend that you buy *Managing for Innovation* as well.

But now . . . on to the how-to chapter.

4.1   ENSURING CREATIVE APPROACHES IN INFORMATION SYSTEM DESIGN*

J. Daniel Couger

Introduction

More than 4000 articles have been published on the subject of creativity (Rickards, 1985). Only five have been published in journals related to the field of information systems (Elam & Mead87; Eliot87; Nunamaker *et al.*87; Telem88a, b). The paucity of articles concerning creativity in IS is enigmatic. Certainly, creative approaches need to be used to develop information systems. Creativity is needed in developing strategic IS plans, in the management of IS personnel, and in implementation of computer applications. Yet, for some inexplicable reason, IS practitioners and academicians have neglected to write about creativity in IS—its planning, its organization, or its operation.

The objective of this paper is to demonstrate the widespread applicability of creativity theory to the information systems field. It uses the inductive method, by focusing on the use of creativity approaches in system development, then generalizing applicability of creativity techniques to all areas of IS.

Definitions of Creativity

There are more than a hundred definitions of creativity in the literature (Seiffge74). At one end of the continuum is the simplistic view (Guilford67; Crovitz70; Getzels62; Csikszentmihalyi75) that creative thinking is a form of problem solving. At the other end of the continuum is the view that, to be truly creative, the innovation must demonstrate 'radical newness' (Hausman75; Morgan23).

The most comprehensive definition is provided in the landmark paper on 'The process of creative thinking', by Newell and Shaw (1962).

*Excerpted from an article in *Managerial and Decision Economics II*, pp. 281–295, used with permission (1990).

They believe that to be creative a solution must satisfy one or more of the following conditions:

(1) The product of the thinking has novelty or value (either for the thinker or for his or her culture).
(2) The thinking is unconventional, in the sense that it requires modification or rejection of previously accepted ideas.
(3) The thinking requires high motivation and persistence, taking place either over a considerable span of time (continuously or intermittently) or at high intensity.
(4) The problem as initially posed was vague and ill-defined, so that part of the task was to formulate the problem itself.

The Newell-Shaw definition is one of the most comprehensive. Although it clearly states that only one 'or more' of the conditions must be met, it implies that all four conditions are important. The reference containing the more than a hundred definitions is in German, so we have not been able to make a direct comparison of all those definitions. Of the more than 30 definitions reviewed, the most frequently mentioned factors were 'newness or uniqueness' and 'value or utility'. A concept that includes those factors is quite powerful; if the IS field utilizes a creative approach that includes those outcomes, substantive results can be expected. The discussions of this paper are based on a concept of creativity that is characterized by uniqueness and utility.

Ensuring Creativity in System Design

Past approaches to system design have led to early convergence toward solutions. The traditional design approach has been to: (1) request a statement of system requirements from the user, (2) develop a logical design to meet those requirements, (3) develop a physical design for processing, and (4) develop a program design. Until recently, however, few users knew enough about computing capabilities to fully utilize the computer potential. Therefore their statement of requirements was limited to their view of computing capabilities. The typical approach is for the system designer to provide only what the user requests. Using this approach, user satisfaction is high; there is little reason to consider anything beyond the original system specifications. There is little incentive for the designer to evaluate requirements in a creative manner in order to produce an optimal system. Doing so might delay completion of a system. For the same reason, there is little incentive to consider a variety of approaches for the logical, physical and program design phases. A graphical representation of this process of rapid convergence toward a single solution would be a funnel-shaped process, as shown in Fig. 4.1. The outer bounds identify the more desirable approach, widening each development phase to consider a wider range of alternatives. Figure 4.2 also depicts the use of special creativity techniques to generate alternatives.

Even today, with users much more knowledgeable about computing capabilities, they cannot be expected to be aware of the full range of capabilities. The turnover of knowledge in this dynamic field occurs so rapidly that it is difficult for a full-time practitioner to remain abreast of the technology, much less a user who must maintain currency in his or her own discipline.

To avoid rapid convergence, and the strong possibility of suboptimization, we suggest that the system design be re-evaluated at strategic points. Creativity techniques can be used at those points to ensure that the system is innovative.

There are natural stopping points at which creativity evaluation could take place: requirements definition, logical design, physical design and program design. Figure 4.2 represents this emphasis toward delaying convergence, that is, keeping an openness to new approaches, new alternatives. In each phase of development, the design is held open until a variety of alternatives have been considered. For example, in the requirements phase the development team is not content merely to meet the user's request, knowing that users are not aware of the full potential of the computer to facilitate their function. The development team explores a variety of alternatives to optimize the system.

For example, assume that the manager of our company's order-processing department has come to us, the IS department, requesting that the order entry system be revised. She wants us to accommodate requests from several large customers to enter their orders directly into our computer, to speed up delivery time. Say, our company is a wholesale supplier with about 500 firms as customers. We can meet the request as stated, alter the system accordingly, and receive high marks on client satisfaction with our response to her system revision request. Assume instead that we use a creativity technique to generate other alternatives that *both* meet the client request and provide the company with a better overall order-processing system. Figures 4.1 and 4.2 represent such a situation. In Fig. 4.1 the widening of the requirements phase represents the consideration of a broader range of alternatives, not just those originally submitted. Figure 4.2 shows that convergence on the selected solution occurs later in each development phase. Those two changes, widening the range of alternatives considered and delaying selection until those alternatives have been evaluated, may

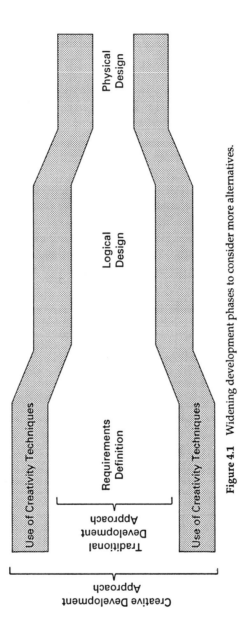

Figure 4.1   Widening development phases to consider more alternatives.

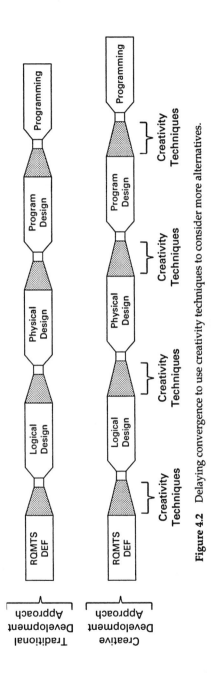

Figure 4.2 Delaying convergence to use creativity techniques to consider more alternatives.

produce an improved solution. Continuing the example, the creativity sessions might have derived an approach that not only allows a few large customers to enter orders directly but also enables other customers to do the same. It even includes providing them with a terminal to encourage their doing so. The opportunity to order on-line provides customers with products several days sooner than our competitors, using conventional technology. It also enables them to reduce inventory costs; they do not have to have as many units on hand, since they can get fast response when their sales increase faster than expected. It saves our company the cost of entering orders and enables us to improve order accuracy since customers are entering orders using our system and our procedures.

Increased Cost-Effectiveness

Figure 4.2 also depicts the additional time required to accomplish each phase, the time needed to generate and evaluate additional alternatives. As shown by the above example, the added delay is more than justified—the expanded system is quite cost-effective. In addition to the benefits previously stated, there is another benefit that should be entered into the cost-effectiveness evaluation. Now our customers are locked into our system; the cost for them to change to a competitor's system is much greater than before. A routine order-processing system has been changed to a competitive weapon system. In an actual case in the hospital supply industry, the cost of the system enhancement and the cost to provide terminals to customers was well below the increased sales revenues. This approach enabled the company to move from tenth to second place in the industry.

The time added to generate and evaluate other alternatives is insignificant compared to the total system development time. Using two sets of data, one from organizations applying the creativity techniques and another on system development time for typical computer applications, we calculate that use of the creativity techniques should expand development cost by less than one half of 1%. Unfortunately, we cannot acquire actual data on use of creativity techniques in IS development. The author has not found any organization using them—hence the reason for this paper!

Pursuing the model suggested in Fig. 4.2, the design team has the potential to increase the cost-effectiveness of the systems in the logical, physical and program design phases as well as the requirements phase example cited above. In each of these phases a variety of approaches might be used.

For example, the choice of the logical design is typically transparent to the client—whatever it takes to produce his or her desired results is the only matter of interest to the client. To a large extent, the same is true of the IS manager responsible for the system. For the set of applications under development in his or her area of responsibility the manager's primary concern is meeting client requests. Therefore, there has not been a lot of motivation for the design team to explore a variety of alternatives. Selecting a workable approach has been the principal criterion. Yet there are many alternative approaches. Shall a data-driven or a process-driven logical design methodology be used? Should the system be completely on-line or should some components be batch processed? In the physical design phase there are questions of which database methodology to utilize and in the program design phase questions of optimizing processing time or program development time. Use of a creativity generation/evaluation technique before converging on one approach will ensure that the system is being optimized in each phase of development. In the next section we will examine some of the creativity techniques that might be used.

Techniques to Facilitate
the Process of Creativity

A variety of techniques (methods) have been developed to facilitate the process of creativity. These techniques originate primarily from the discipline of psychology, although there are contributions from other disciplines such as engineering, science, and education.

Creativity techniques for requirements definition. The objective of the CRC has been to transport to the IS arena some of the creativity techniques proven in other disciplines. To provide readers with a wider range of techniques than just those five described previously, a different set of techniques will be illustrated.

One technique that has proven useful in several fields is the 5Ws and the H. By asking 'Who? What? Where? When? Why?' we have greater assurance that we are covering the full set of alternatives to be considered. The response to the H (How?) question provides approaches to implementing the ideas generated with the Ws.

In the example mentioned above, using computer systems to gain a competitive advantage for a firm, a designer can ask the following questions:

(1) How might an application be used for other purposes? Could it be used, not just to support internal clients but company customers as well?

(2) Why would we want to provide the service to our customers? How can it provide us with a competitive advantage?

(3) Who could best use it? Which customer category?

(4) Where could it be used? Customer management, customer purchasing agents, customer accounting, etc.?

(5) What is necessary to reorient the application to this new purpose?

(6) When would it best be installed to provide optimal competitive advantage?

The 5Ws/H technique is one of the most useful of all creativity techniques when applied to IS because it can be used after each phase of the development cycle.

Creativity technique for the logical design phase.   The 5Ws and the H technique would be useful for logical design as well. Consider, for brevity, only the 'why' questions. 'Why is this set of logic the most appropriate for the system? Why have we selected this specific methodology for portraying the system specifications? Why are we dividing the logic among modules in the manner chosen?'

Another creativity technique useful for the logical design phase is 'Checklist', developed by Polya (1971). The design team would work through the following checklist of questions, relating them to the system being developed: 'Have you seen this problem before? Or have you seen the same problem in slightly different form? Do you know a related problem? Do you know a theorem that could be useful?' Look at the unknown! Try to think of a familiar problem having the same similar unknown.

'Here is a problem related to yours and solved before. Could you use it? Could you use its results? Could you use its method? Should you introduce some auxiliary element in order to make its use possible? Could you restate the problem? Could you restate it still differently?' Go back to definitions.

'If you cannot solve the proposed problem try to solve first some related problem. Could you imagine a more accessible related problem? A more general problem? A more special problem? An analogous problem? Could you solve a part of the problem? Keep only a part of the condition, drop the other part? How far is the unknown then determined? How can it vary?'

'Could you derive something useful from the data? Could you think of other data appropriate to determine the unknown? Could you change the unknown or the data, or both, if necessary, so that the new unknown and the new data are nearer to each other? Did you use all the data? Did you use the whole condition? Have you taken into account all essential notions involved in the problem?'

Creativity techniques for the physical design phase. The 5Ws and the H would work well in this phase also, as illustrated below using only the 'why' question: 'Why are we using traditional life-cycle development methodology instead of prototyping? Why have we chosen to use on-line processing (or batch) instead of batch processing (or on-line)? Why are we using the database access methodology chosen instead of (relational, direct)?'

Another creativity technique useful for generating alternative approaches for the physical design of the system is the 'Manipulative Verb' technique suggested by Koberg and Bagnall (1981). They have devised a set of verbs to manipulate the problem in order to come up with new perspectives. The verbs are:

Multiply	Distort	Fluff-up	Extrude
Divide	Rotate	By-pass	Repel
Eliminate	Flatten	Add	Protect
Subdue	Squeeze	Subtract	Segregate
Invert	Complement	Lighten	Integrate
Separate	Submerge	Repeat	Symbolize
Transpose	Freeze	Thicken	Abstract
Unify	Soften	Stretch	Dissect

For example, if the designers of the order-processing system illustrated previously were going through this list, they might come up with the following responses to the first three verbs:

Multiply—can we derive a set of transaction types for large customers, then generalize them for all customers to simplify maintenance and enhancement of the system?

Divide—can we divide users into levels of sophistication for menu screen design and HELP and tutorial modules, yet keep the main procedure standard for all users?

Eliminate—can we eliminate some of the special tailoring that at first appearance seems necessary in order to standardize on a data-access procedure? Can we design a data-storage procedure to standardize on one storage medium to eliminate the need for both tape and disc storage?

Creativity techniques for program design. The 5 Ws/H technique is also useful for this phase of the system development cycle, as illustrated by the following questions for just the 'why' question: 'Why have we chosen to partition system functions into this particular set of modules? Why not use other optimization techniques for data processing? Why have we selected this programming language?'

Another technique appropriate for this phase is 'Attribute Listing', developed by Crawford (1954). The goal might be to list the attributes needed in the program set for the computer application under investigation. The procedure is to state the problem and its objectives. (Almost all techniques begin with this set, which is useful regardless of where you are in the system development activity, to make sure all persons involved have a uniform understanding of the problem.) The second step is to list the characteristics (attributes) of a product, object or idea related to the problem. The third step is to withhold all evaluation, systematically modifying the attributes to meet the objectives of the problem. The desired program design attributes have changed significantly over the past 15 years. In the period prior to that time, considerable emphasis was upon optimization techniques, to minimize computer processing time for the program. During the next era, hardware costs declined so much that emphasis was shifted to reduction of programming time. As a result, program optimization was an attribute that became much less important, replaced by an attribute almost the exact opposite—simplification of program procedures. Structured methodology was developed to accomplish this objective.

Automatic code generation is still several years away from widespread use, so the interim emphasis is on the attribute of program robustness, the ability of a program to be revised easily. The present economic environment is so dynamic that systems must be much more responsive to change, thus must be more changeable. The Attribute Listing technique can be used to generate the factors in program design that might produce a more robust program.

Conclusion

Figure 4.3 depicts how clients and designers can interact to a greater extent to enrich the system development process. Their interaction should produce a greater range of possibilities than their working alone. Using this approach, designers are involved early in the requirements definition phase to make sure that the full potential of computer capabilities is exploited. Likewise, clients are involved in logical design, not just in the normal approval activity after the logical design is complete but early enough to provide suggested improvements.

This same result is the objective of prototyping, an iterative process where client/designer interact continuously to produce a more complete

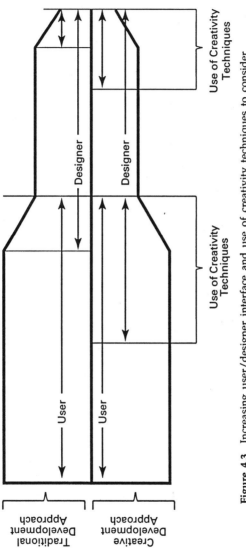

Figure 4.3 Increasing user/designer interface and use of creativity techniques to consider more alternatives.

solution than that produced by traditional development approaches. This paper concentrates primarily on traditional development process, still used for the majority of development work, but the suggested approaches would work equally well for prototyping. Moreover, Fig. 4.2 identifies an activity that is not normally included in prototyping, inserting creativity techniques to ensure that more alternatives are considered. The potential for improving the development process through these approaches appears significant. Their use can be facilitated through automation, as well. IS can also increase its cost-effectiveness by using creativity techniques in areas other than system development. The techniques described above, plus other techniques proven in other disciplines, can be used throughout the IS function. Some of the areas targeted for use of the techniques by the CRC are:

(1) *Creative marketing of IS products and services.* The goal of this project is a procedure for enhancing marketing of IS products and services, both commercial and internal to a company.

(2) *Generation of creativity for those persons assigned less creative jobs.* Some areas of IS are considered to be much less challenging and to provide little opportunity for creativity. Examples are operations, quality assurance and maintenance programming. Since over 50% of the human resource budget of the typical IS department is allocated to maintenance, the need for enhancing creativity/productivity is paramount. This area will be the pilot for research on enhancing creativity in each of these areas perceived to provide little opportunity for creativity.

(3) *Creativity in strategic IS planning.* In contrast to the areas considered to have little opportunity for creativity, the strategic planning area of IS has little constraint on the creative process. A recent survey revealed that less than 40% of IS departments have a strategic IS planning activity. Creativity is needed to show the relevance of strategic planning. Next, techniques for creative planning need to be developed and promoted.

(4) *Individual versus group creativity for system development.* The literature is replete with contradictory articles concerning the degree to which group creativity is possible. This research project will derive experimental tests on individual versus group creativity in system development.

The dearth of articles on creativity in the IS field is enigmatic. This field needs creativity just as much as other fields—perhaps more so.

Computer systems are a prime way for the USA to forestall its declining competitive edge in international competition. The simple computer applications have been computerized. The more complicated lie ahead. For these reasons, US system designers need to be even more creative in the future. 'It is my belief, based on my experience, that it [creativity] exists in every individual and awaits only the proper conditions to be released and expressed' (Carl Rogers).

REFERENCES

R. P. CRAWFORD (1954), *The Techniques of Creative Thinking*, Englewood Cliffs NJ; Prentice-Hall

H. F. CROVITZ (1970), *Galton's Walk*, New York; Harper and Row

M. CSIKSZENTMIHALYI (1975), *Beyond Boredom and Anxiety*, San Francisco CA; Jossey-Bass

J. ELAM and M. MEAD (1987), "Designing for Creativity; Considerations for DSS Development," *Information and Management* 13 (5), 215–22

L. B. ELIOT (1987), "Creativity Management and Analogical Thinking," *Data Management* 25 (4), 20–21

J. W. GETZELS and P. W. JACKSON (1962), *Creativity and Intelligence*, New York; John Wiley

J. P. GUILFORD (1967), "Creativity Yesterday, Today and Tomorrow," *Journal of Creative Behavior* 1, 3–14

C. R. HAUSMAN (1975), *A Discourse on Novelty and Creation*, The Hague; Nijhoff

D. KOBERG and J. BAGNALL (1981), "The Universal Traveler: a Soft-Systems Guide to Creativity, Problem-Solving, and the Process of Design"

C. L. MORGAN (1923), *Emergent Evolution*, New York; Holt

A. NEWELL, J. C. SHAW and H. A. SIMON (1962), "The Process of Creative Thinking." In H. E. Gruber et al. (eds) *Contemporary Approaches to Creative Thinking*, New York; Atherton Press

J. NUNAMAKER, L. M. APPLEGATE, and B. N. KONSYNSKI (1987), "Facilitating Group Creativity: Experience with Group Decision Support System," *Journal of Management Information Systems* 3 (4), 5–19

G. POLYA (1971), *How to Solve It*, Princeton, NJ; Princeton University Press

T. RICKARDS (1985), *Stimulating Innovation: a Systems Approach*, New York; St. Martin's Press, p. 51

I. SEIFFGE (1974), *Problems und Ergebnisse der Kreativitaetsforschung*, Bern; Hans Huber

M. TELEM (1988a), "Information Requirements Specification I: Brainstorming Collective Decision-Making Approach," *Information Processing and Management* 24 (5), 549–57

M. TELEM (1988b), "Information Requirements Specification II: Brainstorming Collective Decision-Making Technique," *Information Processing and Management* 24 (5), 559–66

4.2   USING A BOTTOM-UP APPROACH TO CREATIVITY IMPROVEMENT IN IS DEVELOPMENT*

J. Daniel Couger, Scott C. McIntyre, Lexis F. Higgins, and Terry A. Snow

A number of publications in the computer field contain articles that conclude with something to the effect of "for this important approach to be successful, top management support is essential." Top-down has become a buzzword for modern IS organizations. In this article, we discuss an important opportunity for improvement that can be implemented from the bottom-up. Certainly, approval by top management would be useful. Nevertheless, the creativity improvement program that we are describing can be successfully implemented from the bottom-up. In fact, the program has a higher probability of success if it is introduced bottom-up.

We will describe the program successfully introduced at UTMC (United Technologies Microelectronics Center), then generalize the approach to show its value in any IS organization.

Very little research has been published on the use of creativity generation techniques in information systems organizations. A six-month review of the IS literature revealed that, in the 35-year history of the IS field, only five publications include more than one page on the topic of creativity. We decided to introduce to IS some of the techniques proven successful in other disciplines. An IS unit in UTMC was selected as the target organization. Selection of a single work unit (nine people) permitted close observation of the results for each individual.

Background on the Organization

UTMC is headquartered in Colorado Springs, CO. It is a subsidiary of United Technologies Corporation of Hartford, CT. UTMC was established in 1980 to assist other UTC divisions with the integration of custom and semicustom microelectronics into their military and defense systems. In 1985, UTMC expanded its charter to market semicustom and military-

*From *Journal of Systems Management*, Sept. 1991; used with permission.

standard integrated circuits to other high-reliability military and aerospace companies. UTMC also engages in government and customer funded research and development contracts. The company employs approximately 500 people and is housed in a 280,000-square-foot facility that includes wafer fabrication, assembly, research and development, test engineering, marketing and administration.

The work unit selected for the creativity improvement program is responsible for the development and maintenance of the computer applications used in management of the company. The CAD activities and computer processing activities are in different reporting units. The unit consists of nine programmer/analysts (P/As). UTC's corporate IS organization provided a grant to the University of Colorado Center for Research on Creativity and Innovation with the agreement that a program for creativity improvement would be implemented in the UTMC IS department.

The unit is considered by its "users" (the managers in other units of UTMC) to be quite effective. The most recent annual survey of users rated the IS department above average on all eight of the rating factors: meeting commitments, training of users, timely output, minimal errors, solving problems, easy in use, providing status, and an overall rating. The rating of excellent or near excellent was given in five of the categories. If a creativity improvement program proved useful for an IS organization already considered to be excellent, the program would have widespread applicability.

Design of the Program

A two-pronged approach was selected for the program:

1. Improvement of the environment for creativity and innovation.
2. Training in specific techniques for creativity generation and evaluation.

Two phases were identified for the first six months of the program:

Phase I: Training workshop to establish an environment to facilitate creativity and to teach a variety of creativity generation and evaluation techniques.

Phase II: Reinforcement of the concepts/principles taught in the workshop, with opportunities to discuss experience in application of the techniques and to test the degree to which the environment for creativity had been enhanced. Additional techniques were also introduced during this period.

Training on Creativity Generation/
Evaluation Techniques

Arnold Toynbee, in *Widening Horizons In Creativity*, warns that "potential creative ability can be stifled, stunted and stultified," and states that society has "a moral duty to ensure that the individual's potential ability is given free play." In *Climate For Creativity*, Abraham Maslow says that "general creativeness, holistically conceived, emanates from the whole system, generally improved." Following these admonitions, one-third of the workshop was devoted to discussing how to improve the climate for creativity in the IS organization. This was accomplished by asking the employees to identify positive and negative contributors to the creativity environment.

The remainder of the workshop was devoted to gaining a familiarity with the following creativity generation/evaluation techniques: metaphors, Crawford blue-slip writing, 5 Ws and the H, problem reversal, wishful thinking, peaceful setting, extrapolation and brainstorming (see sidebar on page 223 for an explanation of these techniques). Participants were involved in exercises using each of these techniques, both to gain familiarity in use and to generate questions about applicability in the UTMC setting.

Follow-Up Sessions

Reinforcement occurred in two ways. First, in staff meetings, employees were invited to identify results of creative activity. During two of these meetings, an additional creativity technique was introduced and illustrated—force field analysis and progressive abstractions. Second, the vice president of operations, to whom the IS organization reports, asked the IS manager to conduct training for two other organizations within his area of responsibility: materials control (purchasing and inventory) and production control. The IS manager involved two of his supervisors in the training, giving all three an opportunity to reinforce their own training.

Results

A survey instrument was selected to administer to each employee before the program began to obtain perceptions on the environment for creativity and innovation. The same instrument was administered at the end of Phase II as part of the measurement of results. The post-test revealed a significant improvement (.05 level of probability). Individuals estimated their own improvement at 23% (range 10%–40%); they estimated the improvement for the whole department to be 27% (range 20%–40%). But the real "proof of the pudding" was a creativity log, in which the P/As kept track of their creativity improvements. Creativity techniques were successfully used on the four major IS projects underway in the unit, as well as on many other tasks. Table 1 provides a brief description of each improvement and designates whether the result was primarily an efficiency or effectiveness improvement.

Cost/Effectiveness

The creativity program more than paid for itself in the efficiency improvements alone—in savings in computer processing time and computer programming time. For example, the reduction in processing time for each CAM (computer-aided manufacturing) database expansion now only takes four hours instead of the previous 60 hours. Processing time on year-to-date (YTD) overhead computations was reduced from 24 hours to 45 minutes. The bookings forecast report processing time reduction was from six

TABLE 1   Results of Use of Creativity Techniques

	Type of improvement	
Creative Approach	Efficiency	Effectiveness
Develop integrated enterprise		X
Develop new CAM system structure		X
Evaluate CASE tools		X
Devise new CAM database expansion approach	X	
Devise new GL report structure	X	
Use of RDB engine for INGRES	X	X
Concoct CAM file-based system	X	
Design more user-friendly report driver		X
Integrate product data		X
Design new file structure to book orders		X
Determine approach to quickly revise sales forecasts		X
Revise INGRES code to improve user interface		X
Reduce time to calculate YTD overhead	X	
Devise new file access approach for booking forecast	X	
Design more usable enterprise modeling output		X
Devise CAM disk recovery approach		X
Circumvent restriction in vendor package for CAM		X

hours to six minutes. The CAM report distribution improvement reduces programming maintenance time by 10–15 hours per month.

The improvements in effectiveness are even more important. The improvements in product management reports and the sales forecasting system are producing significant results. The introduction of more "user-friendly" approaches for access to computer applications encourages users to utilize the power of the computer for more in-depth analysis in their areas of responsibility. Moreover, the integration of seven planning techniques into a unified enterprise modeling system appears to be a highly significant improvement. UTMC's president believes that the new enterprise modeling system will have a major impact on the corporation's planning effectiveness in integrating systems. The improvements summarized in Table 1 are described in more detail in the following section. In addition to these major improvements, there were dozens of smaller improvements in the day-to-day activities of the P/As.

Another indication of the value of the creativity program comes from the person to whom IS reports, the vice president of operations. He asked the IS group, based on the results in the IS area, to conduct training on creativity techniques for the other departments reporting to him.

Creativity Improvements in UTMC IS Department

The following descriptions were developed by the analysts and programmers; the first person "we" was retained to show the pride of authorship of personnel in reporting their team's creative accomplishments.

1. *Enterprise Modeling:* The MIS department was examining approaches for an enterprise model for the company. While we were conducting discussions with vendors and consultants about different approaches, UTMC's CEO attended a seminar on seven planning techniques for solving business problems. He wanted to create a UTMC culture to use this methodology. Picking up on his interest, the MIS department utilized "what if" questions to modify and integrate these planning techniques into a unified methodology for an enterprise model. We also deviated from the normal procedure of modeling the current business to modeling the "ideal" business. This approach should identify opportunities to re-engineer the UTMC business process flow. The MIS department is teaching these techniques to a large number of UTMC managers who will participate in enterprise modeling

2. *CAM Restructure:* Earlier in the year, we had a project to work with Production Control to bring up a manufacturing planning module that was part of our vendor-supplied CAM (computer-aided manufacturing) sys-

tem. This CAM system had first been brought into UTMC seven years ago when our business was completely different. For instance, we did not have our own wafer fab facility and only built products for UTC. We now supply products to commercial customers, as well as UTC customers, resulting in a very different focus. Thus, we were having difficulty in getting the manufacturing planning module to work properly with our existing route and facility structure. Instead of trying to force-fit a system that would never work properly, we decided to step back and completely redo our CAM system structure to prepare us for the 1990s. We used the "5 Ws and H" and brainstorming creativity techniques to conduct structured interviews of all functional groups utilizing the CAM system. We developed a three-year plan for a major upgrade to our system in support of company business objectives for the 1990s. We presented the plan to senior management, got approval and have begun work on the project.

3. *Evaluation Of CASE Tools:* The MIS department needed to evaluate different CASE (computer-aided software engineering) tools to improve our productivity and software quality. We used the "problem reversal" creative technique to list the factors that were causing poor productivity and quality in MIS. This allowed us to quickly select the major factors that needed to be addressed by the CASE tool and generate a CASE tool comparison matrix that narrowed our selection evaluation to three tools.

4. *CAM Database Expansion:* Our CAM database contains all of our manufacturing data and is constantly expanding. In order to maintain good response time for database accesses, the database must be periodically reorganized. Previously, we would unload the database, make the changes, and then reload the database. This process took around 60 hours to complete. One of the MIS section managers was looking at ways to improve system performance; he discovered a new way to modify the CAM database size without having to unload/reload the database. We were able to apply these techniques to our specific site and reduce the database expansion task to four hours (resulting in 46-hour time savings). This is a good example of extrapolation, using a proven solution approach in a new application area.

5. *Automated GL Report Structure Cleanup:* Our GL (general ledger) report structure needed to be cleaned up because it contained reporting structures that were obsolete, had missing reporting structure entries, and had centers that would sum to the wrong summary center. The financial department planned to manually conduct this clean up project. The process would have taken several personnel-months to complete. Instead, we suggested that use of the "wishful thinking" technique to help the finance people identify how they desired the GL report structure to be. We then wrote a computer program to automatically clean up the reporting structure. As a

result, more than 40,000 obsolete reporting structure entries were deleted, more than 10,000 missing reporting structures were added and 2,505 errors were corrected to properly summarize the reporting structures. Automation of this process not only saved Finance many months of manual activity, but it also ensures consistent reporting across UTC, UTMC, and for government reports.

6. *Use of RDB To Replace Ingres:* Currently, most of our financial systems use the INGRES (vendor name) relational database software package; we are also developing a major marketing system on INGRES. We like the flexibility that the relational database gives us, but it is expensive to license on multiple VAX systems. We currently have a VAX cluster but only have INGRES running on one VAX 8650. As more and more applications run on INGRES, it will become necessary to add the software to more machines. Additional INGRES licenses will cost us significant dollars. By asking "what if" types of questions (5 Ws and H technique) and brainstorming, a suggestion resulted that may provide a cost effective way of using existing INGRES implementations on multiple machines. DEC has an RDB (relational database software package) whose engine is supplied free on all VAXes. INGRES frontend tools can use the DEC RDB engine. We will test the feasibility of using this INGRES-RDB combination to allow our IN-GRES-developed systems to run on all computers on our VAX cluster.

7. *CAM Report Distribution:* CAM reports are automatically produced monthly, weekly or daily depending upon frequency requirements. The system determines the frequency by using hard-coded command procedures to indicate when the report was to run, as well as for whom the report was being generated. While this procedure worked, it required programmer time to keep it current. Using the "what if" question (5 Ws and H technique), a file-based system was developed. We created a file that contains all the required information to run the reports. The result is a reduction in programmer maintenance time by 10–15 hours a month. The output also provides visibility to the user community on who gets what reports— which is especially useful when someone goes on vacation.

8. *STAR Screen Driven/Report Driver:* We are developing a new sales order system named STAR. We needed to introduce some "user-friendly" features, such as the capability to move directly from one function to another function without going through the menu structure. We also needed a friendly front-end to reports to more easily select criteria and specify desired sorting for reports. We used brainstorming techniques with senior MIS analysts from different groups to derive a solution that was easy to maintain. We repeatedly asked the question "what could we do . . . " to arrive at the ultimate solution. We developed several powerful tools that can be used on any INGRES application.

DESCRIPTION OF CREATIVITY TECHNIQUES

Analogy/Metaphor—An analogy is a statement about how objects, people, situations or actions are similar in process or relationship. Metaphors are figures of speech. Metaphors and analogies can be used to create fantasy situations for gaining new perspectives on problem definition and resolution.

Brainstorming—This technique is designed to produce a large quantity of ideas in a short period of time by a process that stimulates ideas. Idea generation is separated from evaluation as a means to encourage ideation.

Blue Slip—Ideas are individually generated and recorded on a 3"x5" sheet of blue paper. By anonymous recording and sharing of ideas, people feel more comfortable about expressing ideas. Using a single slip to record ideas facilitates sorting and grouping of ideas.

Extrapolation—A proven technique or approach is applied to a new problem.

Progressive Abstraction Technique—Alternative problem definitions are generated by moving through progressively higher levels of problem abstraction until a satisfactory definition is achieved. When a problem is systematically enlarged in this way, new definitions emerge that can be evaluated for their usefulness and feasibility. Once an appropriate level of abstraction is reached, possible solutions then can be more easily identified. The major advantage of the technique is the degree of structure provided to the problem solver for systematically examining problem substructures and connections.

5Ws and the H Technique—The Who-What-Where-When-Why-How questions aid in expanding an individual's view of a problem or opportunity to try to make sure that all related aspects have been considered.

Force Field Analysis Technique—The name of this technique is derived from the technique's ability to identify forces contributing to or hindering a solution to a problem. The technique can stimulate creative thinking in three ways: 1) define direction (vision), 2) identify strengths that can be maximized, and 3) identify weaknesses that can be minimized.

Peaceful Setting—The objective of this approach is to enable people to mentally remove themselves from present surroundings to enable a less cluttered, more open mental process. They visualize themselves in a favorite, relaxed setting such as beachside or mountainside.

Problem Reversal—Sometimes it is useful to reverse a problem statement to provide a different framework for analysis. For example, in trying to improve the climate for creativity, it is useful to consider the opposite—how to "ruin creativity."

Associations/Images Technique—This approach builds on the natural inclination of humans to associate things. The linking or combining process is another way of expanding solution space.

Wishful Thinking—This technique is particularly useful for people who typically take a very analytical approach to problem solving. It enables them to loosen their analytical parameters to consider a larger set of alternatives than they might ordinarily consider. It is designed to permit a degree of fantasy in the solution process, and this loosening-up may result in some unique approaches. By taking unusual positions to start the problem solving process, a perspective might arise that would not ordinarily be brought forth.

9. *Program Management Reports:* A user came to MIS requesting help on his personal computer inventory program that he was using to manually track information about key UTMC programs. We used the "wishful thinking" creative technique to determine that he desired a report pulling data from our general ledger, labor collection and the Viewpoint program management system. We were able to accomplish his "wish" by using the UDMS (User Data Management System) report writer tool. So for the first time our company can base key decisions on integrated UTMC program data.

10. *12-Month Window:* UTMC needed to implement a business practice that allows the booking of an order only if its customer-request-date was within a 12-month window. A previous attempt to implement this capability had been unsuccessful because the programming logic was difficult in the existing Order Entry System. We used the brainstorming technique with senior MIS analysts to evaluate what went wrong last time and how we could successfully implement the window this time. The result was a sound design with a completely different file structure concept.

11. *Forecast Projection System:* UTMC needed salesmen to be able to

update their forecast projections from the field in order to improve the accuracy and timeliness of sales forecasts. Resources were committed to other projects and were therefore not available to undertake this major upgrade to the forecasting system using normal procedures. Instead we used the prototyping technique with the INGRES RDB and UDMS report writer, then hired a contract programmer for two weeks to provide an interim capability until the major upgrade can be performed. This approach provided UTMC with a timely solution; it also provided valuable input into the requirements for the ultimate system. The "what if" approach, along with an emphasis on a creative environment, fostered teamwork among personnel from MIS, marketing, sales and our vendor-contractor.

12. *User Interface For INGRES Scrolling Region:* INGRES has a built-in capability that does not work the way a user would normally scroll areas. Instead of using the TAB key to move from field to field, the user has to use the Enter key. This feature is not "friendly" for the user and made the system difficult to use. By asking "what if" questions, we were able to develop a clever modification to our INGRES code to allow the interface to work "normally" within a scrolling area. This modification made the STAR system more friendly and reduced potential operator errors.

13. *Year-to-Date (YTD) Overhead:* UTMC needed to be able to calculate YTD overhead during its normal closing cycle, but since it took 24 hours to run the program it was not possible to do so without delaying the output of other important jobs. MIS needed to step back from the way that we were using YTD overhead to come up with a new solution approach. We used the "5 Ws and H" technique and determined that, since this was a set-oriented problem, we could convert two major COBOL programs to DCL (digital command language) and SQL (structured query language) and reduce the run time to 45 minutes.

14. *Bookings Forecast Report:* Because the booking forecast report extract normally requires six hours of elapsed time to run, the information is not available in a timely manner for the forecast projection business cycle. To find a better solution, we used the "5 Ws and H" creative technique. It produced the suggested use of INGRES instead of RMS (records management services) files. The elapsed run time was reduced from six hours to six minutes, and the CPU time was reduced from 15 minutes to seven seconds, enabling a timely forecast projection.

15. *Postscript Printing:* To produce more readable enterprise model charts, we used the "wishful thinking" creative technique to ask the question, "could we print the Freelance PC graphics on a new VAX Postscript laser printer?" This approach led to development of the capability to print reports generated from a PC on the laser printer connected to a VAX. It also led to encoding print characteristics into a file name so the users

would not have to know the details of generating a report or graph. This capability is used in the forecast projection reports.

16. *CAM Recovery:* A disk failure destroyed a major CAM disk, making our CAM system non-operative. Our manufacturing process is heavily dependent upon this system, so we had to recover as quickly as possible to minimize the impact on our business. An MIS analyst and a key user used the brainstorming technique to come up with procedures to automatically update the missing data instead of entering the data into the system by hand. These procedures saved many hours of manual data entry, provided an explicit audit trail and avoided many hours of CAM system downtime.

17. *CAM Reporting:* In attempting to use a vendor reporting package to develop reports needed by Production Control, we ran into a major program restriction. We used the "5 Ws and H" creative technique to get around the restriction on accessing DBMS group keys that contain numeric values by "borrowing" an unused DBMS record field to parse the correct search field.

Improved Environment for Creativity

The program proved successful from two standpoints. The principal evidence is the quantity and quality of ideas generated by the systems development group. The more important, yet less tangible, result is the creative environment that now exists. A post-mortem interview conducted with the group revealed that the group is more cohesive, more open to ideas and more supportive of colleagues' ideas. There is both a supportive attitude within the group that fosters generation of ideas and a nurturing climate that helps colleagues flesh-out and improve their ideas. The following sampling of the group members' comments are indicative of the positive environment for creativity.

Comment 1: "I used to have to be more secretive about the time I spent on coming up with 'far-out' ideas—I felt that I should be working on very practical solutions. Now I don't worry about people getting the impression that I am day-dreaming—we have the confidence of management that we are good at generating good ideas."

Comment 2: "In our meetings many of us hesitated to bring up a 'wild idea,' not certain if it would be ridiculed. Now we feel comfortable with generating 'wild ideas.' The ideas are sometimes met with laughter but we know it is more a spirit of playfulness than criticism. We feel comfortable in responding to laughter with a comment like, "Hey! I'm just trying to be creative!'"

Comment 3: "When I've scheduled a meeting with our users, I try to think if one of the creativity techniques might be appropriate for some portion of the agenda."

Comment 4: "I'm not comfortable yet in suggesting the use of a creativity technique with a group of people who have not been through the creativity workshop. But when a group gets stuck, unable to come up with a solution, I find myself suggesting one of these techniques to get us unstuck, to get back on track."

Comment 5: "One of the surprising outcomes for me was a new tolerance for some of my users who I always considered to be uncreative. Now I tend to tell myself 'Be patient, let them come about it using their own approach.' I find they are more creative than I thought—they just use a less logical approach to reaching a solution."

Comment 6: "In response to the question, 'Would I have come up with those creative solutions on our list without the introduction of the creativity program?' I'd respond that some of them—undoubtedly. However, now I tend to be on the lookout for more creative solutions."

Comment 7: "Within the new creative environment, we find ourselves less constrained in our thinking. For example, yesterday Theresa came up with a solution that was a quantum jump ahead in thinking. That is not untypical for any one of us in the new environment."

Comment 8: "One measure of our creativity is the improvements we've made in the accounting package. We've been able to identify and implement some improvements that the experts—the developers of the package—were surprised about. Their technical staff is many times the size of ours and yet we introduced some significant changes."

Superiority of the Bottom-Up Approach

Why do we believe that the bottom-up approach is superior to the top-down approach for introducing a creativity improvement program? The principal value of the bottom-up approach is the work unit going through the entire program together. The manager is in the workshop and, therefore, goes through the same change process as his team. That manager, in turn, is more open to new ideas and to facilitating their implementation. We found that approximately 90% of the improvements can be implemented without having to obtain approval from the next level of management. Therefore, team members experience a sense of empowerment—they see quick results and are motivated to integrate creative approaches into their everyday work habits. As voiced by one employee, "This has been the most exciting period of my career."

With the typical top-down approach, management is trained then is expected to convince subordinates of the value of the program. Subordinates are less likely to respond positively because they did not go through the change process with their manager.

It is valuable for management to have half-day presentations on the ingredients of the creativity program. As a result, management is more likely to be supportive of the program and to be responsive to the other 10% of the ideas that need higher level approval. Nevertheless, the program could be introduced by a first-line manager—achieving excellent results on the large majority of the suggested improvements without having to go to his manager for approval.

What's next? The next phase of the UTMC program is continual reinforcement of concepts and principles and continual updating upon new developments in creative processes by reading and discussing creativity articles and papers. The discussion leader rotates each time with the following emphasis:

1. Assurance that everyone attained an equivalent understanding of the content of the paper.
2. Application of the ideas in the paper to the UTMC IS environment.

Conclusion

The manager of IS states: "In the near term the benefits have included creative improvements in systems development, business systems processes, employee hiring, cost effectiveness and system efficiency. The long-term benefits are even more exciting. Creativity is now a part of our culture. We have become significantly more effective as a change agent within UTMC and have already begun to enhance the way the company works."

4.3 MANAGING FOR INNOVATION

Watts Humphrey is best known for his work on software process at the Software Engineering Institute. His *Managing the Software Process* is probably one of the most significant books in the field of software engineering, and his work on process has been at the heart of most important discussions of software engineering topics for at least a decade. We have already dealt with the topic of process earlier in this book; why is Humphrey's name arising here as well?

Two years before his 1989 process book, Watts wrote another book, *Managing for Innovation*. This latter book has attracted almost no attention over the years, and yet in many ways it may be just as important as the better-known one.

The subtitle of the innovation book is "Leading Technical People," and the idea behind the book is that people matter a lot in building software product. The book is about innovative technical software people and the role of managerial leadership in enabling that innovation. That makes the book a fascinating juxtaposition with Humphrey's later process work, since in that later work he has taken the position that process (not people) is the key to software success.

But back to the earlier Humphrey book. What is the relationship between innovation and creativity? The relationship is discussed at more length elsewhere in this book, but Humphrey—quoting Theodore Levitt—puts it very succinctly:

"Creativity is thinking up new things. Innovation is doing new things."

Humphrey goes on to add, "While innovation requires creativity, it also involves a great deal of hard work."

The book is about both creativity and innovation, although Humphrey is clearly more interested in the latter, because it is in the "doing," the "hard work," that management's role comes to the fore.

What does Humphrey have to say about the intricate relationship between management and the creative technical person?

Regarding control, he reports findings from the literature that "managers who tightly control the way their people work generally get significantly less creativity than those with a looser and more informal style."

Regarding management technical knowledge, he reports other findings that "when the manager's ability was limited, innovation was highest when the group was given the greatest freedom.

"When the manager was highly skilled in administration, personnel, and technology," Humphrey went on, "the results were mixed; sometimes freedom helped, but sometimes it did not." Humphrey concludes with an old saying: "If you don't know what you're doing, then stay out of the way!"

Looking at the matter from a different point of view, Humphrey examines studies of successful and unsuccessful groups. "In the most innovative the managers personally involved themselves in the work and maintained close technical contact with their people. For the least innovative the managers were less active and more remote."

Is there a lesson to be drawn from this material? Perhaps it is "the most innovation comes when (a) the manager has technical skills and involves himself or herself in the group's work, while (b) maximizing the amount of freedom given his technical people."

Is technical creativity the most important factor in successful innovation? According to Humphrey and the studies he cites, the answer is "no." In fact, the "persistent tendency of technical people to confine themselves to the laboratory and not to seek a detailed understanding of the user's needs" is one of the foremost reasons for research and development failure, he says.

What is the alternative to the laboratory-confined technologist? "Successful product development depends more on market astuteness than on technical competence," he says, quoting a University of Pennsylvania study. The most innovation, in fact (according to another study), comes "when the users were technically competent." That is, users, understanding the application problem to be solved, are more likely to produce innovation than computer technologists, who understand only the computing problem to be solved. Humphrey goes on to cite another study that found "75% of all innovations . . . came from market sources, but the highest percentage of technically driven innovations given by any single study was only 34%." That is, customer need, rather than technological progress, determines whether an innovation is likely to be successful or not. (Sounds familiar, doesn't it? It's a new variation on the old theme, "necessity is the mother of invention.")

An interesting aside in the book deals with the issue of "how age affects creativity." Although there is a common belief that creativity and innovation peak at a fairly early age (it has been cited as being anywhere from 21 to 29), Humphrey says there is "an increasing body of evidence that points the other way." In one study, the researchers found that "performance peaked at an early age but declined very slightly thereafter." "The precise point at which this peak occurred depended on the technical field; it was earlier in the more abstract fields of mathematics and theoretical physics and later in such pragmatic specialties as biology and geology. The initial peak fell in the mid-30s, but they also found a late peak in the mid- to late-50s. This double peak phenomenon occurred in all the groups of engineers and scientists . . . studied, and the dip between these two peaks was not very significant."

Humphrey summarizes with an encouraging thought: "For creative people, the late 30s and early 40s is a highly stressful period. Once they pass this hurdle, however, many engineers and scientists will continue their creative work for many years . . . many of Thomas Edison's 1100 inventions were produced late in his 84-year life."

From the point of view of "managing for innovation," then, the good leader must know that any of his people, of any age, may contribute creativity and innovation.

There is one strange and somewhat jarring part of Humphrey's book.

Before he joined the SEI, Humphrey spent a number of years with IBM. Many of Humphrey's anecdotes, and much of the focus of his acknowledgment section of the book, is about his IBM heritage. In an era when IBM's troubles are well known, and every computing columnist feels free to pontificate on "what went wrong with IBM," it is a little strange to read a book with statements like "IBM is a leading example of corporate technological success. It has demonstrated a remarkable ability both to make the right decisions and to make its decisions right." It is important to get past this early impression of the book, however, because what Watts Humphrey has to say here about innovation—and creativity—is well worth reading.

REFERENCES

HUMPHREY 1989 - *Managing the Software Process*, Addison-Wesley, 1989; Watts S. Humphrey

HUMPHREY 1987 - *Managing for Innovation*, Prentice-Hall, 1987; Watts S. Humphrey

5

A BRIEF LOOK AT
CREATIVITY IN
OTHER FIELDS

> *"Students of the creative process have long distin-*
> *guished between two kinds of thinking: analysis and*
> *synthesis. Sometimes the latin word* cognito, *mean-*
> *ing 'I think' in the sense of analyzing or taking apart,*
> *is contrasted with* intelligo, *meaning 'I understand'*
> *in the sense of gaining insight into the nature of*
> *something . . . We can look at the world and see how*
> *things differ (make distinctions) or how they are the*
> *same (make analogies). The first approach usually re-*
> *sults in the creation of new categories, the second*
> *usually involves shifting contexts."*

—Ellen J. Langer, in *Mindfulness*, Addison-Wesley, 1989
(© 1989 by Ellen J. Langer, Ph. D. Reprinted
by permission of Addison-Wesley Publishing Company, Inc.)

There is something fascinating about the field of software. It consumes our
energies, our talents, our interests. We can make a career out of doing nothing but software-related things, and be quite happy in the doing.

But people who focus their attention only in one direction begin to realize, after a while, that their horizons have become narrow and their
judgements impaired. Do those of us who focus too long and too hard on
software suffer from that malady?

I think the answer is yes. In this chapter, we will take a brief tour of
the role of creativity in other fields. Some interesting lessons can be learned
in doing so.

One field that particularly deserves our attention is the ages-old field
of problem-solving. There is a strange history to this field. Although
problem-solving is, of course, as old as the human race and has been writ-

ten about sporadically through the centuries, it took the advent of computers to spur renewed interest. In the early 1960s some remarkable new work in problem-solving took place.

There are three particularly interesting findings from that new spurt of interest in problem-solving:

1. The thing we call the software life cycle is really a universal problem-solving approach (this theme is elaborated in section 5.5, to follow).
2. As problems increase in complexity, heuristic methods become more and more important, and formal approaches begin to break down (this theme was elaborated in chapter 3).
3. General problem-solving approaches, which have led to so much success in the field of computing to date, are characterized as "weak" approaches to problem-solving, whereas special-purpose approaches are characterized as "strong" (contrast the role of an adjustable wrench vs. specific-sized wrenches in loosening a nut, for example).

Taken both individually and as a whole, these three findings suggest some dramatically different approaches to both software practice and software research in the future. One might imagine a future, for example, that looked at variations within the life cycle rather than trying to scrap it entirely, as some in computing suggest; focusing away from formal approaches and toward heuristic ones, which is substantially at odds with much conventional wisdom in computing today; and moving from generalized, cure-all software solution approaches toward application-focused ones: application-specific methodologies, tools, languages, and perhaps even computers, for example.

What's the point here? That looking beyond our own field can lead us to a place where our own field is seen in a much clearer perspective. That in so doing, we may spot some fundamental problems with the contemporary directions of our field. That is the purpose of this chapter.

In the first two sections to follow, we look at creativity as both an organizational and individual trait. (In the world of the next century, it is easy to imagine that both individual brilliance and organizational innovation will be required to address the massively increasing problems we in our field tackle.)

Next, we look at the issue of using the computer to enhance the creativity of people in other fields (this is the ultimate form of looking outward!). The results of experiments in this area to date, we see, are surprising—and disappointing.

Perhaps some of that disappointment is related to some fundamental paradoxes in the field of creativity. Those paradoxes are defined and discussed in the next section.

Finally, to add perspective to this section that is already focusing on perspective, we do a reprise of the subject matter of this book from the point of view of how it all fits in with the experiences of other disciplines. One author tells us about "the classical contradiction between control and creativity." "'Twas always thus," we say at this point. The fundamental underlying concept of this book—that software must use a combination of control-oriented and creativity-enhancing approaches—is not a new idea at all!

And that's probably the strongest lesson to be derived from a brief look at creativity in other fields.

5.1   ORGANIZATIONAL CREATIVITY

The subject of creativity has been around for a long time. That should mean that here is a topic that can lean heavily on the findings of other researchers in other disciplines, right?

The surprising answer to that question is a qualified no. According to a comprehensive survey of creativity issues in the broader workplace (not just software) there has been a "limited amount of research on creativity in organizations," but "decades of research on organizational innovation" [Woodman93]. The paper elaborates on that theme: "researchers still know surprisingly little about how the creative process works;" and "from the applied side, we also know little about how organizations can successfully promote and manage individual and organizational creativity."

Part of the problem, the authors say, is that "organizational researchers have done a relatively poor job" of "disaggregat[ing] the construct of creativity from the broader construct of innovation." How do they distinguish between creativity and innovation? "We frame the definition of organizational creativity as a subset of the broader domain of innovation. Innovation is then characterized to be a subset of an even broader context of organizational change . . . even though creativity may produce the new product, service, idea or process that is implemented through innovation . . . innovation can also include the adaptation of preexisting products or processes . . . " In other words, creativity conceives novelty, and innovation puts creative and/or modified ideas into usage.

But let's step back a little and look at the picture being painted in [Woodman93]. The subject that interested them, and forms the basis for their paper, is something they call "organizational creativity." Organizational creativity comes about, they say, through interactions involving individual creativity and group creativity. "Organizational creativity is a function of the creative outputs of its component groups and contextual influences (organizational culture, reward systems, resource constraints, the larger environment outside the system, and so on) . . . Group creativity is a function of individual creative behavior inputs, the interactions of the individuals involved, group characteristics, group processes, and contextual influences." In other words, although individual creativity plays an escalating and important role in organizational creativity, there are other factors that also play a role.

Since individual creativity is a key building block, the authors look at it a little more deeply. They see it as consisting of both personality traits and cognitive factors. To be specific:

- Personality traits
  - High valuation of esthetic qualities in experience
  - Broad interests
  - Attraction to complexity
  - High energy
  - Independence of judgment
  - Autonomy
  - Intuition
  - Self-confidence
  - Ability to resolve apparently conflicting traits in one's self-concept
  - A firm sense of self as creative
  - Persistence
  - Curiosity
  - Energy
  - Intellectual honesty
- Cognitive factors
  - Associative fluency
  - Fluency of expression
  - Figural fluency
  - Ideational fluency
  - Speech fluency
  - Word fluency
  - Practical ideation fluency
  - Originality

That apparent laundry list of creative traits emerges from an interesting history of exploring creativity. "Much of the early research on creativity," the authors say, "was characterized by catalogs of biographical and historical information on eminent creators." However, analyzing that information didn't bear much fruit: "Attempts at empirically keying these measures resulted in factorial complexity that makes theoretical interpretation . . . virtually impossible." To overcome that problem, as well as to fill in the apparent missing gaps in a biographical approach, other researchers began including the interaction of personality data with the biographical data. According to the authors, some of those researchers have "demonstrated that personality data interact with biographical data to predict creativity."

The main contribution of the paper, in addition to supplying a strong foundation of references to the earlier creativity literature, is to postulate a set of beliefs about creativity in the form of hypotheses. The paper, unfortunately, does not go on to test the hypotheses, leaving that as an exercise for future researchers! Here are the hypotheses.

About individual creative performance:

1a: It will be increased by group norms that support open sharing of information.

1b: It will be decreased by group norms that create high conformity expectations.

1c: It will be increased by organizational cultures that support risk-taking behaviors.

1d: It will be decreased by reward systems that rigorously evaluate creative accomplishment and link these outcomes tightly to extrinsic rewards.

About group creative performance:

2a: It will be increased by group diversity.

2b: It will be decreased by autocratic styles of leadership.

2c: It will have a curvilinear relationship to group cohesiveness.

2d: It will be increased by the use of highly participative structures and cultures.

About organizational creative performance:

3a: It will be increased by the availability of slack resources.

3b: It will be decreased by restrictions on information flows and communication channels within the system.

3c: It will be increased by the use of organic organizational designs (e.g., matrix, network, collaborative groups).

3d: It will be decreased by restrictions on information exchanges within the environment.

Many of the hypotheses, although unevaluated within the paper, emerge from the writings of previous creativity scholars. For example, the authors point out that "motivational interventions such as evaluations and reward systems may adversely affect intrinsic motivation toward a creative task because they redirect attention away from the heuristic aspects of the creative task and toward the technical or rule-based aspects of tasks performance." Note that hypothesis 1d directly evolves from this finding.

Note also the apparent underlying assumption on the researchers' part that creativity is harmed by "technical or rule-bound aspects" and helped by "heuristic aspects." This provides some justification for the positions taken in other essays in this book that formal, methodological, disciplined approaches to building software may indeed get in the way of the creative processes also needed.

Other findings cited by the authors that tend to support the hypotheses include these:

"The number of formal supervisory levels and the number of R&D employees were negatively correlated with innovation [not creativity], whereas the [small] size of the research project teams . . . was positively correlated . . . "

"We expect creativity to be enhanced by adaptive, flexible organizational structures . . . "

"A reasonable conjecture is that when *functional managers* control rewards, engineers fear that nonroutine behavior will be evaluated negatively by those managers. However, when *project managers* control rewards, the overall outcome is evaluated regardless of the means used to accomplish the task."

Interestingly, and harking back to an earlier section of this book, this suggests that too much emphasis on process can get in the way of creativity, and that a product focus—the goal, after all, of the project manager—is more likely to allow employees the freedom to be creative.

What do the authors of the paper see as *their* bottom line? "To understand creativity in a social context necessitates an exploration of creative processes, creative products, creative persons, and creative situations. A useful theory of organizational creativity must provide a framework of sufficient complexity and richness to integrate these four components."

That sets the stage for future research very nicely. But a great deal of it still needs to be done.

REFERENCE

WOODMAN 1993—"Toward a Theory of Organizational Creativity," *Academy of Management Review*, Vol. 18, No. 2, 1993, Richard W. Woodman, John E. Sawyer and Ricky W. Griffin

5.2   THE CREATIVE PERSON

What constitutes a creative person?

That turns out to be a hard question. It's hard partly because there are a lot of different studies that give a lot of different answers, but it's also hard because there is enormous debate about whether there is, in fact, such a person.

The latter issue—the debate about whether there is such a thing as a creative person—centers on the issue of whether creativity can be learned. The answer to that question is, of course, extremely important. Given that we have already seen that some portion of software's tasks demand creativity, the question boils down to this: "Must we hire people who are inherently creative to build software, or can we train creativity into those we already have?"

If only a few are creative, that is an important but also depressing answer. First of all, that answer enormously complicates the task of hiring software specialists, since the role of creativity in the skill mix of new employees suddenly becomes critical. It is also a depressing answer because it means that only a chosen few can perform those software tasks that are creative.

Fortunately, most students of that question have come down on the side that says creativity can be learned. That is especially good news to people who offer courses in improving creativity, since of course such an effort would be pointless if creativity is one of those things you either have or don't have. But it is also good news to all of us, because it means that we don't have to worry about whether there is a creativity barrier in our lives that we are either able to overcome or not.

Be all of that as it may, let us pursue a related issue at this point.

Suppose that some people are dramatically more creative than others. This does not force us to assume that the others cannot be creative, only that there are people who are really good at it. What are the characteristics of these creative people?

There are lots of interesting studies of that question. Here are a couple of sets of answers from some particularly interesting sources.

"One trait I quickly noticed," according to David Johnson [Johnson90], writing in an unusual publication called *Midnight Engineering* (it's a journal for people considering starting their own technical business), "was their intense concentration on their work. At times they seemed to be in another world, taking little or no interest in the activities around them. Although I would not call them anti-social, they did prefer to work with their computers or test equipment than with other people."

Johnson went on, "When they were not concentrating on a problem they were very easy to get along with and they had a keen sense of humor. However, I did notice them to be much less tolerant of disturbances. When working on an especially difficult problem, loud music, clerical work, group meetings and report writing were all viewed as interruptions or distractions . . .

"When they did allow themselves a break it was to read. They seemed to have an unquenchable thirst for knowledge . . . It didn't seem to matter what the subject was, as long as it was interesting . . . Perhaps this general interest is why few of the individuals I knew had advanced college degrees and why many crossed over from one technical area to another . . .

"The generalist attitude of many creative people I knew was also displayed in their problem solving techniques. I noticed that they did not rely heavily on detailed mathematical tools when solving problems. If calculations were needed only ball-park figures were used . . . They relied much more on trial and error methods. For them it was faster to wire up a circuit and test their design than wait for a paper study . . . "

Johnson's informal analysis of creative people gives us a lot of practical, deeply felt insight. But are there more rigorous, scientific studies of the same issues?

As you might expect, there are. In an interesting series of studies, [Barron58] offers us an analysis of "The Psychology of Imagination."

The bottom line of Barron's studies is this: "Creative individuals are more at home with complexity and apparent disorder than other people are." How did that manifest itself in his studies? Here is a particularly interesting answer:

"When confronted . . . with the Rorschach inkblot test, original individuals insist to a most uncommon degree upon giving an interpretation which takes account of all details in one comprehensive, synthesizing image. Since some of these blots are quite messy, this disposition to synthesize points up the challenge of disorder. It also illustrates the creative response to disorder, which is to find an elegant new order more satisfying than any that could be evoked by a simpler configuration."

Barron also found that creative people resisted giving in to group consensus. In a series of contrived experiments, he set up a situation in which the majority under test gave an agreed-upon false answer, and the real test subjects, knowing what the majority had chosen, had to make their own choice. Only about 25% of the real subjects were able to resist the erroneous consensus. Barron tested those subjects further, and found they expressed their independence in such statements as:

"I like to fool around with new ideas, even if they turn out later to be a total waste of time."

"Some of my friends think that my ideas are impractical, if not a bit wild."

"The unfinished and the imperfect often have greater appeal for me than the completed and polished."

As a result of these and other tests, Barron came to these conclusions about creative people:

"They are especially observant, and they value accurate observation."

"They often express part-truths, but this they do vividly; the part they express is the generally unrecognized . . . and unobserved."

"They see things as others do, but also as others do not."

"They are thus independent in their cognition, and they also value clearer cognition. They will suffer great personal pain to testify correctly."

"They are motivated . . . both for reasons of self-preservation and in the interest of human culture and its future."

"They are born with greater brain capacity; they have more ability to hold many ideas at once, and to compare more ideas with one another—hence to make a richer synthesis."

"They are by constitution more vigorous and have available to them an exceptional fund of psychic and physical energy."

"They usually lead more complex lives, seeking tension . . . [and] the pleasure they obtain upon its discharge."

"They have more contact than most people do with the life of the unconscious—with fantasy, reverie, the world of imagination."

"They have exceptionally broad and flexible awareness of themselves."

"The creative person is both more primitive and more cultured, more destructive and more constructive, crazier and saner, than the average person."

Now let me ask you an odd question. As you read those statements, did you do a little self-analysis, measuring your own creative instincts? I know that I did. And I suspect that all of us feel within ourselves some sense of the creative, and thus some kinship with that elusive "creative person." In other words, we may or may not view ourselves as creative people, but we know that we can be creative when the need arises. That's a nice feeling, of course, but also an important one. We have met the creative person, and he (or she) is us.

REFERENCES

BARRON 1958—"The Psychology of Imagination," *Scientific American*, Sept. 1958; Frank Barron

JOHNSON 1990—"The Creative Person," *Midnight Engineering*, January/February 1990; David Johnson

5.3   COMPUTER SUPPORT FOR CREATIVITY

Most of this book is inward-focused. That is, it is about the role of creativity in *building* software; the inward focus is on the field of software itself.

However, this section is outward-focused. It is about the role of computers and software in helping others to be creative. It is included because there is quite an active community within the computing and software field, looking at creativity issues outside the field.

For example, in the spring of 1993 an international symposium was held in England with the theme "Creativity and Cognition." The title itself does not express what was unusual about this conference, but the subtitle does:

"Artists, musicians, designers, cognitive scientists and computer scientists present ideas on creativity and cognition that cross the boundaries of art and science."

This was a truly interdisciplinary conference, where experts from both "soft" and "hard" fields met to share ideas. A book based on the symposium was published by MIT Press in early 1994.

Themes of the conference were:

- Concepts, processes, and computational models
- Art and science: intersections and boundaries
- Computer technology: methods and tools
- Reflections on art practice; studies in design practice

The interaction of the different disciplines came through nicely in the titles of some of the papers presented: "Towards Artificial Creativity," "Using the Computer to Augment Creativity: Computer Choreography," "Culture, Knowledge and Creativity: Beyond Computable Numbers," and "Tamed Equations." The image of Computer Choreography through Tamed Equations is especially wonderful!

There is a fundamental concern beneath all of this disciplinary interaction, however: Does the use of a computer really enhance the creative efforts of those in other disciplines? It is easy to imagine that the answer ought to be yes, especially from the point of view of us computer folk who are used to the many and diverse wonders that computers can work. But is there any hard evidence to support that intuition?

There are two recent studies that address this issue. Interestingly, these studies come not from the world of the arts, where we might expect the most interest in creativity, but from the world of business. In [Elam 1990] and [Durand 1992] we find studies of the value of creativity-enhancing software packages in the decision-support application domain.

Traditionally, decision-support systems (DSS) are focused on a particular problem, and on the structuring of solution approaches through a database and a model base specific to that problem. Notice that the traditional DSS is, in some ways, the exact opposite of what a creativity-enhancing DSS might be, since it is specific-problem-focused and provides a structured solution approach, whereas a creative DSS might be expected to be applied to a number of different problems, and facilitate different, freewheeling, creativity-enhancing skills.

The First Study

In the first referenced study [Elam 1990], the authors found a commercially available creativity-enhancing DSS and set up an experiment in its value. The software chosen (ods/CONSULTANT, by Organization Development Software) had not yet been announced in the marketplace at the time of the study, but it seemed to the authors that what it offered was closer to their study goals than any other available package. (For a more complete discussion of available creativity-enhancing software packages, see [Thierauf 1993]). The tool offered facilities for encouraging idea generation, facilitating brainstorming, provoking questions, and combining idea fragments, as well as quantitative support for prioritizing/grading ideas, identifying interdependencies among ideas, and allowing for categorizing ideas along user-selected dimensions.

The study involved three groups, assigned a common set of problems but using three different approaches to solving them:

1. No computer support
2. ods/CONSULTANT support using the following model (called Version 1):
   - Describe problem
   - Gather candidate facts
   - Assess relevance and validity
   - Organize facts
   - Develop explanations
   - Identify solutions
3. ods/CONSULTANT support using the following model (called Version 2):
   - Gather candidate facts
   - Determine objectives
   - Assess relevance and validity
   - Identify obstacles
   - Inventory resources
   - Generate ideas
   - Edit and translate ideas
   - Make decisions
   - Test decisions

What was the fundamental difference between the two versions? The authors saw Version 1 as focusing on underlying causes, moving from causes to explanations and then solutions. Version 2, by contrast, focused on practical solutions at every step. The authors summarized the two by saying, "Version 1 looks backwards for causes and depth of understanding while Version 2 looks ahead for practical solutions."

The subjects of the study were practicing professionals with similar backgrounds from a Big Eight accounting firm. The tasks assigned included a business problem and a public policy problem. The results of the problem solution were judged for their creativity by a panel of expert judges who were asked to use their own subjective definition of creativity. The expectation was that the judges would evaluate results on the novelty and appropriateness of the problem solution. Judges were people like corporate presidents, management consultants, college professors, and directors of national funding agencies.

What were the results? They were quite surprising and, in fact, somewhat unsettling. Using a rating scheme in which lower numbers indicated greater creativity, the results were:

- Version 1: 8.0
- No Software: 12.7
- Version 2: 16.8

That is, there was considerable difference between the two software versions (this difference was the only one the authors considered statistically significant), and the creativity of those who used no software aids at all fell between the two software-supported versions. The authors called the results "intriguing," noted that "we expected both software treatments would result in more creative responses than no software," and summarized: "The difference in the results for the two software treatments is an important one for DSS designers . . . software environments can both enhance [and] . . . inhibit desired outcomes."

The authors also obtained user perceptions of the two versions of the software tool. Version 1 was seen as more fun to use and more helpful than Version 2, but more difficult to use.

And the authors, who did not consider time taken by the subjects in evaluating creativity, noted that the Version 1 users took more time than the others.

The authors do not say so, but the implication seems to be that creative solutions may take more time than less creative ones, but generate more fun during the doing.

The Second Study

In the second referenced study [Durand 1992], a similar experiment was conducted. The area in which creativity was sought was in the decision-support domain, and a commercially available software package—in this case, Idea Generator—was employed. (The package is said to increase the ability of its user to brainstorm, generate alternatives, defer judgement about alternatives until a sufficient number are available, and select among the alternatives.)

Hoping to improve on some of the limitations of the first study, the researchers chose 88 subjects (MBA students with about two years of work experience), premeasured the subjects for innate creativity, assigned them two short case studies to perform, and used independent judges to evaluate the results on a comprehensive set of criteria, only a few of which were related to creativity. (Neither the judges nor the subjects knew the experimental subject was creativity.)

Subjects worked the case studies either using the software or with no software support.

And what were the results of this second study? For 28 measurement techniques, only five of which were related to creativity, *the software-supported subjects scored more poorly in every single category.* Let's say that again: Software not only did not help induce creativity (or any of the other possible improvements in the assignment), it actually hurt.

What possible explanation can there be for such a surprising finding? Did the subjects fail to use the software properly? No, the researchers gathered information that said the subjects using the software accomplished the kinds of things the software was designed to support (a high quantity of ideas, fleshed out in detail and depth).

Was there some sort of bias caused by people with inherent high or low creativity? No, the software diminished the performance of both!

What then? The authors admit to being "puzzled," and call the findings "clear and unexpected." In their discussion section, they conclude that "solutions developed with the aid of the software were judged less creative." And they provide, as perhaps the only possible conclusion, "creativity inducing software appears to need further development before it can contribute meaningfully to improving Decision Support Systems."

We have seen, throughout much of this book, that creativity is an elusive thing to define, discuss, and measure. Even when we succeed in defining, discussing, and measuring, if we test for creativity we get considerable variance in our responses. (See the section on creative vs. intellectual and clerical tasks, for example.)

The findings of these studies simply echo that theme. We can still hypothesize, for example, that computers can be used to enhance creativity; but we must quickly add that we don't understand very much about how to do that, and that badly done computer-enhanced creativity can have a negative, not positive, impact on our goals.

That's not a very satisfying finding. However, it does appear to be an accurate assessment of the state of the art in computer-aided creativity.

REFERENCES

DURAND 1992—"Creativity Software and DSS: Cautionary Findings," *Information and Management* 23, 1992. Douglas E. Durand and Susie H. VanHuss

ELAM 1990—"Can Software Influence Creativity?" *Information Systems Research,* March 1990; Joyce J. Elam and Melissa Mead

THIERAUF 1993—*Creative Computer Software for Strategic Thinking and Decision Making: A Guide for Senior Management and MIS Professionals,* Quarum Books; 1993. Robert J. Thierauf

5.4   CREATIVITY PARADOXES

Creativity, we have already seen, is a difficult subject to pin down. It has been defined perhaps a million times, and its definitions differ depending on the definitionist. Its effects have been described over and over again, and yet it is hard to say precisely when an effect is creative and when it is not. Can creativity be learned? Many say it can, some say it can't. There seems to be something magical about this elusive notion of creativity.

Because of all of the above, it probably should not surprise us that there are significant paradoxes involved in creativity. At least two can be found in the literature:

Creativity paradox number 1: The more a creative person knows about the subject of focus, the less the need for creativity.

Creativity paradox number 2: In order to think originally, we must familiarize ourselves with the ideas of others.

And, fascinatingly enough, the juxtaposition of those two paradoxes creates a third:

Creativity paradox number 3: Creativity paradoxes 1 and 2 do not agree with each other.

Let's elaborate on each of those paradoxes in turn.
The more a creative person knows about the subject of focus, the less the need for creativity.

Suppose you are presented with an extremely complicated problem to solve, but also suppose that you have solved similar problems many times before. Your approach to solving this current problem, naturally, is to examine your successful past solutions and begin to find one or more to modify to match the new problem.

However, in the act of reusing past solutions, you are short cutting some of the facets necessary to allow an act to be labeled creative. If we accept the [Newell62] definition of creativity used earlier in this book, creativity must involve novelty or value, use unconventional thinking, be a product of high motivation and persistence, and deal with vague and ill-defined problems. Your reused solution certainly has value, but its reuse has stripped it of the notion of novelty; yesterday's unconventional thinking is rapidly becoming today's conventional thought; high motivation and persistence are certainly less needed now; and although the initial problem may have seemed vague and ill-defined, familiarity is beginning to breed a sense of understanding and definition.

Perhaps it was said best in [Sasso 1989]. "What part does *creativity* play in the design process?" the authors ask. "From our perspective, it does not fit neatly in at a particular point in a certain process. Rather, we see creativity as permeating each of [its] . . . activities . . . The extent to which this occurs is largely determined by the interaction of the designer's experiences and the design space—if his experience includes an overall solution obviously adaptable to the current design space, very little creativity will be needed. If, on the other hand, the design situation is entirely foreign to the designer, practically every aspect of the design process will require creative thinking."

How ironic! In a problem-solving situation, the potential is there for the most creative solutions to be provided by those who understand the problem least. Isn't that fairly unsatisfying? In fact, can that make any sense at all?

In order to think originally, we must familiarize ourselves with the work of others.

This thought, too, represents a paradox. Doesn't the very act of familiarizing ourselves with the work of others detract from the originality of what we produce?

Those who have identified this paradox see it emerging from what they have called the "four phases of creativity": preparation, incubation, illumination, and verification. Creative thought, according to this "life-cycle" view of creativity, cannot occur in a vacuum. It must be stimulated (preparation and incubation) before it can bring forth fruit (illumination). And it is during this stimulation, when the problem-solver is exploring the subject area of the problem, that stimuli are ingested that can later drive the creative force. For example, [Henle 1962] (as quoted in [Couger 1990] says:

> "It seems that creative ideas do not occur to us unless we spend a great deal of time and energy engaged in just the activity that makes their emergence most difficult . . . It may be that immersion in our subject matter is a condition

of creative thinking not only because it gives us the material with which to think but also because it acquaints us with the difficulties of the problem."

Not all creative ideas, of course, emerge from a four-phase process. The notion of the "aha," or serindipitous solution, is well-known. Yet even with situations where solutions appear to fall out of the blue, a little thought usually suggests that some part of the brain has been ingesting input and mulling over the problem, even without a formal identification of those activities.

This paradox, unlike the first, is more satisfying. It seems to match our western ethic, that those who work at a problem are more likely to solve it satisfactorily than those who do not.

And that brings us to the third paradox:

Creativity paradoxes 1 and 2 do not agree with each other.

How can it be true that we must immerse ourselves in a subject area in order to be creative, and yet to the extent that we draw from our mind past solutions we are not?

Perhaps a resolution to this dilemma can proceed something like this:

Paradox 1 presents us with the situation in which the problem-solver has already immersed himself (or herself) in the problem, and (at some point in the past) come up with a solution. The act of creating that solution is what moved the problem-solver past the stages of novelty, unconventional thinking, and the need for persistence, and moved the problem toward being one that is well-defined.

Paradox 2, on the other hand, presents us with the situation in which the problem-solver is at an earlier stage in the creative process for this problem. Preparation and incubation must precede illumination. No ready-made past solution is available.

Thus, the differences seems to be one of degree. A little exposure to the problem at issue is vital to the instantiation of creativity, but a lot moves us past the need (and, of course, into a different phase of that creativity life cycle).

Seen in this way, the third paradox, although interesting as a semantic exercise, is probably less significant than the first two. And that's probably just as well. There are enough difficulties with understanding the nature of creativity without the need to deal with conflicting paradoxes!

REFERENCES

COUGER 1990—"Ensuring Creative Approaches in Information System Design," *Managerial and Decision Economics*, Vol. 11, pp. 281–295, 1990. J. Daniel Couger

HENLE 1962—"The Birth and Death of Ideas," in *Contemporary Approaches to Creative Thinking*, Atherton Press, p. 43, 1962; M. Henle

NEWELL 1962—"The Processes of Creative Thinking," in *Contemporary Approaches to Creative Thinking*, Atherton Press, 1962; A. Newell, J. Shaw and H. Simon

SASSO 1989—William C. Sasso and Monte McVay. "The Constraints and Assumptions Interpretation of Systems Design: A Descriptive Process Model," submitted to the *Journal of Systems and Software* in late 1989 but never published.

5.5   'TWAS ALWAYS THUS

We in software like to believe that the problems we encounter are fresh and new, just like our profession.

That is a tempting belief. It is fun to employ this marvelous new technology to solve problems, and it would be fun to think that the problems we are solving are just as new.

Some of them are, of course. Space exploration and automated flight control were areas of speculation before the computing era, but they were not real problems capable of being solved in any meaningful way.

However, most problems that we solve are not new. Information systems and financial systems and manufacturing systems were possible and existed long before computers. They may be enormously more efficient and effective now, but the problems themselves are not new.

Many attempts have been made, in the field of computing, to capitalize on this past history. People examine ideas from the rich past of other disciplines to try to identify those ideas that could be useful in the new era of computing and that, of course, is a worthy endeavor.

But along the way, something odd has happened. We have tried to borrow ideas from the solution domain of other disciplines, but we have ignored what we have learned about the problem domain.

What do I mean by that?

With the advent of the field of software engineering, many attempts have been made to use analogy as a vehicle for identifying traditional engineering approaches that might be useful in software. We have examined manufacture by parts, for example, and statistical quality control. These kinds of approaches have been problematic in software, however. There are some fundamental differences about software that make these kinds of solution analogies difficult to employ. The uniqueness and weightlessness and spacelessness and near-zero manufacturing cost of software products mean that many ideas simply do not transfer well into its world.

Perhaps, however, we have been looking at the wrong side of the analogy picture. The topics we mentioned above were about solution approaches. What could we learn if we focused, instead, on past understandings of addressing the problem itself? The field of problem-solving, although eons old, is not as rich in concepts as we might like, but it still offers some worthwhile analogies to the software problem-solver.

The Life Cycle as Universal Problem-Solving Algorithm

Take the idea of the software life cycle as an example. Although notions of the life cycle differ, most would agree that the life cycle consists of something like this:

1. Identify a problem.
2. Define the requirements of the problem.
3. Design a solution to the problem.
4. Implement the design.
5. Test the implementation.
6. Use the implemented product.

To those of us in software who are used to reading, and sometimes arguing, about the life cycle, the discussion above probably seems simplistic and rather boring. But let's take another look at this life cycle from the more traditional point of view of problem-solving.

Those steps above are, essentially, a universal problem-solving algorithm. None of them is intrinsically software-specific. If you look at the traditional great books on applications of problem-solving, like Polya on mathematics or Alexander on architecture, you will find something resembling this same life cycle as a part of what they present. And that's not all. Writers use this same approach. Artists use the approach. I have even been told that, at a meeting of a business and professional women's club, something akin to this life cycle was presented as the proper approach to starting a business!

If we in software could only see the life cycle as an analogy borrowed from the problem-solving past, we could save ourselves a lot of arguments about whether the life cycle is appropriate or not. Of course it is appropriate—we in software are not about to rewrite the history of problem-solving. What we have sometimes failed to see, in our often-endless arguments about the appropriateness of the life cycle, is that the basic framework of the life cycle can be bent to include a lot of variations. Spiral life cycles and prototyping, for example, are simply variations on the basic life-cycle theme. The fact that iterations occur within the life-cycle stages should not be a problem to any but the most pedantic of life-cycle believers.

The life cycle as a universal problem-solving algorithm is only one benefit we can achieve by focusing on the problem domain instead of on the specifics of solution domains. The real purpose of this chapter of the book is to focus on another.

The underlying message of this book has been that there are two approaches to building software. One is management-driven, control-oriented, formal, and disciplined. The other is skill-driver, creativity-focused, informal, and freewheeling. Which of the approaches we choose can have a profound effect on both the process of building software and its product. The suspicion with which we began the book, reinforced in various ways throughout, has been that the appropriate construction approach to software must somehow include a blending of these two approaches. The theme of the book has been to emphasize the importance of the second approach, primarily because the forces that bear on the world of software have concentrated almost exclusively on the first, and some important things have been lost along the way.

But wait. The message of this chapter has been that an examination of the historic notions of problem-solving can be useful. Is that true of this dichotomy of approaches, as well? Do we find anything about the Roman vs. Greek, management-driven vs. technologist-driven, dilemma in older information sources?

Mechanistic versus Romantic; Hard versus Soft; Rational versus Empirical

The answer is, as you might expect, yes. In fact, this dichotomy is ages old. Perhaps the best description of the history of this difference is given in [Dahlbom 1992].

Dahlbom identifies these same two very different approaches as the Mechanistic approach, characterized by a focus on representation, formalization, program, order, and control, and a Romantic approach, characterized by individual artistic expression, genius, and creativity. "The Romantic reaction to the Mechanistic world view," Dahlbom says, "made much of the difference between organisms and machines, wanting to defend nature and everything natural against the machines and everything artificial."

Dahlbom goes on: "The Romantic philosophers were not interested in taking the universe apart like a machine, in analyzing it into its smallest atoms. No, they wanted to contemplate, understand, interpret, feel and see through the world to its hidden meaning, like you do with a poem or painting."

Dahlbom labeled this dichotomy as "the classical contradiction between control and creativity." He then evolved this dichotomy into a discussion that he (and many other authors) characterize as "hard" and "soft" approaches. Here, the two words have meanings that differ somewhat from what our intuition might suggest. Hard means objective, algorithmic, consisting of facts, with the world being representable in an exact and true way. Its history rests in the Mechanistic. Soft means fuzzy, consisting of ideas, subject to interpretation, emphasizing cultural differences. Its history rests in the Romantic. Hard subjects are easily taught—they can be memorized, they can be tested via multiple-choice or true/false approaches. Soft subjects are difficult to teach—memorization is not possible; testing must be by discussion or essay.

Educational institutions, especially in the United States, tend to focus on hard subjects. There is even an expression about academe: "hard drives out soft." (That is, those who espouse hard subjects tend to reject those who espouse soft ones. Tenure battles, for example, are all too often fought along these lines.) There is something satisfying (and easy!) about teaching and testing a collection of facts. There is something unsettling (and difficult!) about teaching a collection of ideas, where today's ideas may be significantly different from those of yesterday or tomorrow.

Students tend to be more comfortable with hard subjects. We are taught, starting in the lowest grades, that a learning experience consists of accumulating facts. If the student does not make the transition, as he or she moves up the learning ladder, that the mature person must add idea-based concepts to a fact-based mindset, the student is very uncomfortable in a class where what is learned is soft. Not only is this true for the traditional soft subjects, like philosophy and sociology, but it is true in software-related pedagogy as well. Management topics, for example, are inevitably soft. Software engineering, in the sense that there is no fixed formula that is best for all problems, is soft. (Some computer scientists try to convert it into a hard subject by teaching formal ways of building software, but the bias of this author is that it is at best premature to teach formal approaches exclusively, since these approaches have yet to be shown to be a demonstrated improvement over informal ones through evaluative research. Further, this seems about as imaginative as teaching history as a collection of dates, a sure way to spoil the subject of history!)

The notion of mechanistic vs. romantic, now evolved into hard vs. soft, takes one more turn of the evolutionary wheel in Dahlbom's book. He makes a distinction between "rationalism" (the theory that reason is the foundation of certainty in knowledge) and "empiricism" (the doctrine that knowledge is obtainable by direct experience through the physical senses). He then elaborates that distinction into one between systems construction, which he says "belongs to the rationalist tradition," and problem/solving, which is "an expression of more empiricist ideas." "The main concern in the systems construction approach is complexity," he says, "whereas the main concern in the problem-solving approach is uncertainty. This suggests the following principle: In situations where the complexity of the problem is high and the uncertainty is low we should choose a systems construction approach and in situations with high uncertainty and low complexity we should prefer a problem solving approach."

Be that as it may, Dahlbom does offer one interesting gleam of hope in this spectrum of dichotomies. "The fierce antagonism between rationalists and empiricists has mellowed over the years," he says. "In this century science has arrived at a somewhat loose, but healthy, combination of the two methods. The kind of inductivism stressing the need for unbiased observation has been abandoned as impossible in favor of theoretically based hypothesis testing. You use induction to infer the empirical implications of your theories and you then test these implications by collecting data, using induction to order the data. It is [just] such a healthy mixture of deduction and induction that we would like to see in the problem solving approach."

What does all of this mean? That the dichotomy between Roman and Greek, management and technology, mechanistic and romantic, hard and soft, rational and empirical, or whatever one chooses to call it (or them)— that this dichotomy is not unique to software, and it dates back to antiquity. Remember that Dahlbom called it "the classical contradiction between control and creativity."

'Twas always thus. It is unlikely that we in software, like our brethren in much older disciplines, are going to solve the problem, to blend the dichotomies, to end the contradiction, in our lifetime. But perhaps, using the vision of Dahlbom, the "fierce antagonism" can, as it has in those older fields, "mellow over the years." One of my hopes is that this book, exhibiting much sympathy for the creativity required in software but at the same time acknowledging the need for discipline and formality as well, will help move us toward the "mellowing" that we in software need so badly.

REFERENCE

DAHLBOM 1992—*Struggling with Quality, The Philosophy of Developing Computer Systems*, pp. 16–17, 52–55, 94–95, 142–143, Academic Press, 1992; Bo Dahlbom and Lars Mathiassen

6

SUMMARY

"Learning takes place when we are receptive to information that does not fit and creates conflict with our models. Complacency thrives on harmony."

—Moshe F. Rubinstein, in *Tools for Thinking and Problem-Solving*, Prentice-Hall, 1986

A reviewer of one of my earlier books provided a piece of important insight. After getting to the end of that manuscript, his reaction was, "Remind me now, where was the beef?" There are a lot of different ideas in a collection like this, and it's kind of nice for the author to do a tatting up at the end.

I followed that reviewer's advice for that previous book, and I was pleased with the summary section that ended the book. It provided not just the reader, but myself as well, with a clearer picture of just where the book had taken us.

Because of that, I set about to do the same for this book. This chapter is the result of that effort.

6.1 A SYNERGISTIC FINDING

As I struggled to wrap a gestalt over the varied pearls on the necklace of software creativity this book represents, I was surprised at what began to happen. I began to get the feeling of synergy; the gestalt began to become more than just the sum of the individual parts of the book.

As I reprised the material, several themes played hauntingly in my mind. There was the theme of Jeff Offutt, closing the door of his laboratory and discarding all the formal methods he had just finished teaching his students, resorting to *ad hoc* and—yes—creative solutions instead. There was the theme of David Parnas, acknowledging that true top-down design was simply not possible, advocating instead that we "fake it" in our final documentation efforts. There was the theme of Bill Curtis, expecting to find balanced and controlled evolution in design activities, finally coming to the conclusion that design is instead an opportunistic process. There was the theme of Douglas King, quoting Herb Simon as saying that solving well-understood problems via formal approaches is very different from solving ill-understood problems, using weakly structured, heuristic approaches. There was the theme of Bruce Blum, who told us that software process optimized for fun was only good when the tasks were small and the motivation for quality was based on an individual's insight, and that software process optimized for phased compliance is only valid when there are firm and stable requirements.

There was a common theme running through all these separate ones, I began to see. And that common theme, as I thought about it some more, began to take this form:

We in the academic world of computing have been trying to treat the construction of software as a monolithic entity. We define and advocate one-size-fits-all methods, languages, computers, and tools. We expect each new methodology to solve all problem types. We construct a process evaluation model and expect to apply it to all software projects.

I believe the message of all those haunting themes is that our one-size-fits-all approach is wrong. No, it is worse than that. It is WRONG! It is important that we in computing begin to address software projects with the nature of the project itself as one of the determiners of how we go about running the project, how we go about solving the problem.

This was not an entirely new thought to me. I had already done some research work in the application-domain dependence of solution approaches, and realized that—far more than we yet understand—different domains require different solution approaches. But that was another neat and tidy compartment in my mind, the subject of another set of essays and research papers, and I had not yet seen that there was a relevance to this software creativity material.

I had also done some work on the size and criticality aspects of software projects. My Prentice-Hall book *Building Quality Software*, for example, contains as appendices recommendations for quality solution approaches that are dependent on the size and criticality of the project in question.

However, what seemed to be emerging from these haunting themes on creativity was a whole new dimension, the dimension of "Innovativeness of the Problem to Be Solved." Thoughtful writer after thoughtful writer had said, each in his own way, "formal approaches lose their effectiveness as we move in the direction of more innovative problems," and "disciplined approaches must at least be blended with creative ones for problems that tax the mind."

I began to struggle with the notion of a way to represent software projects, based on some essential criteria. It was clear, for example, that project size played an important role in the techniques to be used in the solution. It was equally clear that project criticality played the same kind of role. The new thought emerging here was that Innovativeness of the Problem also played the same sort of role. There were a lot of different dimensions, in short, that should have an effect on the methods we use to solve problems in software.

Remember, this struggle was happening at the same time that the Software Engineering Institute was advocating a Capability Maturity Model, and a five-level management maturity rating scheme, that was being applied across the board to all software projects. It was happening at the same time that each new formal method and methodology that came along from both computer science researchers and vendor salespeople was being advocated for all projects.

I expect, in years to come, that people will see the hard-won insight I am describing here as something that should have been obvious all along. But in the era in which I extract these notions from the haunting threads of my contributors, this was radical thinking indeed.

What am I trying to say here? That each new approach to building software must be evaluated as to its appropriateness along several project characteristic dimensions:

- The nature and need of the application domain
- The size of the project
- The criticality of the solution
- The innovativeness of the problem

There may be other appropriate dimensions; this is still evolving thinking. For example, other candidates might be the knowledge/style of project managers, or the quality/capability of the technical project members.

It is interesting to note, in fact, that these candidates emerge from an organization/focused, as opposed to a project-focused, view of approach selection. For a fascinating look at an elaboration of that concept, see [Constantine 1993], which offers these organizational paradigms for different kinds of projects:

- Closed (the traditional hierarchic organization—Constantine says this approach is best for "routine, tactical projects")

- Random (based on innovative independent initiative—Constantine says this is best for projects requiring "creative breakthrough")
- Open (adaptive and collaborative—best for "complex problem-solving")
- Synchronous (efficient, harmonious alignment—best for "repetitive, critical performance")

[Hyman 1993] is a nice case study of the applications of some of these concepts.

But let's stay with the previously mentioned project-first set of project approaches for the moment.

Let's apply the various issues of Chapter 2 of this book against each of these dimensions.

Discipline: Strong discipline is needed for super-large and/or critical projects. For other projects, it decreases in importance.

Formal methods: Formality is appropriate for small projects (perhaps large ones, after appropriate research is done); we do not yet know if it is important for critical projects, although many advocates believe it is essential; and (most important) it is only useful for projects where the problem is not very innovative. Heuristic approaches seem to be more effective for complex projects. (Rettig and Simons, for example, take the position that an "iterative strategy," involving divide-and-concur approaches, a spiral life cycle, object technology, rapid prototyping, and incremental testing, are best when the problem is complex [Rettig93].)

Optimizing solutions: Optimization may only be possible for small projects. It is relatively independent of project criticality (we would like to obtain optimal solutions for critical projects, but that does not make it possible) or problem innovativeness.

Quantitative reasoning: In spite of the desirability of quantitative approaches, it is probably true that they are only applicable to relatively small and not very innovative projects.

Process: Process probably should move hand-in-hand with discipline. That is, the more the need for discipline, the more the need to define the process on which discipline will be applied. See the discussion of discipline above.

Intellectual, creative tasks: The need for intellectual and creative approaches increases with project size, solution criticality, and especially the innovativeness of the problem.

Fun: The role of fun is probably the inverse of the role of discipline. That is, it happens most on small projects that are non-critical but represent at least somewhat innovative problems.

Now, there's a problem here. It took a lot of words to say all those things. And those words will tend to obscure the simplicity of the underlying idea. I tried to draw a graphic that would simply and cleanly represent these several dimensions playing across these creativity issues, but it quickly got out of hand. So, before I move on here, let me underscore the underlying idea one more time:

The one-size-fits-all approach to software problems and solutions prevents us from seeing some important truths. Those important truths take the form of helping us see when certain solution approaches will work well and when they will not. Such highly touted approaches as disciplined methods, formal methods, and defined processes, which have been advocated for all projects no matter their nature, are fairly limited in applicability to a certain subset of all problems. It is important to begin a discussion about when each such approach is appropriate (and, perhaps more important, when it is not). This section suggests a first cut at that discussion.

In the field of human relations, and especially its subset interested in civil rights, it is popular to talk about "celebrating the differences" among human beings. What that means is that, although we humans differ in race and sex and religious preference and certain other key parameters, those differences are things to be explored and appreciated, not feared and avoided. It is time for the field of computing to celebrate its differences. And the dimensions we discuss above—application domain, project size, criticality of solution, and innovativeness of the problem—define the types of differences that the field of computing and software ought to be beginning to understand—and celebrate.

REFERENCES

CONSTANTINE 1993—"Work Organization: Paradigms for Project Management and Organization," *Communications of the ACM*, Oct. 1993; Larry L. Constantine

HYMAN 1993—"Creative Chaos in High-Performance Teams: An Experience Report," *Communication of the ACM*, Oct. 1993; Risa B. Hyman

RETTIG and SIMONS 1993—"A Project Planning and Development Process for Small Teams," *Communications of the ACM*, Oct. 1993; Marc Rettig and Gary Simons

6.2   OTHER FINDINGS

That celebration of differences through the varying dimensions of the software project is, I think, the most important thought I would like you to take away from the reading of this book; but there are some others.

First of all, the creation of the book, as you recall, represented a personal odyssey for me, as I moved from a view of software as creative art to a more balanced view of software as disciplined and creative art. Perhaps you have had some sort of odyssey of your own as you have read what I have written.

Underlying that odyssey, I would like to believe, are some other interesting thoughts.

There are major cultural differences in the ways we approach the construction of software. Whether those differences are called Greek vs. Roman, technology-driven vs. management-driven, or assembly line vs. craftsmen; or whether they take the much older form of mechanistic vs. romantic or rational vs. empirical, those differences become very real when we consider their implications for *how* we build software.

There is little data to show that one culture is better than the other. However, there are a few findings, scattered along the fringes of the chasm between them, which suggest that on some occasions each side might be right.

Perhaps the most interesting data in the book results from a couple of experiments into the nature of software tasks. Breaking those tasks down into their creative, intellectual, and clerical natures, one experiment demonstrates a consistent finding that roughly 80% of software's tasks are intellectual, and only 20% clerical. Regarding the degree of creativity in the tasks, the other experiment is less conclusive. Expert judgements vary, some saying that only 6% of software's tasks are creative, with others putting the figure as high as 29% (the average is 16%). Whatever else the findings mean, certainly they show—in a quantitative way—that software's tasks are a considerable intellectual challenge.

For which tasks is creativity needed? Although there is disagreement here, it seems fairly clear that it includes at least these activities:

- Translating business needs into problems for creative solution (strategic planning and competitive advantage tasks come in here)
- Resolving problem statements defined by multiple and conflicting enterprise organizations
- Designing solutions to complex and new problems
- Establishing a necessary and sufficient set of test conditions and cases

- Making a major enhancement to a software system where the enhancement is outside the design envelope of the original system

Given that creativity must be part of producing software solutions, what does that mean in terms of staffing? We have seen throughout the book support for the notion that all of us have the capability to be creative. We also saw, through the findings of Dan Couger, that the cost of training approaches to enhance that inherent creativity need be no higher than 0.5% of project costs; we further saw that there are a lot of well-known techniques for enhancing creativity; and finally, we saw that those techniques can raise individual creativity by a perceived 23%, and the creativity of the organization in which those individuals function by 27% (according to one informal study).

Interestingly enough, we also learned that software tools for enhancing the creativity of non-software people have mixed, if not negative, success. It looks like we can make more progress, at this point, focusing creativity on software tasks, rather than focusing software on creative tasks.

There is one more set of ideas that I, at least, will retain from my odyssey in the creation of this book. They are the pithy quotes I obtained related to the role of creativity in software. Here are some of my favorites:

On quantitative approaches: "If you torture the numbers long enough, they will tell you anything you want to know."

On "you can't manage what you can't measure": "We do it all the time."

On the role of discipline and process: "We follow all the rules, and fail."

On the war between theory and practice: "Weak theory gets laughed out of the halls of practice," and "Stuck practice does not upgrade to match the legitimate findings of theory," and "When theory and practice battle, it's a sure sign that something is wrong."

On researchers who believe they are entitled to government support but produce work that no one ever references: "They are welfare queens in white coats."

On generic vs. *ad hoc* approaches: "Generic approaches are 'weak' in the sense that they solve no problem really well; ad hoc approaches are 'strong' in that they focus on the problem at hand."

On the conflict between creativity and discipline: "They are an 'odd couple' in that both are necessary."

That last pithy quote brings us full circle. Should software approaches be formal and disciplined or freewheeling and creative? In the final analysis, the message of this book is clear. The answer is simply:

"Yes!"

APPENDIX

Many of these essays were previously published, perhaps in one of my regular columns ("Software Reflections" in *Managing System Development* or "Editor's Corner" in *The Journal of Systems and Software*), or in the journal I edit and publish (*The Software Practitioner*, or elsewhere. The past history of the essays contained in this book is shown in the table below.

Essay			*Was Previously published in*
Ch. 1.	Why Software Creativity?		MSD, JSS
	1.1	Greece versus Rome:	
		Two Very Different Software Cultures	OI
	1.2	Control and Corporate Culture	—
Ch. 2.	Of Two Minds: An Informal Look at Software Creativity		
	2.1	Discipline versus Flexibility	
		• Will the Real Henry Ford of Software Please Stand Up?	TCF, SS
		• Software Automation: Fact or Fraud	MSD, JSS
		• Are Programmers Really "Out of Control"?	MSD, JSS
		• Discipline Is a Dirty Word: A Story About the Software Lifecycle	MSD, JSS
		• The Faking of Software Design	MSD, JSS
		• The Strange Case of the Proofreader's Pencil	MSD, JSS
		• Structured Research? (A Partly Tongue-in-Cheek Look)	SC, MSD,JSS
		• The Falutin' Index	ESP
		• The "Odd Couple" of Discipline and Creativity	MSD, JSS
	2.2.	Formal Methods versus Heuristics	
		• Formal Methods versus Heuristics: Clarifying a Controversy	SP, JSS
		• A Guilt-free Approach to Software Construction	MSD, JSS
		• Formal Methods: A Dramatic (Success, Failure) Story	MSD, JSS

LEGEND:

ESP - Embedded System Programming

HIC - Proceedings of the Hawaiian International Conference on

         System Sciences

I&M - Information and Management

ISM - Information Systems Management

JSM - Journal of Systems Management

JSS   - Journal of Systems and Software

MDE - Managerial and Decision Economics

MSD - Managing System Development (formerly System

         Development)

OI   - *The Olduvai Imperative*

SC   - *Software Conflict*

SS   - *Software Soliloquies*

SP   - The Software Practitioner

TCF - *Tales of Computing Folk*

In each case, the essays were used with the permission of the appropriate
publisher.

INDEX